Civilized Creatures

Animals, History, Culture

Harriet Ritvo, Series Editor

CIVILIZED CREATURES

Urban Animals,
Sentimental Culture, and
American Literature,
1850–1900

Jennifer Mason

The Johns Hopkins University Press
Baltimore and London

Printed in the United States of America on acid-free paper
2 4 6 8 9 7 5 3 1

The Johns Hopkins University Press
2715 North Charles Street
Baltimore, Maryland 21218-4363
www.press.jhu.edu

Library of Congress Cataloging-in-Publication Data

Mason, Jennifer, 1972–

Civilized creatures : urban animals, sentimental culture, and American literature, 1850–1900 / Jennifer Mason.

p. cm.— (Animals, history, culture)

Includes bibliographical references (p.) and index.

ISBN 0-8018-8071-8 (hardcover : alk. paper)

1. American fiction—19th century—History and criticism. 2. Animals in literature. 3. Animal welfare—Moral and ethical aspects—United States. 4. Animal welfare—United States—History—19th century. 5. Human-animal relationships in literature. 6. City and town life in literature. 7. Sentimentalism in literature. I. Title. II. Series.

PS374.A54M37 2005

813'.309362—dc22 2004023001

A catalog record for this book is available from the British Library.

Philosophers have always been puzzled to contrive such a definition of man, as should completely distinguish him from every other animal. We are not aware that, among the many attempts of this sort, he has ever been described as an animal that gets on horseback. Yet this is one of the most peculiar characteristics of the human race.

[NATHANIEL HAWTHORNE], "Wild Horsemen," *American Magazine of Useful and Entertaining Knowledge* (1836)

"Ah, I tell ye what," said Candace, looking mysterious, "dogs knows a heap more'n dey likes to tell!"

HARRIET BEECHER STOWE, *The Minister's Wooing* (1859)

CONTENTS

ACKNOWLEDGMENTS

WHILE WORKING on this project I received generous assistance from people I deeply respect and admire. Chief among these are Evan Carton and Ann Cvetkovich, who directed the dissertation out of which this book developed, and dissertation committee members Phil Barrish, Shelley Fisher Fishkin, and Michael Winship. Evan Carton and Phil Barrish also read and offered valuable feedback on portions of the manuscript written after the dissertation. Every chapter of this book has benefited from conversations with and careful readings by Eric Lupfer, whom I am grateful to have as a friend and colleague. Harriet Ritvo, Mason Stokes, and two anonymous reviewers from the Johns Hopkins University Press offered suggestions that proved valuable during the later stages of revision. For their feedback on early versions of the book's chapters, I would like to thank Alyssa Harad, Robert Levine, William Scheick, Paige Schilt, Sandy Soto, and members of the Dallas Area Social History Group. My work on this project was also sustained in less direct but nonetheless important ways by the many colleagues who provided me with a sense of intellectual community. Among these, I would like to thank, in addition to those named above, Daniel Brownstein, Andreas Killen, Sean Quinlan, Cary Wolfe, and Joanna Wolfe.

Librarians at the Harry Ransom Center, the National Sporting Library, the American Antiquarian Society, the Folger Shakespeare Library, and the British Library provided patient and much-appreciated assistance while I worked with their collections. The interlibrary loan departments at the University of Texas at Austin and Skidmore College cheerfully, quickly, and repeatedly found me materials that I needed. Robin Bledsoe and John Seaverns shared with me their extensive knowledge of books on the horse, and they each introduced me to texts that became important sources in this project. I would also like to thank my research assistants Naomi Gutierrez and Christina Harris; John Cosgrove, humanities librarian at Skidmore College; Faith Herbert of the Constitution Island Association; Georgia Barnhill, the Andrew W. Mellon Curator of Graphic Arts at the American Antiquarian Society; Iris Snyder of the University of Delaware Library Special Collections Department; Diane

Wald and Carter Luke of the Massachusetts Society for the Prevention of Cruelty to Animals; copy editor Michael A. Baker; and Robert J. Brugger, Courtney Bond, and Amy Zezula of the Johns Hopkins University Press.

My work on this project was funded by an Andrew W. Mellon Postdoctoral Fellowship at the UCLA Humanities Consortium in 2000–2001 and by a William S. Livingston Fellowship from the University of Texas at Austin in 1999–2001. Skidmore College provided funding for travel and for my research assistants. I am grateful to the Regents of the University of California for permission to reprint those portions of chapter 1 that appeared as "Animal Bodies: Corporeality, Class, and Subject Formation in *The Wide, Wide World,*" in *Nineteenth-Century Literature* 54:4 (March 2000).

I wish to thank Barbara Angelis Mason, Roland Mason, Mary and George Angelis, and Maria Mason Kaperonis for their support of all my academic endeavors. I reserve my final thank you and deepest gratitude for Pete Blum. His companionship has brought a tremendous amount of joy to my life, and his constant and enthusiastic support has sustained me throughout all phases of my work on this book.

Life in the Built Environment

Nature has long been reckoned a crucial ingredient of the American national ego. Ever since an American literary canon began to crystallize, American literature has been considered preoccupied with country and wilderness as setting, theme, and value in contradistinction to society and the urban, notwithstanding the sociological facts of urbanization and industrialization. The critical urge to explain this preoccupation in terms of a general theory of American culture is almost as long-standing.

LAWRENCE BUELL, *The Environmental Imagination*

IN AMERICAN literary and cultural studies, the second half of the nineteenth century is universally understood to be a period of intense interest in animals and their relationship to people.[1] Explanations of why this is so, however, have been subordinated to a particularly resilient critical narrative about the importance of the nation's wild nature—a narrative that links the importance of such nature to its absence from most people's daily lives. This book proposes, first, that between 1850 and 1900 the most powerful influence on Americans' understanding of their affinities with animals was not increasing separation from the pastoral and the wilderness, but rather the population's feelings about the ostensibly civilized creatures present in the built environment.[2] Second, it argues that understanding the dynamic relationship between people's lived relations with animals and the multiple, species-specific, and often markedly affective discourses relating to these animals is essential for understanding the contests for power in the human social order played out in literary texts—even in texts that do not appear to be "about" animals per se.

Although urbanization and industrialization severed certain connections to the nonhuman world, these forces also brought people into new proximities with animal life. This claim is borne out by Nathaniel Hawthorne's "Little Annie's Rambles" (1835, 1837), a sketch first published nine years before the 1844 journal entry that Leo Marx places at the center of the introduction to *The Machine in the Garden* (1964).[3] An urban-based version, in many ways, of Wordsworth's "Tintern Abbey," the story opens as its unnamed narrator observes Annie, the five-year-old daughter of a friend, standing on her family's doorstep with "that impulse to go strolling away—that longing after the mystery of the great world—which many children feel, and which I felt in my childhood."[4] Seized by the urge to relive those dizzy raptures of youth, the narrator spontaneously takes Annie by the hand and the pair sets out on a ramble that proves as restorative as Wordsworth's sylvan one, even though it takes place "in the most crowded part of town." On their excursion, Annie and the narrator encounter streets thronged with horses; a parrot, canary-bird, and squirrel in cages in storefronts; "a big, rough dog . . . in search of his master" who "touch[es] little Annie's hand with his cold nose"; "a very corpulent and comfortable cat, gazing at this transitory world"; a wheelbarrow full of lobsters; a cart of fresh fish; and, at a menagerie exhibiting in town, an elephant, a lion and lioness, a tiger, several monkeys, a polar bear, a trained pony, a wolf, "a hyena from Egypt," and "a black bear from our own forests" (125–27).

As this brief story suggests, nineteenth-century cities and towns teemed with animal life. Every urban center required thousands of horses to transport people and move goods to the local or national market. The need for horse-drawn transportation increased rather than diminished with the rise of the railroad. In the year 1900, there were 3.5 million horses in the nation's cities and 82,000 in Chicago alone.[5] Those who could not afford to keep horses for their own transportation or recreation were often employed to drive or care for the horses of those who could. In the days before modern refrigeration, animals used for food were, by necessity, kept close by the populations that ate them. Well into the latter part of the century, cattle and sheep could be found grazing in and around cities, while chickens and other small livestock populated the back or side yards of middle-class homes as well as the recesses of the densest urban slums. Companion animals were ubiquitous. Wherever there was a sufficient population density, one could find racetracks, riding academies, exhibitions of trained animals, traveling menageries, circuses, and (later in the century) zoological gardens ready to absorb the population's leisure time and disposable income. As efforts to exterminate predatory wild animals had, by the mid-1800s, effectively extirpated many of these species from the Eastern seaboard, living in an area populated enough to attract traveling menageries probably increased the frequency of encounters with native wild animals as well as the range of species (both native and exotic) to which one was exposed.

But if the animals on which this study focuses—those that were not only present in the built environment but believed to share humans' affinities for civilized life—have not been central to studies of U.S. cultural, intellectual, and literary history of the nineteenth century, it is not primarily because scholars did not know they were there. Indeed, commonsense reflection on the technological, alimentary, and economic realities of life at this time convinces us that this must necessarily have been so. The problem, instead, lies in the perversely durable notions of American exceptionalism that continue to pervade discussions of America's (and in particular nineteenth-century America's) relation to the nonhuman.

It is true that in the past three decades no critical assertion has been subject to more, or more vigorous, challenges than the early- and mid-twentieth-century claims about the centrality of the wilderness romance to American literature. These myriad critiques and revisions have, however, sustained and even extended several assumptions fundamental to the original articulation of this thesis. Among these is the notion that animals became important to the American literary imagination precisely at the point they became absent from most people's everyday lives. This idea has generated two now widespread critical assumptions, which, though they certainly appear to be mutually sufficient if not mutually exclusive alternatives, have most often been held in conjunction with each other. The first assumption is that the animal presence in literary texts should be read as a construct of the human imagination uninformed in any meaningful way by people's interactions with actual animals. The second assumption is that writing about nonhuman nature required the writer's at least temporary location at or beyond the periphery of civilization. The revisions of this second idea have been accomplished not so much by negating it as by promoting its secret double. For, in the early- and mid-twentieth-century critical accounts of nineteenth-century U.S. culture and nature, what was the heroic white male's location in the wilderness but the most potent of symbols for his ideological distance from, if not outright disdain for, mainstream, sentimental American culture? The inclusion over the past thirty years of people other than white men in the critical conversation about nature has been accomplished by asserting the possibility of maintaining an ideological distance from mainstream culture in the absence of a geographical distance from it; that is, by arguing that it was possible to possess a modified or muted form of that vague loathing for conventional life expressed so ardently by Ishmael in the opening of *Moby Dick* (1851) even if you lived—by choice or necessity—within the civilized world.

Thus, even (and perhaps especially) in the feminist literary criticism aimed at revaluing women's sentimental and domestic fiction, identification with or romanticization of nonhuman creatures remains (as in its original masculine version) cognate with scorn for the civilized or domestic.[6] And we continue to believe that, if wild animals whose existence was untrammeled by civilization became interesting to people as embodiments of individualism and self-reliance, then domesticated animals were either meaningless to "Americanness" or meaningful only as symbols of enervation, subordination, or dependency—in short, of that which is opposite from or despised within the American point of view.[7] In "America and Its Studies," Djelal Kadir observes the persistence of "the dominant imaginary . . . that would have the United States be a perpetually unique and unprecedented historical phenomenon in disconformity (usually righteous) not only from the rest of the world but also from itself."[8] There is no better evidence of the power that this fantasy of American exceptionalism retains over American studies than the now ubiquitous acceptance of the critical paradigm according to which having something "American" to say about nonhuman nature in the period between 1850 and 1900 remains predicated on having a nonstandard relation to American culture—one that takes the form of a rejection (however qualified or submerged) of the sentimental and domestic cultural formations associated with mainstream life located in the built environment.

Admittedly, existing ideas about American attitudes toward domesticated and wild animals are not without explanatory power. They capture accurately, for example, the position of Henry David Thoreau. In *Walden* (1854) wild animals function as a veritable walking dram of that "tonic of wildness" that Thoreau says we need.[9] "As I came home through the woods," he writes, "I caught a glimpse of a woodchuck stealing across my path, and felt a strange thrill of savage delight, and was strongly tempted to seize him and devour him raw; not that I was hungry then, except for that wildness which he represented" (210). This impulse for violent appropriation is uncharacteristic of Thoreau, who subsequently renounces flesh eating entirely. Typically, he consumes animals' "wildness" through his eyes and ears rather than his mouth, as he does when he spends an entire afternoon pursuing a loon with his boat, not to catch the bird but to relish the bird's ability to evade capture. Thoreau delights in the loon's "long-drawn unearthly howl, . . . perhaps the wildest sound that is ever heard here," because he associates it with the bird's unassailable freedom: "I concluded that he laughed in derision of my efforts, confident of his own resources" (236). Conversely, domesticated animals appear in *Walden* primarily as metonyms for the noxious and vitiating effects of civilization. The keeping of animals enslaves men—threatens to make one into a "horse-man or herds-man merely." "No nation of philosophers," Thoreau contends, "would commit so great a blunder as to use the labor of animals" (56). Just as humans now require heated houses in the winter, he notes, dogs and cats have become similarly dependent on artificial warmth. The very thought of the dog's bark sparks a diatribe against domesticity: "Who would live [in a farm house] where a body can never think for the barking of Bose? And O, the housekeeping! to keep bright the devil's door-knobs, and scour his tubs this bright day! Better not keep a house" (223). Later, he remarks that the "village Bose" (or dog) is now "fit only to course a mud-turtle in a victualling cellar." When the dog does venture into the woods, his "heavy quarters" make him sluggish; he sniffs "ineffectually" at foxes' burrows; though he imagines he trees the squirrel, the spry squirrel has really "treed itself" to better observe the dog (232).

The notion that views such as Thoreau's governed thinking about animals in the second half of the nineteenth century can be sustained only through the magical thinking of American exceptionalism, by which Thoreau can symbolize the rejection of mainstream American culture yet somehow simultaneously represent it.[10] Recent examinations of the reception and promotion of nature writing in the nineteenth century have demonstrated conclusively what many Thoreau scholars had long surmised on more anecdotal evidence: that Thoreau, in addition to being regarded as an eccentric crank in his own lifetime, continued to be regarded as such (to the extent that he was regarded at all) after his death in 1862.[11] At this time, Eric Lupfer points out, "Thoreau was regularly described as 'obscure,' 'eccentric,' 'morbid,' and 'idiosyncratic.' "[12] An 1865 review of the posthumously published *Letters to Various Persons* describes Thoreau as "so peculiar a person that everything that relates to him must be read with interest by any one who likes to study what is abnormal in human development."[13] Though the editors at Houghton Mifflin managed to drum up interest in his work at the end of the century, they succeeded by promoting previously unpublished works that were more cheery and less caustic than *Walden* and by assiduously downplaying (both by their selections and by editorial framing) Thoreau's hostility toward civilization. Lupfer's analysis of Houghton Mifflin correspondence reveals that even among editors at this firm there were "serious questions about the merits of Thoreau's work." In an 1880 introduction to Thoreau's essays in *American Prose,* Houghton Mifflin editor Horace Scudder complained about the "protesting attitude" of Thoreau's work and maintained that his method "was against the common order of things, and therefore the results reached could not be relied upon as sound and wholesome."[14] Throughout the final third of the nineteenth century, Lupfer finds, the country's most popular nature essayist was not Thoreau but John Burroughs, whose writings were praised most often by contemporaries for their "home-like" quality.[15]

As late as the middle of the twentieth century, the perception that Thoreau's elevation of nature over civilization was quintessentially "American" was not accompanied by the belief that Thoreau's views were "representative" of contemporary thought in the usual sense of the term. Consider an essay by Perry Miller that first appeared in 1955 and was later republished in *Nature's Nation* (1967), whose title has become a shorthand for assertions about the primacy of wild nature to the "American literary imagination." Assuming a facile equation between "nature" and "wilderness," Miller argues that the "the problem of American self-recognition" in the nineteenth century was "an essentially irreconcilable opposition between Nature and civilization," "with the assumption of all virtue, repose, dignity are on the side of 'Nature' . . . against the ugliness, squalor and confusion of civilization."[16] Although this claim may seem unremarkable to us, Miller did not believe that his readers would find it so. After laying out his thesis, he interjects: "The reader may object that I am talking nonsense. This was the expanding, prospering, booming America of the 1840's; here, if ever in the annals of man, was an era of optimism, with a vision of limitless possibilities, with faith in a boundless future. . . . Surely this society was not wracked by a secret, hidden horror that its gigantic exertion would end only in some nightmare of debauchery called 'civilization'?" Miller then observes, "The most cursory survey of the period does indeed display a seemingly untroubled assurance about the great civilization America was hewing out of the wilderness. This faith, with its corollaries of belief in progress and republican institutions, might be called the 'official' faith of the United States" (198). He admits quite directly, "The issue I am raising—or rather that the writers themselves raised—*may have little to do with how the populace actually behaved*" (201, emphasis added). Miller even concedes that "possibly there were, in sum, no more than three Americans" who allied themselves with the wild over the civilized "and in their time they were largely ignored by their countrymen." Thus, when Miller proceeds to argue, "Yet Whitman, Thoreau, and Melville speak for this society, and to it, in great part because, by making their choice, they thrust upon it a challenge it cannot honestly evade" (207), his argument rests not on a principle of direct representation but rather on the peculiar calculus of American exceptionalism, in which the "real" story about America and nature cannot equal the " 'official' faith" but must instead involve an explicit repudiation of it.

In the fifty years since Miller first published his essay, we have moved beyond the assumption that the writing of three men (or of any number of men—or of any group defined by one gendered, ethnic, socioeconomic, or regional affiliation) can be said to "speak for this society." But to the degree that we have ascribed Thoreau's position or its variants to as many and as many kinds of people as possible instead of truly questioning its representativeness, we have not really transcended the exceptionalist fantasy at the heart of Miller's essay. Neither have we succeeded (despite valiant efforts) in vanquishing his equally central opposition between nature and culture. Since the mid-1990s, scholars in and outside of literature and environment studies have delineated the jointly theoretical and practical problems of imagining either "nature" or "wilderness" as places free of human beings and human influence.[17] These efforts, however, have not produced a critical apparatus that would enable us to think about nonwild animals apart from "debauching artificiality."[18] To date, the urban turn in ecocritical studies has materialized primarily in the substitution of "wilderness" with a concept of "wild" that tolerates sustained proximities between human and nonhuman yet leaves domesticated animals invisible as ever. A brief review of recent titles underscores my point: *The Suburban Wild; Urban Nature: Poems about Wildlife in the City; City Wilds: Essays and Stories about Urban Nature.*[19]

In the introduction to *A Sand County Almanac* (1949)—a text often hailed as the twentieth-century analog to *Walden*—Aldo Leopold declares his intention of waking up readers to the superiority of "things natural, wild, and free" over that of "things unnatural, tame, and confined."[20] That Leopold felt compelled, in 1949, to attempt such an awakening suggests that the elevation he proposes must not have been at that point axiomatic; nonetheless, within present-day scholarly treatments of America's animal nature, being "tame," "confined," and "unnatural" are all of a piece. It is only by excluding animals that are not free or wild from the category of nature that no less an authoritative source than the recent *Columbia Guide to American Environmental History* (2002) by Carolyn Merchant can proclaim in the first sentence of the chapter "Urban Environments, 1850–1960" that "living nature disappeared from everyday experience for most Americans by the mid-twentieth century." There are, for example, currently 5 million companion animals living in New York City. Merchant mentions that 3.5 million horses were present in U.S. cities in 1900, but only to highlight the problem of disposing of the resulting manure. Thus, the *Columbia Guide*'s most substantial discussion of domesticated animals appears under the heading "Garbage."[21] Domesticated animals have remained a critical blind spot in American studies, even in the work of those most committed to rejecting the dichotomized view of nature and culture, in which humans exist "outside" of nature and contact between human and nonhuman renders the nonhuman "unnatural."

To construct a critical narrative more accountable to "how the populace actually behaved"—to the ways in which people living in the nineteenth century actually experienced, thought about, and wrote about their connection to other animals—we need first to consider this subject in the context of that strain of Western thought that regarded domesticated animals as both more "natural" and less "debauched" than wild ones. In the Christian tradition, wildness was long understood to be a condition visited upon animals as punishment for Adam and Eve's disobedience toward God. According to the reading of Genesis that was ex officio in the early modern period and espoused by many theologians well into the nineteenth century, *all* animals were tame (and, like Adam and Eve, noncarnivorous) when first created; humans coexisted peacefully with the animals and exercised dominion over them.[22] People of the early modern period inherited "the long-established view . . . that the world had been created for man's sake and that other species were meant to be subordinate to his wishes and needs." It was believed that with the Fall, "man forfeited his easy dominance over other species. The earth degenerated. Thorns and thistles grew up where there had been only fruits and flowers (Genesis, iii.18). The soil became stony and less fertile. . . . Many animals cast off the yoke, becoming fierce, warring with each other and attacking men. Even domestic animals had now to be coerced into submission."[23] Attributing wild animals' ferocity to the Fall enabled people to sustain belief in their centrality to creation in the face of the undeniably vexed state of relations between humans and animals in the postlapserian world, where animals not only defied humans but even attacked and ate them. From this perspective, the degree to which an animal was wild, fierce, or implacable to human desires indicated the degree to which that animal had degenerated from an original and ideal state. Puritans opposed blood sports such as bearbaiting because, in the words of one sixteenth-century theologian, "The antipathy and cruelty which one beast showeth to another is the fruit of our rebellion against God, and should rather move us to mourn than to rejoice."[24] Conversely, domesticated animals were seen as animals whose degeneration had been less extreme and who had retained, as Andrew Willet remarked in 1605, some of their "natural instinct of obedience" toward humans.[25]

Like other aspects of the Christian worldview, ideas about the original nonwildness of animals extended well beyond the reach of organized religion. This belief animates Edward Hicks's *Peaceable Kingdom* (c. 1834), which presents Native Americans' peaceful submission to European settlers as the fulfillment of a divine plan by juxtaposing William Penn's treaty with the Delaware Indians with a scene in which feline, ursine, and bovine predators—along

Edward Hicks's *Peaceable Kingdom* (c. 1834) depicts humans and animals restored to peaceful coexistence. The formerly wild animals are now tame, and the lion is eating straw to signal the renunciation of his carnivorous ways. Gift of Edgar William and Bernice Chrysler Garbisch, Image © Board of Trustees, National Gallery of Art, Washington, DC.

with the prey species on which they were known to feed—submit peacefully to children. The same conviction informs the passage in *Nature* (1836), in which Emerson links humans' alienation from God to our alienation from wild animals. "We are as much strangers in nature, as we are aliens from God," Emerson writes. "We do not understand the notes of birds. The fox and the deer run away from us, the bear and tiger rend us."[26] Ideas about the original tameness of all animals is equally in evidence in the "Happy Family" exhibits that first appeared in traveling menageries and later became a permanent and popular feature of P. T. Barnum's American Museum (1841–68). However, the ultimate referent of these exhibits—in which predator species (having been well fed before the show) were exhibited in cages full of the animals they often ate—was neither the original beneficence of the Creator nor the sinfulness of man. Instead, they celebrated humans' growing mastery over creation by presenting an ostensible restoration of the natural world to its prelapserian state through human (as opposed to divine) agency.[27]

Equally relevant to nineteenth-century understandings of animals is the long history in Western science of regarding domesticated animals as the link between humans and the rest of creation. In *History of Animals,* Aristotle grouped human beings with domesticated animals.[28] Following this logic, Pliny the Elder's *Natural History* "affirmed the existence of intermediary species between man and animals, men with dog's heads or tails. Their existence was so well accepted that Jesuit missionaries believed they had found these strange beings in California."[29] When Buffon, who admired Pliny as well as Aristotle, even if he did not agree with all of their findings, produced his monumental and enormously popular *Natural History, General and Particular* (1749–89), he too placed domesticated animals between humans and wild animals.[30] The logic of this placement becomes clear in Buffon's chapter on dogs, which begins, "Neither majesty and elegance of form, strength of body, freedom of movement, nor other external qualities, constitute the principal dignity of animated beings. In man, we prefer genius to figure, courage to strength, and sentiment to beauty; and, therefore, we are induced to think, that the chief excellence of an animal consists also of internal qualities."[31] In eighteenth-century natural history, no less than in Christian theology (or the Platonic idealism on which it was based), the unseen "spiritual" reality counts as more real than the merely material one, and thus moral and intellectual qualities were seen as more meaningful than morphological traits. It was this principle that Buffon and virtually all other natural historians through the end of the nineteenth century used to defend their placement of the dog in a separate species from the wolf. After conceding that the dog was physically indistinguishable from the wolf and other wild canines, the nineteenth-century zoologist Edward Bennett nonetheless supported the classification of dogs as a separate species, explaining, "It is to the moral and intellectual qualities of the dog that we must look for those remarkable peculiarities which distinguish him."[32]

As historian Harriet Ritvo has shown, the belief that domesticated animals were fundamentally different from and superior to wild animals shaped eighteenth- and nineteenth-century natural history writing in a variety of ways.

Zoological writers "often . . . treated the distinction between wild and domestic animals as primary rather than contingent, the basis for taxonomic discrimination rather than the occasion for description and explanation."[33] In 1763 Richard Brookes stated that "the most obvious and simple division . . . of Quadrupedes, is into the Domestic and Savage."[34] Ritvo observes that many naturalists similarly "used domestic animals as taxonomic models, typically claiming that 'each class of quadrupeds may be ranged under some one of the domestic kinds'; thus domestic animals both exemplified and limited the range of mammalian possibilities."[35] Belief that the condition of being or not being domesticated represented a fundamental difference among animal species manifested itself in less direct ways as well. The author of *A Comparative View of the State and Faculties of Man with those of the Animal World* (1772) claimed that "all Animals, except ourselves . . . are strangers to pain and sickness" but then quickly qualified this statement, noting, "We speak of wild animals only. Those that are tame . . . partake of our miseries."[36]

Nineteenth-century interactions between humans and animals were also shaped by new beliefs about nature's spiritual but this-worldly benefits and the elevation of personally obtained knowledge of nature over the knowledge offered in books. The emergence of these ideas in U.S. society is traditionally attributed to, more than any other influence, the writings of Ralph Waldo Emerson. In *Nature* Emerson rejected natural theology's insistence that as the one goal of this life was attainment of the next, the only legitimate reason for interest in the natural world was that it could help us attain the afterlife. As Arthur O. Lovejoy has explained in *The Great Chain of Being* (1936), the discipline of natural theology evolved from the belief that, since all of the earth's creatures formed a linear, hierarchical chain of increasing perfection whose apex was God, contemplating those "steps in the stairway up to perfection" might assist humans in their efforts to ascend those stairs. Even so, natural theology afforded "the lower grades of being . . . only the use that belongs to steps, that of things to be spurned and transcended"; "their chief office [was] to remind us of their own transiency and insufficiency, or to serve as sensible symbols of supersensible attributes of deity, and thus to show that 'all things other than God are vanity and vexation of spirit, . . . and do not afford solace, but only affliction.'" Thus, the "ascent of the ladder of created things," Lovejoy explains, is "only another name for a progressive *contemptus mundi.*"[37] Rejecting this sort of "hostility and indignation towards matter," Emerson emphasized the presence of God in nature. "I have no hostility to nature, but a child's love to it," he wrote in *Nature* (35). In contrast to the natural theologians, Emerson recommended contemplation of nature for the ways it would help and sustain us in the here and now. He also roundly rejected the principle that made natural theology and natural history books such great sellers: the notion that while the Book of Nature was theoretically open to all, to attain the best understanding of nature as a manifestation of God's excellence, the average person would do well to consult a critical guide. Instead, Emerson argued that the best way of knowing nature (and hence the deity) was not through books but experience.

However, the ways in which people interacted most often with nonhuman creatures suggest that the popularity of Emerson's ideas owed less to their originality (even within an American context) than to Emerson's ability to articulate—albeit in a particularly eloquent, rhetorically powerful form—ideas driving the changes already taking place in human-nonhuman interactions (in both Europe and the United States). By the time Emerson published *Nature,* the historical privileging of book-based knowledge about the natural world was being undermined by the notion that individuals' everyday encounters with nonhuman life could offer valuable moral lessons and cultivate the virtues—such as discipline and benevolence—valued by the middle class. The promotion of animal menageries in the antebellum United States offers the clearest illustration of how people in the early nineteenth century drew on and transformed eighteenth-century ideas about the moral benefits of a print-based practice of natural history to promote practices based not on reading but experience. Menagerie owners deliberately presented the act of looking at live animals as an extension of reading about them in theology-affirming natural history books. The mission statement of the Zoological Institute, a joint stock company created in 1835 through a merger of nine existing U.S. menagerie companies, declared that its formation would enable "knowledge of natural history [to] be more generally diffused and promoted." Most early menageries distributed booklets that described the animals' natural habitat, diet, longevity, and behavior and cited Buffon and other natural scientists who insisted on the moral dimensions of their research. The Van Amburgh menagerie, which operated in the United States for four decades, often advertised itself as a "strictly 'moral show.'"[38]

But as popular as animal menageries (and later circuses) were throughout the century, and as important as zoological gardens, natural history museums, and sport hunting became in the 1890s and after, practices focused on wild animals were not the only or even the primary way in which Americans of the second half of the nineteenth century responded to postrural transformations in their relationship with the nonhuman world.[39] To the minds of many in this period, the success of an urban and suburban society depended less on periodic exposure to wilderness and untamed nature than it did on the proper care and keeping, within the built environment, of animals who participated in civilization. This belief animated the middle class's interest in recreational equestrianism and it explains why the keeping of companion animals and the prevention of cruelty to animals became national obsessions.[40]

The connection between the popularity of pet keeping and the rise of a market-oriented economy is often explained in terms of the rising class's desire to appropriate the behavior of their socioeconomic betters. Throughout the early modern period, the keeping of animals with no economic value was associated with the aristocracy, and possession of beautiful or expensive animals became one way for the bourgeoisie to display their aesthetic sensibilities and wealth. By the latter part of the nineteenth century, the demand for distinguished pets had produced a substantial market for purebred dogs whose bizarre physiology advertised their nonutility. In *The Theory of the Leisure Class* (1899), Thorstein Veblen speculated that the value of such "canine monstrosities" to their owners "lies chiefly in their utility as items of conspicuous consumption."[41] While conspicuous consumption may have driven the market for high-end pets, it does little to explain the spread of pet keeping throughout all social classes or the prominent affective dimensions of this phenomenon. Highly bred "monstrosities," of course, made up only a small percentage of the pet population. Certainly, some people paid enormous prices for dogs. But there has never been a shortage of puppies or kittens (this was even more true before the availability of surgical sterilization than it is now), and the majority of companion animals were most likely obtained for little or no charge. The growth of pet keeping's popularity owed less to a middle-class desire to resemble the upper classes than it did to the construction of a middle-class identity based on interior qualities of mind, a process, as Nancy Armstrong has explained, that enabled the middle classes to define themselves over and against the aristocratic value system based on wealth, heredity, and physical appearance.[42] The American home (which became synonymous in this period with the middle-class home) was opposed not only to the aristocratic home (identified, midcentury, as European) but also to the marketplace. In contrast to both of these spaces, the (proper) American home became defined as the one place where beings are cared for regardless of their economic value. Thus the direction of tender loving care toward an animal with no economic value demonstrated that a home was functioning as it ought to.[43] It is in this period that the proper keeping of companion animals came to stand as a reliable indicator of good moral character and, in particular, a person's ability to care well for others.

Because of the connection between pet keeping and successful adult living, companion animals also came to assume an important place in the discourse of child development. Especially in the final two-thirds of the century, child-rearing authorities as well as regular citizens advocated pet keeping as a means of cultivating empathy, self-discipline, and other virtues. In an 1887 article in *Harper's Bazaar,* Thomas Wentworth Higginson writes, "A dog is of itself a liberal education, with its example of fidelity, unwearied activity, cheerful sympathy, and love stronger than death; nay, love that is triumphant over shame and ignominy and sin—influences that so often wear out human love or make it change to hate." He goes on to observe that "those petted dogs we see carried in the arms of young girls in fashionable equipages are rarely a substitute for the natural object of such emotion, they are rather a preparation or intermediate possession that precedes it; something that is more than a doll and less than a human child." After detailing the case of one such young lady, Higginson adds that "the care given by the young girl [to her dog] was simply the anticipated tenderness of a mother for her child."[44]

The argument Higginson advances was also presented visually in the countless images of children interacting with animals that appeared in periodicals, lithographs, children's books, and advertisements. In 1842 *Graham's Magazine* published one such image under the title "True Affection." At the center of the scene a neatly but not opulently dressed mother is seated on a sofa. With one arm, she embraces an infant daughter, who clings to the mother's neck, pressing her cheek to her mother's face. With the other arm, the mother embraces an older daughter, whose head rests against her mother's body. At the center of the scene, on the mother's lap, is a dog nestled in the arms of the older daughter, pressing its cheek to hers, and gazing with ardent devotion into the mother's face. In addition to reflecting the primacy in mid-nineteenth-century culture of the mother-child bond, "True Affection" expresses two ways that dogs were identified, in the second half of the nineteenth century, with feeling and virtue. On one hand, the feelings the people have for the dog tell us something about the feelings they have for other human beings. Their inclusion of the dog within their literal circle of affection testifies to their commitment to the affective priorities of home life rather than the economic principles of the market. In addition, the centrally positioned dog literally and figuratively links daughter and mother. While all four figures in the engraving are embracing one another, they actually form two parallel pairs, with the mother and infant's cheek-to-cheek embrace mirrored in that of the older daughter and dog. Thus, the positioning of the dog in this scene identifies this home as a place where feelings predominate and indicates

"True Affection," by E. T. Parris. Engraved by Rawdon, Wright, Hatch and Smillie and published in *Graham's Magazine* in December 1842. Courtesy of the American Antiquarian Society.

that this domestic pattern will be reproduced when the girl grows up to embrace her own daughter as she now embraces the dog—a message underscored by the fact that the dog looks to the cuddling mother and infant, his gaze pointing directly to the place where their faces meet.

By the end of the century, good parenting and good pet keeping became, in some contexts, nearly synonymous. In his childhood memoir entitled *A Boy I Knew, and Four Dogs* (1898), Laurence Hutton describes his juvenile self as "the friend and confidant of Four Dogs who have helped to humanize him for a quarter of a century and more." In Susanna Louise Patteson's *Pussy Meow: The Autobiography of a Cat* (1901), the book's central human character is a mother who considers pet keeping so important to her son's development that she willingly changes residence several times so that the family can keep its animals. "Many parents would have less cause to mourn over selfishness and ingratitude in their children," Patteson writes, "if they would set a more generous and unselfish example before them in their own treatment of dumb and helpless creatures."[45]

Perhaps the most stunning indicator of the importance assigned at this time to humans' custodial relations with animals is the American crusade to prevent cruelty to animals. The first society devoted to this cause was founded in Britain in 1824. Similar organizations did not appear in the United States until after the Civil War, for, as one contemporary supporter explained, "a reasonable people could not have listened to the claims of dumb animals while human beings, held in more ignoble bondage, were subjected to greater cruelty and added outrage."[46] Henry Bergh of New York City founded the nation's first animal welfare organization in 1866, and before the decade's end there were Societies for the Prevention of Cruelty to Animals (SPCAs) in Massachusetts, Pennsylvania, California, Illinois, and Minnesota. (Though Bergh named his organization the American Society for the Prevention of Cruelty to Animals, or ASPCA, it and most other SPCAs focused their activities on the city or region in which they were founded.) By 1879 an article in *Scribner's Monthly* magazine declared Bergh "a stalwart hero, a moral reformer worthy of an enlightened and practical epoch. This is easily said and maintained now that a denial of the beneficence of his work would be accepted by most persons as a confession of moral turpitude."[47]

Given the neglect of the animal protection movement in existing historiography, it is difficult to illustrate in a study not devoted exclusively to this topic the speed and force with which this cause pervaded American culture. But some idea can be gathered from a brief examination of the career of George Angell, one of the nineteenth century's most tireless and charismatic animal advocates. Immediately after charting the Massachusetts Society for the Prevention of Cruelty to Animals (MSPCA) in 1868, Angell conscripted more than one hundred of Boston's political, social, and intellectual elite to serve as its honorary vice presidents. He convinced the mayor and the chief of police to lend him, for three weeks, seventeen police officers whom he impressed into the duty of soliciting members and funds for the new organization. On June 2, 1868, Angell brought out 200,000 copies of the first issue of the MSPCA monthly *Our Dumb Animals* (a feat even more remarkable given that, as late as 1885, only four general monthly magazines had a circulation of more than 100,000). Thirty thousand of these were promptly distributed free of charge to "nearly every house in Boston" by police officers walking their beats. From that issue onward, thousands of complimentary copies were sent regularly to teachers' associations, school committees, school and university libraries, editors of periodicals, clergy, lawyers, public libraries, and hotel and steamboat reading rooms.[48] Like other SPCAs, the MSPCA had police powers that enabled it to enforce animal protection laws and arrest those who violated them. But "the prosecution of cruelists was only one branch, and not necessarily the most important, of its activities."[49] Like other reformers in this period, Angell regarded education as the surest means of effecting enduring social change. From the 1880s on, educational programs—particularly those aimed at children—became the center of Angell's attention.[50] In 1886, Angell's assiduous campaigning persuaded the Massachusetts Board of Education to incorporate humane education into the official school curriculum. In January 1890 alone, Angell "succeeded in having some thirty-six thousand compositions written on kindness to animals by the pupils of the Boston Grammar schools."[51] Unlike the leaders of other SPCAs, however, Angell had national and even international ambitions. Throughout the 1870s, '80s, and '90s Angell delivered lectures across the country, leaving a trail of new SPCAs in his wake. Not satisfied with this, Angell and some of New England's "most respected citizens" founded, in 1889, the American Humane Education Society (AHES) "to carry humane education for the prevention of every form of cruelty . . . into all our American schools and homes."[52] The AHES made inexpensive or free humane education materials available to teachers throughout the nation, and it fostered the formation of "Bands of Mercy," juvenile clubs whose members pledged "to be kind to all harmless living creatures, both human and dumb" and "to protect them from cruel usage."[53]

One factor facilitating the precipitous rise of the U.S. humane movement was increasing awareness (resulting in part from popular interest in anthropology and prehistory) that Western civilization could not have attained its current form without domesticated animals. Nathaniel Southgate Shaler, the dean of Harvard's Lawrence Scientific School, makes this point clearly in *Domesticated Animals: Their Relation to Man and to His Advancement in Civilization* (1895), which was written for a popular audience. Shaler acknowledges the tangible benefits of animal food, labor, and fiber, but he argues that the most important product of humans' custodial relationships with animals was the development of the psychological qualities essential to civilization. He writes: "Although no discreet person will venture to determine the relative weight which should be given to the influences which have made for civilization, there can be no doubt that the care of domesticated animals has been one of the most potent of these agents. Not only has this employment served to develop the motives of care-taking that result in the postponement of the momentary satisfaction of indolence or of hunger for the prospect of security or wealth to come, but it has served to arouse and broaden the sympathies given men, that humane spirit without which the best of our higher culture cannot be attained." Rather than limiting the salutary benefits of caring for animals to the prehistorical past, Shaler insists that "man's contact with the domesticated animals has been *and is ever to be* one of the most effective means whereby his sympathetic, his civilized motives may be broadened and affirmed" (emphasis added).[54]

Such ideas clearly inform the rhetorical strategies that enabled Angell and other humane leaders to generate support, membership, and funding for their organizations. In a speech delivered in 1869 (and reprinted several times over the following decades), Angell urged people to support the humane cause because its success or failure would mean "the difference between peace and war, national prosperity and national ruin."[55] When announcing the creation of the AHES in 1889, Angell declared, with his characteristic aplomb,

> The future historian will tell his readers that the most important discovery of the nineteenth century—more important than all discoveries in the art of war, all armor-clad vessels, all guns, fortifications and cannon—more important than all telegraph wires and all the applied powers of steam and electricity—more important than all prisons and penitentiaries—was the discovery of the simple fact that the tap roots of all wars and murders and cruelty and crime could be cut off by simply teaching and leading every child to seize every opportunity to say a kind word or do a kind act that should make some other human being or dumb creature happier; that on the continent of North America, in the city of Boston, on the 16th day of January 1889, was organized the first incorporated society in the world—The American Humane Education Society—for the specific object of awakening the world to the importance of this discovery.[56]

Elsewhere, Angell went so far as to suggest that kind interactions between children and animals could at least partially offset the deleterious effects of bad parenting:

> There are hundreds of thousands of parents among the depraved and criminal classes of this country, whom no child can be "taught to love," or ought to be. There are hundreds of thousands of homes where the name of the Almighty is never heard except in words of blasphemy. But there is not a child in one of those homes that may not be taught in our public schools to feed the birds, and pat the horses, and enjoy making happy all harmless creatures it meets on the street, and so be doing acts of kindness forty times a day, which will make it [the child] not only happier, but better and more merciful in all the relations of life.[57]

By the end of the nineteenth century, the daily practices that put people in contact with animals led to significant changes in the understanding of these animals' ontological status. In the late eighteenth century and early nineteenth century, even those books that urged compassionate treatment of animals or insisted that studying them was morally improving repeatedly stressed the absolute inferiority of animals to people.[58] Such beliefs became gradually more difficult to sustain over the next hundred years. New methods of animal training (such as the horsemanship methods discussed in chapter 1) rendered control invisible and produced animals that seemed to be not just self-regulating but even more malleable than humans to the forces of civilization. Once highly affective forms of pet keeping became widely sanctioned, these practices directed people's attention to their companion animals' inner lives. In this context, it grew increasingly easy for people to believe that the animals they encountered through these practices possessed or had the capacity to develop some of the intellectual, emotional, and moral qualities previously held to be exclusively human. The importance of pet keeping to the discourse of child development rested on the belief (reflected in the essay by Higginson quoted above) that companion animals—and especially the dog—exhibited the qualities parents wished to inculcate in their children. By the 1870s (as I explain in more detail in chapter 4), dogs came to be regarded not just as bona fide participants in scenes such as the one depicted in "True Affection," but possessors of the most genuine and durable feelings of all. As the century progressed, books and articles in the nation's most respected periodicals—including "Have Animals Souls?" (1856), "Are the Lower Animals Approaching Man?" (1887), and *Where Is My Dog? Or, Is Man Alone Immortal?* (1892)—challenged assumptions about human uniqueness with increasing intensity.[59]

This rising esteem for nonhuman animals coincided with growing disillusionment with human nature. In the decades after the Civil War, Americans perceived unprecedented levels of greed and self-interest in their now thoroughly urban, industrial, capitalist society. Indifferent to the wealth and prestige that increasingly stratified social relations, the animals people encountered in the built environment seemed to many to be more honest, more generous, more loyal—in short more civilized—than many of the people who lived there. By the end of the century, it became more and more common for writers to explicitly challenge if not the principle of linear gradation built into the Great Chain of Being, then at least placement of humans at its apex. Rush C. Hawkins described the stories contained in his 1896 volume *Better than Men* as evidence "that a certain select number of so-called lower animals [for Hawkins, horses, dogs, and elephants] are better, by nature and conduct, in certain elemental virtues, than men."[60] In the same year that Rush's volume appeared, Mark Twain composed a spirited essay arguing that human rather than nonhuman animals deserved the title "lower animals."[61] Thus, although animals such as horses and dogs came to be regarded as the best of nonhuman animals for the most anthropocentric of reasons, the practices valued and popularized on account of these anthropocentric notions led paradoxically to an eventual questioning of humans' absolute ascendancy over other forms of life.

The following chapters demonstrate in more detail how distinctions between "civilized" and wild creatures and the elevation of the former over the latter affected the material practices through which people interacted with animals as well as the contests for cultural power enacted in literary texts. I have adopted a literary historical methodology because historiography in this area always has been and continues to be buttressed by a particular reading of the American literary historical record (in which "American imagination" and "American literary imagination" have often functioned interchangeably), and thus the most effective way of complicating the existing critical paradigm is to approach it on its own terms.[62]

The book's methodology also reflects my interest in fostering conversation about the difficulties of fully relinquishing—in the humanities in general but in the discipline of literary studies especially—long-cherished notions about nature and culture. Certainly, few who work in cultural or critical theory today would disagree with the idea that, as William Cronon so lucidly puts it, although the nonhuman world obviously exists independently of our mental constructs, "the way we describe and understand that world is so entangled with our own values and assumptions that the two can never be fully separated."[63] But while we have become proficient in demonstrating the entanglements of the kind Cronon discusses, we are far less adept at thinking and writing about the entanglements that occur on the other side of the nature/culture divide. In other words, deconstruction of the nature/culture binary has largely taken the form of showing the first term to be always contaminated and shaped by the second—not the other way around. If poststructuralists in the humanities confidently assert that there is no "natural," they still feel quite certain that there is nonetheless such a thing as culture (no scare quotes around this word), whose features are, by definition, of entirely human design. For the most part what we study in the humanities continues to be conceived as a purely human realm of action, in which the nonhuman enters in the form of passive "matter" (imagined, historically, as feminine) onto which humans exert the shaping and animating force (imagined, historically, as masculine, and without which "nature" would remain homeostatic).[64] Though we have gradually come to accept the notion that the forces actively affecting this thing called "culture" might reside in biologically female as well as male bodies, most scholars remain deeply wedded to the belief that the final boundary beyond which this force cannot be extended is the boundary of the human.

In literary studies (with the exception of the growing but nonetheless delimited subfield of ecocriticism), analyzing the relationship between discourses of animality and literary texts has become coterminous with the theoretical sleight of hand that makes the body of the animal disappear under the smoke and mirrors of "deconstructing the natural." Thus, with Anna Sewell's 1877 animal welfare novel *Black Beauty*, for example, the ticket for admission to the critical conversation has become a scholar's ability to reveal the animal to be no more than a screen for some specifically human concern, such as gender or race.[65] Moves of this kind do not deconstruct the nature/culture binary; they merely switch the side being privileged. Just like claims to an unmediated access to nature made under the banner of objectivism, these arguments operate with an "either/or" and not a "both/and" between the terms "nature" and "culture."

One of my goals in writing this book has been to find a way of talking about both nonwild animals and literary texts in terms that acknowledge "culture" to be as tangled up with nature as "nature" is with culture. To that end, I have focused this study on literary texts that do not appear to be (in the common sense of the term) "about" animals and that were written by and about people who wanted not to escape civilized life but to obtain a modicum of power within it. My readings find people's beliefs about their affinities with the nonhuman world to be central, not ancillary, to the existing critical debates about the texts' cultural politics. However, my position is not just that we cannot understand the ideas about the human social order located in these texts unless we understand their authors' ideas about particular kinds of nonhuman animals; I am arguing that such ideas have been shaped by the presence of actual, animate nonhuman bodies that circulate in and co-create with us this thing we call culture. For me, examining "how the populace actually behaved" is concomitant with thinking about these behaviors as part of a dynamic interplay of human and nonhuman forces. Horsemanship, pet keeping, and animal protection were not merely fantastical dematerialized sets of ideas existing only in the realm of text and imagination; they were transmitted through and predicated upon interaction between human and animal bodies. Neither the obvious asymmetry of power that characterizes these interactions nor the impossibility of accessing a "real" animal essence unmediated by culture negates the active role that the animals themselves play in the creation and transmission of these discourses.[66]

Chapter 1 investigates Susan Warner's use of a newly emerging discourse of female equestrianism to illustrate the ability of horses and middle-class women to transcend a mere bodily existence. In recent criticism, arguments about whether domesticity in *The Wide, Wide World* (1850) empowered or disempowered women, and whether it was embraced or critiqued by Warner and her contemporaries, have been founded upon, or at least buttressed by, essentially figurative readings of horses and horsemanship. The interpretation of Ellen Montgomery's riding lessons as a metaphor for her disempowerment and the ubiquitous denunciation of John Humphreys as "brutal horse-beater," however, have little grounding in the nineteenth-century horsemanship on which Warner drew. Although for centuries horses in Western culture had been associated with human passions and horsemanship with their forcible domination, a combination of new methods for disciplining equines and new forms of recreational riding rendered the equine body, in the nineteenth century, discursively situated to communicate the internalized discipline and self-regulation that was necessary to make a human body middle class. Through horseback riding and other lessons, Ellen attains the particular mental-bodily development necessary for her to become a proper, sentimental, middle-class woman who is inserted into a network of power relations—a network in which Ellen attains power *over* other kinds of women who fail to meet the same standards.

The second chapter focuses on Nathaniel Hawthorne's novel *The Marble Faun* (1860), which after a period of long neglect has recently come to the center of the critical conversation about Hawthorne's racial politics. Governing much of this work is the notion that, by characterizing the racially other Donatello as a human-animal hybrid in *The Marble Faun* and by comparing a group of fleeing slaves to mythological fauns in "Chiefly about War Matters," Hawthorne constructed nonwhite people's cultural differences as permanent, genetic inferiorities. But these arguments about Hawthorne's articulation of race through animality have proceeded without any clear understanding of what Hawthorne understood animality to mean. My reading of the novel argues that *The Marble Faun*'s seemingly anachronistic worrying about the old theological *felix culpa* question is a timely and highly informed novelistic response to and bold, imaginative extension of the current scientific and social debates on the origin of species, the course of evolutionary history, and the uniqueness, supremacy, and security of humankind at the apex of creation. Seen through this historical lens, *The Marble Faun* works more to undo than uphold the logic of racial purity and insurmountable racial superiority, since here (and in "Chiefly about War Matters") aligning people with animals simultaneously marks their distance from norms of northeastern U.S. middle-class culture and their capacity to achieve them. My reading of *The Marble Faun* also problematizes our long history of treating Hawthorne as something of an odd man out among a group of writers passionately interested in the nonhuman world—that is, as the only one of the great architects of the American Renaissance that held the rearguard and not the vanguard of American thinking about nature. Because neither Hawthorne's preference for the comforts of the fireside over the travail of outdoor living nor his focus on animals that inhabited the human community could be assimilated under the conventional definition of nature writing, his interest in animals and the treatment of animality in his work have been largely ignored. But as my examination reveals, Hawthorne's encounters with and preference for civilized creatures actually propelled his thinking about human-animal connections along a trajectory that was in many ways far more radical than that of his wilderness-loving peers.

I am also interested in *The Marble Faun* for what it reveals about the history of evolutionary thought. Studies of late-nineteenth-century human-animal relationships have often considered how the growing acceptance of Darwin's theory of evolution affected the way people thought about and interacted with their animals. Here, I argue that we need to think about this question in the converse. Thus, I examine how people's interactions with animals affected the acceptance of evolutionary theories, Darwinian and otherwise. In the eighteenth century and through the early part of the nineteenth, the assertion that dogs were more similar to humans than were nonhuman primates was one of the strategies used to put out the fires of evolutionary thinking. However, in the nineteenth-century, developments in beliefs about dogs' closeness to humans—generated in large part by the increasingly affective nature of people's relationships with companion animals—eventually shifted the effects of this belief, so that rather than refuting the theory of evolution, ideas about canine nature came to facilitate its acceptance. The case of Hawthorne and *The Marble Faun* provides one illustration of why and how this was so and suggests that nineteenth-century beliefs about dogs and other companion animals did as much if not more than studies of nonhuman primates to facilitate acceptance of the theory of species transformation.

Chapter 3 argues that Harriet Beecher Stowe's theory of "animal nature"—as it applied to humans and nonhumans alike—constitutes an important context for understanding the racial and gender politics of her work. Rejecting her contemporaries' dichotomized views on environment and inheritance, Stowe asserts that humans, like all animals, were products of *both* nature and nurture. Drawing jointly on the rhetorics of natural history (which emphasized animals' innate natures) and the humane movement (which emphasized animals' positive responses to proper treatment), Stowe develops a vocabulary for defending women's and children's efforts at self-determination, confounding contemporary antimiscegenation and antiassimilation arguments, and teaching her readers that the survival of the nation, like the survival of the family, depends upon the recognition and respect of difference.

In chapter 4, I argue that we cannot comprehend fully the arguments Charles Chesnutt makes about race—in "The Bouquet" (1899), "The Passing of Grandison" (1899), and *The Marrow of Tradition* (1901), among other texts—without understanding how those texts assume an audience well trained in and receptive to the discourse of animal protection. In existing historiography, scholars have framed the issue of animal protection in terms that suggest that African Americans were at best indifferent to or most likely strongly alienated by this cause. However, examination of Chesnutt's writing reveals that his understanding of contemporary animal politics and their relation to issues of racial justice differ radically from what existing critical approaches lead us to expect. For Chesnutt, the fantastic successes of the humane movement opened up new possibilities for intervention into the discourse of white supremacy. First, Chesnutt redeployed contemporary ideas about the superiority of canine virtue in the service of his antiracist agenda, creating an ostensibly race-neutral platform for arguing racism to be unnatural as well as immoral. Second, he used contemporary ideas about canine nature to rearticulate black masculinity in terms that transcended the logic of white supremacist discourse, which insistently placed black men in one of two equally undesirable positions—that of the white man's servile best friend or that of the dangerous and undomesticatable brute beast. Finally, Chesnutt capitalized upon the then-widespread belief in the national implications of the humane cause to argue that the outbreaks of violence against African Americans deployed to suppress their civil rights were not just discrete cases of horrible injustice but rather a real threat to the interests of all Americans and even to the continuation of civilization itself.

Once we take seriously those human-animal interactions that took place within the built environment and were strongly "sentimental" or affective in nature, we see that a wide range of authors typically excluded from studies of literature and nature were actively participating in contemporary debates about humans' connection to the nonhuman world. But by now it should be clear that I am not so much trying to direct attention to "voices on the margins" as I am suggesting that the voices I analyze were not nearly so marginal as previous theories have led us to believe. A reexamination of the historical record reveals that, indeed, many of the key figures in the critical paradigm focused on wild nature were in their own lifetimes noted for their affectionate interest in and efforts on behalf of civilized creatures. An 1853 book on wilderness painter Thomas Cole mentions approvingly that he possessed an "extreme tenderness of heart" that manifested itself in "fondness for domestic animals."[67] The century's most prominent spokesperson for nature, Ralph Waldo Emerson, became one of the MSPCA's honorary vice presidents. Mark Twain—who has become so closely identified with Huck's disdain for civilization that a recent book on his influence on American culture bears the title *Lighting Out for the Territory*[68]—wrote animal stories that attacked vivisection, bullfighting, and other animal cruelties and argued that animals, like humans, possessed an immortal soul. (One of these, "A Dog's Tale," was published by the National Antivivisection Society.)[69] Senator George Graham Vest's support for the formation of Yellowstone and other national parks has been frequently cited in recent studies as evidence of the widespread desire to "return to nature."[70] But to his own contemporaries, Vest was best known not for his efforts at conservation, but for his role as the lawyer for the plaintiff, in 1870, in a suit to bring dog-killer Leonidas Hornsby to justice. In his closing argument (which I discuss in more detail in chapter 4), Vest made no reference to Hornsby or his act but instead delivered an extended and emotional encomium for the dog, which William Safire recently described as not only a "sentimental" speech but "the best I can find of its kind." "Swallow hard and read it aloud, standing up, to your family," Safire challenges, "there won't be a dry eye in the house."[71] The speech, which was reprinted in newspapers throughout the United States, turned Vest into a national hero and launched his political career. The animal protection cause was also supported by Henry O. Houghton, whose firm Houghton Mifflin and Company published many of the traditionally canonized U.S. writers and did more than any other publisher to invent and popularize the genre of nature writing.[72] In 1889 Houghton cofounded (along with George Angell and four others) the American Humane Education Society; he subsequently became treasurer of the organization and served for the rest of his life on its board of directors. Shortly before his death, he offered to contribute $1,000 toward the erection of new headquarters for the MSPCA.[73]

The Columbia Guide to American Environmental History summarizes nineteenth-century environmental history as follows: "The advancing market not only devastated nature, but also stirred a widespread hunger for an emotionally compelling spirituality and connectedness that the competitive ethic of profit and loss could not satisfy. For much of the market world's new middle classes, this hunger focused on nature." This claim is followed with the conventional panoply of midcentury nature lovers—James Fenimore Cooper, the transcendentalists, the Hudson River painters—and then the assertion that "when, at century's end, peaking assaults on nature finally aroused a conservationist majority, it would draw inspiration from the tradition of Thoreau and Cole."[74] In proceeding this way, *The Columbia Guide* reproduces the same move made in Nash's *Wilderness and the American Mind* (1967) and virtually all other histories of America's love affair with wild nature: they treat Thoreau as representative of the self that America wanted to be and then slide from Thoreau in the 1850s to the conservation and other wilderness-oriented activities that did not gain a solid purchase in American culture until the turn of the century. Without a doubt, people living in the period between 1850 and 1900 did appreciate wild nature, but to satisfy that "widespread hunger" for an "emotionally compelling spirituality" and a sense of "connectedness" to that which was beyond the human, they turned—in greater numbers and with a greater intensity—to the nonhuman creatures with whom they interacted in the course of their daily urban and suburban lives.

In *Nature's Nation,* Miller speculated, "Probably John Jacob Astor and the builders of railroads gave little thought to the healing virtues of the forests and swamps they were defiling" (201). However, Astor did (along with Horace

Greeley, George Bancroft, and Mayor Hoffman) give enough thought to the healing virtues of humans' quotidian interactions with animals to sign his name to the document that founded the ASPCA and affirmed "the duty of protecting animals from cruelty."[75] By the time the Sierra Club was making its fledgling start in 1892, every major U.S. city and quite a few small towns had a society for the prevention of cruelty to animals. The organizations that promoted hiking, bicycling, and hunting followed by more than half a century the ideas about the morally improving effects of recreational equestrianism that led to the still-undisturbed place of horsemanship at the institutions founded for the education of women. The first bill protecting wild animals (the Lacey Act, designed to curtail the slaughter of birds for the millinery trade) passed in 1900—seven years after the Washington State legislature outlawed vivisection in all state schools and colleges except those training doctors and dentists; six years after George Angell convinced the Massachusetts legislature to prevent the display of vivisection or dissection in the state's public schools; and four years after Senator James McMillan of Michigan introduced a bill that would regulate animal experimentation in the District of Columbia, which one contemporary described as "perhaps the center of animal experimentation in this country at the present moment."[76] On April 28, 1899, a regional meeting of Bands of Mercy held in Kansas City attracted "not less than twenty-five thousand children and ten thousand adults."[77] In 1900, the founding of the Boy Scouts of America was still a decade away; by that same year, AHES efforts had resulted in the creation of 40,000 Bands of Mercy, whose members numbered between one and two million.[78]

At this point, my arguments raise two compelling questions: If not at the time and for the reasons that we have long assumed, then when and why did wilderness-oriented activities become the dominant mode of obtaining morally improving contact with nonhuman nature? Given the enormous scrutiny extended to the subjects of not only nonhuman nature but also social reform by academics over the past hundred years, why has the history I am telling about the nineteenth century not previously been told? These questions deserve to be answered in far more detail than I can provide in this book. I will attempt nonetheless to offer a brief overview of what would constitute a fuller answer to these questions in the conclusion. At the beginning of the last century, a growing number of Americans came to believe that the nation's salvation depended on saving the wilderness from destruction, rather than saving animals from cruelty. This apostasy happened precisely at the time when it became clear that saving the nature with which we regularly had contact would pose a much more formidable obstacle to economic and technosocial development than saving the nature with which no humans (or at least no white humans) interacted. The completeness of the erasure from our official history of the nineteenth-century discourses related to feelings for and the feelings of this urban and suburban animal population speaks both to the cultural power of the economic, political, and scientific interests behind the substitution I have just described—and to our own anxieties about existing relations between human and nonhuman animals which, by virtue of our existence in the late-capitalist social order, we cannot but be complicit.

Animal Bodies

Corporeality, Class, and Equestrianism in Susan Warner's *The Wide, Wide World*

> *Sep. 13th, 1850.* Have just, that is this evening, returned from my second riding lesson [with neighbor W. T. Sprole]. My first left me in a high state of excitement and delight—nothing for a very long time indeed so fired my imagination—and soon I was feverish with the desire to finish so enormous a pleasure. . . . My little book [*The Wide, Wide World*] is just going to press, and Anna [Warner]'s "Reminiscences" has been offered to Appleton. . . . Two delicious pieces of good news—two mercies to be thankful for—and yet this horseback riding did more [to] elate my imagination than they both.
>
> Susan Warner, journal

In 1978 Nina Baym casually noted that at a young age Susan Warner "developed a passion for riding horses, a characteristic of all her heroines."[1] Since then, analyses of horsemanship in *The Wide, Wide World* (1850) have played an increasingly central role in readings of the novel. Most essays published in the past two decades, however, focus not on the pleasure Ellen finds in riding but rather on the negative psychological consequences of her equestrianism.[2] Critics read Ellen's riding lessons as violent, dehumanizing "lessons in submission."[3] Her entire education, insists G. M. Goshgarian, is figuratively "and not fortuitously, a matter of riding."[4] John Humphreys "educates himself a wife," Joanne Dobson writes, "much in the same way as he would break a horse."[5] In these analyses, Ellen and horses are linked by their experiences of abuse and oppression.[6]

Although critics disagree about the gains, losses, and overall success of Ellen's educational program,[7] they unanimously equate "healthy" subject formation with a return to a natural, animal, passionate self, and link "oppressive" subject formation with the societal manipulation of that self. (Ironically, this position recalls that of Leslie Fiedler, R. W. B. Lewis, and other critics of the 1950s and 1960s whose nineteenth-century American literary canon feminist critics have been so interested in refuting.) According to Goshgarian, John's hands "seiz[e] the reins of a plot against Ellen's passion"; he "rides the female animal *in* her"; what he curbs in her is "woman's animal passion."[8] Critics insist that as Ellen becomes more docile and less "animal"—through her education that includes and is figured by riding lessons—she also becomes less herself.[9]

Equally at issue in the critical literature is the horsemanship of John Humphreys, as the interpretation of Ellen's riding lessons as disempowering depends in part upon the now ubiquitous denunciation of her riding instructor and eventual husband as a "brutal horse-beater."[10] The violence of John's horsemanship has become central to debates about *The Wide, Wide World*'s position on domesticity. Jane Tompkins maintains that the novel supports domestic ideology, which—while distasteful to today's readers—offered nineteenth-century women forms of spiritual power in a world that gave them few modes of recourse. John's "prowess as a horse-beater," Tompkins suggests, offered readers one more reason to regard female intimacy of the domestic sphere as the much better "alternative to the brutal sexuality embodied in [Ellen's] male masters."[11] Other critics cite John's horse-beating as proof that Warner (and her readers) critiqued and subverted domesticity.[12] John's propensity for equine abuse, critics suggest, undermines the legitimacy of the patriarchal authority invested in him—and it connects him to Saunders, the villain who, in one of the most traumatic scenes in the novel, whips Ellen's pony the Brownie in order to cause Ellen distress.

Plaguing these critical debates about female power in the novel—and plaguing the readings of horsemanship as well—is a flattening of "women," "animals," and the connections between them. Even those studies most focused on riding deploy essentially figurative readings of horses and equestrianism, making little connection with the actual practices and meanings of horsemanship in nineteenth-century America. Treating "women" as a monolithic group and making no distinctions among the discursive functions of animal bodies, these arguments advance reductive theories about connections between "horses" and "women."[13]

Facing page

Title page from a British edition of *The Wide, Wide World* (London: T. Nelson and Sons, 1853), featuring Ellen Montgomery riding her pony. "Elizabeth Wetherell" is the pseudonym under which Warner first published her best-selling novel. Courtesy of the University of Delaware, Newark, Delaware.

Once off and away on the docile and spirited little animal, over
The roads, through the lanes, up and down the hills, her pony her
Only companion, but having the most perfect understanding with
Him, both Ellen and the Brownie cast care to the winds.
Page 481.

T. NELSON AND SONS LONDON AND EDINBURGH.

Reading *The Wide, Wide World* in the context of a newly forming nineteenth-century discourse of female equestrianism, I argue that understanding Ellen's development and relative empowerment/powerlessness depends upon a rigorous consideration of the construction and class politics of animal "nature." Ellen's subject formation is a process of continual negotiation of particular kinds of equine metaphors and equestrian experiences that became available to Warner and her audience as a result of changing views on female education, women's recreation, recreational horseback riding, and the nature of the middle-class woman. Through horseback riding and other lessons, Ellen attains the particular mental and bodily development necessary for her to become a proper, sentimental middle-class woman who is inserted in a network of power relations—a network in which Ellen attains power *over* other kinds of women who fail to meet the standards that she does.

The Equine Body, the Human Body, and the Body Politic

As a cursory survey of art and literature will evidence, women have been riding horses for centuries even though horsemanship remained—until relatively recently—a characteristically male pursuit. At work in Warner's novel, however, are specifically nineteenth-century female equestrian practices and politics that can be understood only in relation to a larger, historically male tradition of horsemanship.[14] Thus, before I turn to *The Wide, Wide World,* I want to spend some time discussing the history of equestrian cultural politics.

In 1560 Thomas Blundeville, in *The Arte of Ryding and Breakinge Greate Horses,* recommended the following corrective for a mount that refuses to go forward: "Let a footman stand behind you with a shrewed Catte tyed at the one ende of a long pole with her belye upwarde, so as shee maye haue her mouth & clawes at liberty. And when your horse doth stay or go backward, let him thrust the Catte between his thyes so as she may scratche and bite him, somtime by the thighs, somtime by the rompe, and often times by the stones."[15] Like the description of Damiens' torture and execution with which Foucault begins *Discipline and Punish,* Blundeville's punishment elicits repulsion and incredulity from a modern reader.[16] As horrific as these systems of corporal punishment may seem now, in the Renaissance they constituted the acceptable method of controlling equine bodies as well as human ones. Renaissance horsemen saw horsemanship as the "art" of imposing physical control over their mounts. Consequently, Renaissance equine manuals debate the techniques and mechanics of physical coercion. They provide detailed descriptions of various ways of manipulating the reins or applying the long and pointed spur, and they offer blueprints for complex bits that were sharp enough to split open the tongue, gums, and cheeks and strong enough to break the jaw. As John Astley notes in *The Art of Riding* (1584), horses "with rawe noses, bloudie mouthes and sides, with their curbed places galled, turning their bodies one waie, & their heads another waie" were a common sight in sixteenth-century London.[17] While Astley and other contemporaries condemned the brutality that produced such gruesome results, their recommendations always pertained to the *degree* of force to be used; they never challenged the belief that horsemanship was centered on the infliction and cessation of physical discomfort.

Indeed, according to Renaissance beliefs about equine nature, physical bondage was the only way to control equine behavior, as horses were closely linked to passion and the gratification of baser drives.[18] In Shakespeare's *Venus and Adonis* (1593), the lusty goddess advises Adonis to act like his "strong-neck'd steed," who upon seeing "A breeding jennet, lusty, young, and proud, / . . . Breaketh his rein, and to her straight goes he. / Imperiously he leaps, he neighs, he bounds, / And now his woven girths he breaks asunder; / . . . The iron bit he crusheth 'tween his teeth, / Controlling what he was controlled with."[19] External implements of physical bondage (and weak ones at that) are all that stand between the passionate horse and the object of his desire.

The focus on the infliction and withdrawal of pain in Renaissance horsemanship stands in stark contrast to the mystical and affective connections between horse and human currently celebrated in American culture (in "horse whisperer" figures and child-wins-the-heart-of-wild-stallion narratives). But my point here is not merely that we have supplanted physical, punishment-based methodologies of horsemanship with more psychologically oriented ones in a way that parallels Western civilization's move from punishment to discipline of human subjects. Rather, I wish to argue that the technologies and the very actions of controlling horses have always been and continue to be integrated—metaphorically, temporally, and physically—with those that control humans, and vice versa.

In both Western and non-Western cultures, horsemanship originated as a technology of war.[20] The very term "horseman" derives from the word for the mounted soldier. In the fifteenth century, however, riding became an important recreational practice. As the heavily armored knight ceased to be a military asset, tournaments designed to test his skill were gradually transformed into occasions of aristocratic display. Eventually tournaments were succeeded by "a sort of pageant in which gentlemen in fancy-dress tilted at rings, or at the quintain, took part in stately musical rides and performed various feats of horsemanship not in combat but in display, parade, or procession."[21] The cavalry manual of the Greek general Xenophon, like other classical texts, became a site of renewed interest, and French riding masters elaborated on his system of classical equitation to create *haute école* or *manège* riding. In the *manège,* or riding arena, movements created for the battlefield were refined and encoded into a system of training formulated to develop the horse gymnastically and to display the aristocratic rider's control over his horse. *Manège* movements included extended and collected gaits, lateral movements, and "airs above ground"—controlled kicks, rears, and leaps. Many young courtiers obtained tutelage in these complex equestrian maneuvers at elite riding academies such as the one established by Antoine de Pluvinel in 1594, which offered instruction not only in riding but in literature, poetry, painting, and music as well.[22] Others learned from a growing number of books that addressed "horsemanship for gentlemen."[23] In the preface to *The Art of Riding* Astley proclaims that his book is for "euerie one that is desirous to be a professor, or at least a practiser of this Art (as the whole companie of valorous young Gentlemen ought to be)."[24] No longer just a component of military training, horsemanship became the highest of masculine courtly accomplishments.

Yet when the aristocrat's horses became vehicles for recreation, they did not cease to function as military vehicles. Even, and perhaps especially, beyond the realm of military combat, horsemanship remained a battleground for competing class interests. "It may be," Foucault writes in *Discipline and Punish,* "that war as strategy is a continuation of politics. But it must not be forgotten that 'politics' has been conceived as a continuation, if not exactly and directly of war, at least of the military model as a fundamental means of preventing civil disorder" (168). *Manège* pageantry certainly afforded the aspiring nobleman an opportunity to impress his peers, but the movements perfected in the ring were also taken into the public streets, producing a spectacle that emphasized the power connected to the aristocrat and absent in the observing commoner. As Sir William Hope asks in *The Complete Horseman* (1696), "What Prince or Monarch looks more great or more enthron'd, than upon a beautiful Horse with rich Furniture, and waving Plumes, making his Entry through great Cities, to amaze the People with Pleasure and Delight?"[25] On display before the masses, the aristocrat's highly trained mount yielded to the power of bit, spur, and whip. Like the figure of the king, the spectacle of the mounted aristocrat crystallized the embodied nature of punishment. In both cases, not only is power understood to be physical, but it also becomes located in the body of the rider/king.

Concurrent with the development of technologies of postcorporal discipline for humans in the eighteenth and nineteenth centuries, authorities on horse training began advocating less physical methods of controlling equine bodies. "The hopes of recompense," wrote Richard Berenger in *The History and Art of Horsemanship* (1771), "have as great an influence over the understanding of the animal, as the fear of punishment."[26] Rather than developing strategies to control the horse physically, writers in this period tried to devise methods that would make the horse self-regulating. While Renaissance equestrian masters sought out more complex or ostentatious methods of physical control, their nineteenth-century successors endeavored to make control invisible.[27] In 1860, horse trainer A. H. Rockwell went so far as to develop a "mode of driving without reins." After witnessing Rockwell "turning, stopping, and starting" his reinless horses "with perfect success" in a May 1865 exhibition at the Dubois Track, a reporter from the *New York Tribune* wrote that Rockwell had "demonstrated to the persons assembled, the great superiority of mental power to that of physical." Compare Blundeville's recommendation for recalcitrant mounts with the following cure for equine aggression offered by Rockwell in *The Improved and Practical System of Educating the Horse* (1872): "If the colt crowds you upon entering the stall, you will, as you enter, gently caress him, proceeding to assure him he is not being hurt, avoiding any loud or sharp words, and feeding him from your hand."[28]

It is important to note that while they were written in the age of rising interest in animal protection and welfare, most nineteenth-century equestrian manuals advocate less physical means of controlling the horse not because they were less abusive but because they were more effective. Colonel J. C. Battersby carefully distinguishes between "subduing" and "taming" the horse (the former a process of breaking the animal's spirit through torture). This distinction, he explains in *The Bridle Bits: A Treatise on Practical Horsemanship* (1886), amounts to the difference between "an exhibition of physical vs. moral power over the horse." But Battersby's rhetoric remains firmly rooted in utilitarian principles: "by proper mouthing, training, use and treatment [the horse] can be made all the more serviceable, and at the same time more agreeable to his rider or driver in the performance of his work."[29] As Foucault observes, "The elegance of the discipline lay in the fact that it could dispense with this costly and violent relation by obtaining effects of utility at least as great" (137). The modern system of horse management is a nearly perfect manifestation of disciplinary control. Trained in this system, equine bodies are docile bodies.

Inextricably tied to paradigmatic shifts in horse training are revolutions in the practices of recreational riding that situated horsemanship to serve middle-class rather than aristocratic interests. The social role of riding underwent dramatic changes in England in the latter part of the eighteenth century as cross-country riding supplanted *manège* riding as the preferred form of recreational equestrianism. As Anthony Dent explains: "The mid-18th century may well be taken as the end of the supremacy of the High Horse, ridden in a spectacular, highly accurate, and above all, dignified manner by masters of the art and their upper-crust pupils. . . . In my view, the reason for British rejection of this aspect of European court culture was in essence political. Dressage was tinged with its association with absolute monarchy."[30] Although today many associate foxhunting with social elitism, in the eighteenth century the popularization of foxhunting and other forms of cross-country riding constituted a move to a more (though by no means thoroughly) democratic recreational equestrianism. Participation did not require an expensive, specially bred, and highly trained horse, or years of instruction at costly (aristocratic) riding schools. While Renaissance equine manuals attracted aristocratic cognoscenti interested in the finer points of equine control, the nineteenth-century trade in horse books flourished by targeting the expanding population of middle-class riders. Thomas Wise's 1782 edition of *The Newest Young Man's Companion* offered instruction in a number of skills required "to qualify Persons for Business without the Help of a Master," including letter writing, arithmetic, bookkeeping, geography, painting, and "The Management of Horses."[31] In his aptly named *Practical Horsemanship* (1850), Harry Hieover accedes that if people call his book "the hornbook of horsemanship—be it so. If it teaches A B C to those who did not know as much before, it will quite answer my purpose, and I sincerely hope it may theirs."[32]

With its emphasis on the psychological discipline that increasingly defined middle-class power formations in general and domesticity in particular, this new equestrianism (unlike the earlier traditions) no longer conflicted with prevailing definitions of femininity, and throughout the early nineteenth century riding rapidly gained popularity as a feminine accomplishment. Also facilitating women's entrance into recreational riding were eighteenth-century improvements in saddle construction. Riding for genteel women had always been problematic because codes of decorum proscribed the parting of female legs as well as the straddling of large objects. Riding astride—as the Wife of Bath is pictured in the Ellesmere Manuscript—marked a woman as unrefined or unchaste. For women living before the eighteenth century, "riding" most often meant sitting sideways on a pillion, or cushion—a position from which controlling the horse was impossible and merely staying aboard was difficult. Seated thus, a woman could ride only smooth horses at slow speeds; for control she depended on a man who either sat in front of her or led her horse while riding his own. Recognizing the limitations of riding sideways, avid horsewoman Catherine de' Medici invented the precursor to the modern sidesaddle in the sixteenth century. Her design enabled the rider's body to face the direction of travel while both legs remained on the same side of the horse; the right knee hooked around a horn to provide stability, and the left foot rested in a stirrup. In the late eighteenth century saddlers improved on Medici's design significantly, making the sidesaddle rider's experience more comfortable and her position more secure—which in turn enabled longer rides, over rougher terrain, at faster paces.[33]

The rise of female equestrianism certainly depended upon these improvements in sidesaddle construction, but such technological advances could have occurred only in a climate in which riding and femininity were increasingly seen as compatible. In addition to affecting who rode and how, new theories of equestrianism occasioned a radical change in the way equine bodies functioned discursively. Although in the Renaissance the equine body was associated with the passion and recklessness of the human body, in the nineteenth century a combination of new methods for disciplining equines and new forms of recreational riding rendered the equine body discursively situated to communicate the internalized discipline and self-regulation that was necessary to make a human body middle class. For Warner, female equestrianism in particular opened up new possibilities for imagining affinities between horses and domestic women.

Docile Bodies

Cows, birds, sheep, pigs, dogs—*The Wide, Wide World* teems with animal bodies, many of which resist or refuse human control. When Timothy the ox repeatedly infiltrates and plunders Aunt Fortune's garden—despite her stick flailing—Fortune curses his "lawless behaviour."[34] And though a welcome member of the Humphreys' household, the cat Captain Parry routinely defies humans' wishes. Named after the hero of an adventure tale, Parry shuns visitors—and even the Humphreys when he is in the mood. Nothing Alice does can prevent him from following her and Ellen the entire way to Mrs. Vawse's, and the burden of his company on the return trip causes them to become lost in a winter storm. The cat first appears in the novel as he breaks social convention: driven by his bodily hunger, Parry jumps onto Alice's cooking table and "plant[s] his paw directly in the middle of one of his mistress's cakes" (168). Alice tries to nudge him off with her elbow, but he refuses to move, "having evidently no notion that he was not just where he ought to be" (168).

But close analysis of animal corporeality in the novel reveals that all animal bodies are not created equal. As a function of the nineteenth-century discourse of horsemanship based on internalized discipline, equines in *The Wide, Wide World* are animals that possess the distinct capacity for self-regulation. Like the horses described in nineteenth-century training manuals, those in Warner's novel exhibit discipline that results from psychological intimacy.[35] The Humphreys' horse Prince Charlie, for example, "was a fine spirited grey that scarcely ever needed to be touched with the whip; at a word of encouragement from his driver he would toss his head and set forward with new life, making all the bells jingle again" (280). But the most pronounced example of equine self-control is Ellen's pony the Brownie, who in his initial appearance "stood as quiet as a lamb, whether Thomas held him or not" (374). The Brownie does not need to be controlled through force or physical restraint because he is self-regulating. The epitome of a docile body, the trained equine body offers itself up as a trope for the middle-class human body. Yet the figurative function of horsemanship remains permanently saddled with material reality. Humans do not gain self-mastery by being figured as horses but by becoming actual riders. At the same time that it transports the human body from one location to another, the horse becomes a vehicle for the human subject's production through and reproduction of technologies of discipline.

Ellen's development in *The Wide, Wide World* tracks onto the way she is figured through equine metaphor. As a result, in part, of becoming a horsewoman, Ellen is transformed from a young, defiant, untrained horse into a fully trained, docile, self-regulating equine. Before she meets John (i.e., for roughly the first third of the novel), little Ellen is figured as a young horse in need of training:

> With a wild cry she flung her arms round her mother, and hiding her face in her lap, gave way to a violent burst of grief that seemed for a few moments as if it would rend soul and body in twain. For her passions were by nature very strong, and by education very imperfectly controlled; and time, "that rider that breaks youth," had not as yet tried his hand upon her. (11)

> she was a child of very high spirit and violent passions, untamed at all by sorrow's discipline; and in proportion violent was the tempest excited by this first real trial. (63)

Ellen remains in this state, however, only as long as she remains ignorant of horsemanship. When Ellen fails to appease Aunt Fortune with a half-hearted apology, the narrator comments:

> Strong passion—strong pride,—both long unbroken; and Ellen had yet to learn that many a prayer and many a tear, much watchfulness, much help from on high, must be hers before she could be thoroughly dispossessed of these evil spirits. But she knew her sickness; she had applied to the Physician;—she was in a fair way to be well. (181)

Two paragraphs later, as she travels to church with Alice, Ellen receives her first lesson in horsemanship.

As Ellen's education progresses, she ceases to be described as a wild colt. Once on her way to being an educated woman and accomplished rider, she is figured as a docile equine who responds to voice alone. Since Ellen's equestrian training is rooted in the principles of psychologically oriented, nineteenth-century equestrian discipline (rather than a Renaissance horsemanship based on physical and violent coercion), the associations between her riding lessons and her general educational program signify its inherently nonviolent nature.

Furthermore, Ellen's riding lessons serve more than an ancillary function to her development. Some recent scholars of sentimental fiction have argued that nineteenth-century education reformers made a strong case for physical, as opposed to mental, development. Supporting this viewpoint, Lora Romero writes, "the advice offered time and again in educational treatises in the early nineteenth century [is that] more emphasis should be placed upon the cultivation of the juvenile body and less upon the development of the juvenile mind."[36] I find the advice offered by these treatises to take a subtly yet significantly different form. Nineteenth-century education writers do not so much argue for more or less attention to either the body or the mind as they rigorously insist on the complete inseparability of bodily and mental development. In 1836 Charles Butler wrote in *The American Lady:* "So intimate is the connexion, so general the sympathy, between the body and the mind, that the vigour of the former seems not only to remove obstacles to the operations of the latter, but even to communicate to its powers an accession of strength."[37]

Catharine Beecher and Harriet Beecher Stowe also shared this concern. In their widely adopted *Principles of Domestic Science . . . A Text-Book for the Use of Young Ladies in Schools, Seminaries, and Colleges,*[38] recommendations for exercise appear, significantly, in the chapter entitled "Health of Mind": "There is such an intimate connection between the body and mind that the health of one can not be preserved without proper care of the other. . . . In exhibiting the causes which injure the health of the mind, we shall find them to be partly physical, partly intellectual, and partly moral" (222). Beecher and Stowe recommend that "whenever any mind is oppressed with care, anxiety, or sorrow, the amount of active exercise in the fresh air should be greatly increased, that the action of the muscles may withdraw the blood which, in such seasons, is constantly tending too much to the brain" (224). Further, they insist that "every college and professional school, and every seminary for young ladies, needs a medical man or woman, not only to lecture on physiology and the laws of health, but empowered by official capacity to investigate the case of every pupil, and, by authority, to enforce such a course of study, exercise, and repose as the physical system requires" (225). The system of education that Warner illustrates in *The Wide, Wide World* follows the precepts of her contemporaries:

> John walked at her bridle; so kind in his care of her, so pleasant in his talk to her, teaching her how to sit in the saddle and hold the reins and whip, and much more important things too, that Ellen thought a pleasanter thing could not be than to ride so. After that they took a great many rides, borrowing Jenny's pony or some other, and explored the beautiful country far and near. And almost daily John had up Sharp and gave Ellen a regular lesson. (341)

> She wrote [John], however, when he had been gone a few weeks, that his will seemed to carry all before it, present or absent. Ellen went on steadily mending; at least she did not go back any. They were keeping up their rides, also their studies, most diligently; Ellen was untiring in her efforts to do whatever he had wished her, and was springing forward, Alice said, in her improvement. (353)

Ellen's equestrian and intellectual educations are conceptually, and temporally, integrated.

Equal to if not more important than the need for bodily exercise for girls, however, was the need to ensure that it was carried out in a certain way. As Butler explains in *The American Lady,* dancing was "an amusement in itself both innocent and salubrious, and therefore by no means improper, under suitable regulations," yet when unsupervised young ladies frequent the ballroom it could excite "sensations of vanity as to personal appearance," thus becoming very problematic indeed (105). Butler stresses the importance of *appropriate* exercise and other pastimes, explaining, "Conscientious vigilance to avoid an improper choice of amusements, and an undue sacrifice of time to them, is a duty of great importance . . . because, by the nature of the engagements in which the hours of leisure and relaxation are employed, the manners, the dispositions, and the whole character, are materially affected" (94).

Similarly, Beecher and Stowe insist that "occupations must be sought which exercise the muscles and interest the mind; and thus the equal action of both kinds of nerves is secured. This shows why exercise is so much more healthful and invigorating when the mind is interested, than when it is not" (105). The success of bodily exercise for girls depends upon its having an integral mental component.

According to many authorities, horseback riding, more than any other form of exercise, facilitated the mental and physical development necessary to make a female body desirable according to middle-class standards. Books on female equestrianism began appearing in Britain in the early nineteenth century. In *The Young Horsewoman's Compendium to the Modern Art of Riding* (1827), Edward Stanley declares a "knowledge of the Art of Horsemanship . . . essential in a Lady's education."[39] Similarly, *The Young Lady's Equestrian Manual* (1838) maintains that riding is "one of the most graceful, agreeable, and salutary of feminine recreations. No attitude, perhaps, can be regarded as more elegant than that of a lady in the modern side-saddle; nor can any exercise be deemed capable of affording more rational and innocent delight, than that of the female equestrian."[40] By the 1830s, these same views began appearing in the United States in the magazine press. An article called "The Exercise of Riding" that appeared in the *American Magazine of Useful and Entertaining Knowledge* in 1835 proclaimed that, for women who "have lost their health" or "become somewhat debilitated from the long neglect of a proper measure of exercise, *riding on horseback* is probably the best employment which can be resorted to."[41] Within a few decades, Americans began producing monographs as well as articles on recreational equestrianism. In 1878, Ghislani Durant, "MD, Ph.D., member of the American Medical Association, Fellow of the New York Academy of Medicine; Member of the Medical Society of the country of New York, etc., etc.," devoted an entire volume to the praise of riding's merits. In *Horse-Back Riding from a Medical Point of View,* he recommends riding "in preference to any other form of exercise" because "it influences the mental and moral nature to a greater extent than any other."[42]

By the time Warner was writing her novel, literature on female equestrianism was readily available. Between July and December of 1848 (the year that Warner began *The Wide, Wide World*) the popular *Godey's Lady's Book* ran a six-installment feature titled "Hints on Equestrianism for the Fair Sex," written by the "Well Known Lady Equestrian" Mrs. J. Stirling Clarke.[43] Clarke writes that "twenty years ago, or even later, it was a rare sight on the roads to see a lady on horseback, but now there is scarcely a young lady of respectability but enumerates riding amongst her accomplishments, and, whether deserved or not, is proud of being thought by her friends and relatives, a 'splendid horsewoman'" (45). Quoting William Lord Cavendish, Duke of Newcastle, she additionally recommends the practice of riding to her female readers because "this art does not consist only in study and mental contemplation, but in bodily practice also" (46).

But as with dancing and all other physical activity, riding only improved a young lady if conducted in a certain way—that is, if it promoted the psychological characteristics valued by the middle class. As Nancy Armstrong explains, the new ideal of female desirability that was advanced in the eighteenth and nineteenth centuries located a woman's value in her internal, psychological qualities—her domestic and feminine virtues—rather than in the wealth, beauty, and showy accomplishments valued by aristocratic standards.[44] In accordance with this theory, Clarke insists that only certain kinds of riding would improve a young girl:

> Dancing we all know to be an instinctive motion, a natural expression of joy, . . . but mark the dancing of the rustic milkmaid and that of the educated and accomplished lady. The one is a clumsy bound, the other the very poetry of motion. And thus should it be with riding. To be used to a horse, to put on a habit, jump into a side saddle and gallop along a country lane, are the equestrian accomplishments of many a rural hoyden or suburban miss; but to sit a horse through all his paces; . . . to have the animal entirely at command, and as if imbued with one intelligence, without loss of temper on the one side or spirit on the other; to unite boldness with modesty, and employ energy without losing delicacy—these are the qualities peculiar and essential to the lady-like horsewoman, and these can only be acquired by patience and attention to excellent instructions. (45)

In order for riding to make a girl more, rather than less, ladylike, she must be subjected to a systematized, supervised course of instruction. Her riding must be physically demanding, yet not unrestrained. Every act should communicate mental awareness and self-control. In short, a display of physical skill must also display mental strength.[45]

Proper horsewomanship not only made a young woman more desirable, it also tutored her in the skills for shaping others according to her desires. As Clarke explains, women's riding worked according to the principles of discipline through love and gentleness:

> What can more strongly illustrate the power of gentleness over brute force than to see a thoroughbred horse, full of fire, under the complete control and subjection of a gentle, timid woman, and how often of a child? It cannot for a moment be imagined that the manual strength of either can do that which a powerful man cannot

> do by his strength. No—the means employed by them are gentleness, a light hand, and firmness; it is scarcely necessary for me to remark that such means have done more towards taming a high couraged and even vicious horse, than all the *force contre force* that can be used: the one makes the animal totally forget that he is under subjection, by leading him to think he is only following his own wishes, when, in reality, he is obeying his rider's; whilst the other excites all the vicious propensities of resistance, which augment as he feels his own increased strength, contrasted with the insignificance of man's. (169)

Although it necessarily takes women out of the home, horseback riding instilled in them the disciplinary skills essential to running an ideal middle-class household.[46] Since the influence exerted in the saddle mirrored the influence that women were to exercise over their families, good riding trained women to be good mothers.

Through her supervised riding Ellen develops the ability—and earns the right—to supervise both herself and others. After months of education with the Humphreys, she reaches a turning point when she reveals that mourning her mother's death has helped her love Jesus not less but "more." Yet Ellen has trouble shaking her gloom until she begins riding again. John does the grieving Ellen good "as soon as [he] came in," but the renewal of her riding lessons enables her to master her excessive sorrow fully. After she has "an excellent lesson, and her master took care it should not be an easy one," Ellen "came back looking as she had not done all winter" (350). Her breakthrough is confirmed when, shortly afterward, she responds immediately and without complaint to the demands of her now-ailing Aunt Fortune. Even though Fortune has ample means to hire sick-nurses and servants, she insists that Ellen (with the help of Nancy Vawse) execute all of the sick-chamber and household duties. This burden is so heavy, and so inappropriate, for the eleven-year-old Ellen that she becomes ill herself. (Indeed, a miserly refusal to hire household help was the cause of Fortune's illness in the first place.) In addition to criticizing Fortune's maintenance of an economical rather than an affective household, this episode proves Ellen's newfound ability to act unsupervised successfully and selflessly. Promptly afterward, she is rewarded with the gift of a pony from Mr. Marshman, who has witnessed her heroic behavior. In contrast to Fortune's relationship with Ellen, Ellen's relationship with the Brownie is appropriately affective:

> Ellen and her little horse grew more and more fond of each other. This friendship, no doubt, was a comfort to the Brownie; but to his mistress it made a large part of the pleasure of her every-day life. . . .

> At any time, Ellen's voice would bring him from the far end of the meadow where he was allowed to run. He would come trotting up at her call, and stand to have her scratch his forehead or pat him and talk to him. . . . Then throwing up his head he would bound off, take a turn in the field, and come back again to stand as still as a lamb as long as she stayed there herself. Now and then, when she had a little more time, she would cross the fence and take a walk with him; and there, with his nose just at her elbow, wherever she went the Brownie went after her. After a while there was no need that she should call him; if he saw or heard her at a distance it was enough; he would come running up directly. Ellen loved him dearly. (381–82)

Having been properly trained under the watchful eyes of the Humphreys, Ellen now becomes the loving authority figure for her equine charge, whom she regulates with love and surveillance. Ellen and her pony, Warner tells us, have a "most perfect understanding" (383).

Much like her pony, however, Ellen is a "docile and spirited little animal" (382). So if she is amenable to discipline, so too is she capable of error. But the ways in which those errors of bodily passion are corrected highlight the disciplinary function of her equestrian education. Very frequently, when Ellen commits an error in passion, she receives her suitable "correction" on horseback. Feeling angry at having her reading curtailed, having to help Margery wind cotton, and finally having to move from the table before she is ready, Ellen gets in such a fit that she is unable to draw well. As John corrects her drawing errors, "She was vexed again, though she did her best not to show it; she stood quietly and heard what he had to say. [John] then told her to get ready for her riding lesson. . . . She was soon thoroughly engaged in the management of herself and her horse; a little smart riding shook all the ill-humour out of her, and she was entirely herself again" (415). And when Ellen refuses to help the poor and semiliterate Irishman Anthony Fox compose a letter to his mother until she is ordered to do so, it is again "time to get ready for riding" (463). Once she is mounted, John reminds her of the importance of self-discipline and of the connection between self-discipline and riding: "You must not talk when you are riding, unless you can contrive to manage two things at once; and no more lose command of your horse than you would of yourself" (463). The benefits of riding are not only remedial but preventative as well: "If ever Ellen was in danger of bending too long over her studies or indulging herself too much in the sofa-corner, she was sure to be broken off to take an hour or two of smart exercise, riding or walking, or to recite some lesson" (464). Ellen's riding, then, is both a mental exercise in itself and a practice that facilitates other kinds of learning.

As thoroughly as Ellen's horsemanship shapes her into the (middle-class) ideal of the desirable woman, the horsemanship of other women in the novel marks them as undesirable and unfeminine. Working-class women's pronounced absence of equestrian aptitude signifies their inferiority: they fail to appear in the saddle not because of their lack of resources but their lack of interest. (The only other woman besides Alice who rides in Ellen's neighborhood is the upwardly mobile Jenny Hitchcock, who marries the town doctor at the end of the novel.) Since they view the female body as a site not for affective but for physical and economically productive labor, working-class women find no value in horsemanship. So sure is Ellen of Aunt Fortune's negative opinion of riding that she seeks Mr. Van Brunt's intercession rather than dare to ask her aunt herself about keeping the new pony. Fortune's refusal to allow the Brownie to stay on the farm at her own expense reveals that she can think of him only in starkly economic terms. Ellen's pony remains at the farm only because Van Brunt volunteers to pay for the animal's keep (380).

Aristocratic characters in *The Wide, Wide World* demonstrate great interest in riding and horses, but, like that of working-class women, their understanding of riding's worth is overly focused on the body. Because aristocratic women locate the value of riding in the opportunity it provides for bodily display, their time on horseback makes them less truly feminine. As Armstrong explains, "for a woman to display herself in such a manner was the same as saying that she was supposed to be valued for her body and its adornments, not for the virtues she might possess as a woman and wife" (75). For the aristocratic woman, riding constitutes not a discipline but an amusement. From the beginning of Ellen's stay with her wealthy relatives the Lindsays, her battles with them are intertwined with class and with riding. When asked for an account of her previous education, the first and only thing that comes to Ellen's mind is her riding lessons; she says she does not know anything well, "unless riding." Mr. Lindsay, however, is very skeptical of her "country riding," assuming it to be of a debased, lower-class sort: "Riding!—And pray how did you learn to ride? Catch a horse by the mane and mount him by the fence and canter off bare-backed? was that it? eh?" (507).

Despite Ellen's claim to a mastery of equitation, Mr. Lindsay insists on sending her to an elite riding school—a vestige of the courtly academies established by Pluvinel and his aristocratic peers. In this context Ellen most fully differentiates her middle-class method of disciplined and practical equitation from the aristocratic riding designed merely to display the body, its wealth, and its social position. When Miss Gordon asks Ellen how she is enjoying her ride, Ellen confesses that she is tired.

> "Tired? Oh, you're not used to it."
>
> "No it isn't that," said Ellen;—"I *am* used to it—that is the reason I am tired. I am accustomed to ride up and down the country at any pace I like; and it is very tiresome to walk stupidly round and round for an hour." (536)

In a reaction consistent with the theories of Beecher and Stowe, Ellen tires from exercise that does not engage her mind. The other women do not tire, since parading around ostentatiously is presumably their purpose.[47] Although Ellen is placed in a group far below her level, she does not complain or mount Miss Gordon's horse without official permission because she detests any act of "putting of herself forward" (536). Finally, however,

> Ellen was taken out of the ring of walkers and mounted on a fine animal, and set by herself to have her skill tried in as many various ways as M. De Courcy's ingenuity could point out. Never did she bear herself more erectly; never were her hand and her horse's mouth on nicer terms of acquaintanceship; never, even to please her master, had she so given her whole soul to the single business of managing her horse and herself perfectly well. She knew as little as she cared that a number of persons besides her friends were standing to look at her; she thought of only two people there, Mr. Lindsay and her aunt; and the riding-master, as his opinion might affect theirs. (537)

Ellen enjoys riding only as an activity that exercises her inward control and self-discipline, and the equestrian skills she displays are both masterful and functional. She can determine her horse's lead at the canter, switch leads, and perform "standing and running leaps, higher and higher, till Mr. Lindsay would have no more of it" (537). All of these advanced movements have practical value for riding cross-country;[48] none are limited to the confines of the ring or tied to the *manège* riding of the aristocracy.

Ellen's elite acquaintances, however, prove capable of corrupting even the (potentially) more middle-class activity of riding cross-country. Ellen cannot enjoy her rides with Miss MacPherson and her friends because they talk "about partners in dancing,—at least the ladies did,—and dresses, and different gentlemen, and what this one said and the other one said" (550)—subjects with which the proper middle-class woman did not preoccupy herself. The coquetry and frivolous mindlessness demonstrated by Miss MacPherson and company on horseback contrasts sharply with the interior focus and seriousness of purpose Ellen displayed at M. de Courcy's. As if echoing the leading pedagogical reformers, Ellen concludes of her ride with MacPherson: "it wasn't very amusing to me" (550).

But while Miss MacPherson's mindless riding marks her as less truly feminine, John's sometimes highly physical riding does not mark him as villainous. We need seriously to reconsider locating subtextual or unconscious resistance to domestic ideology either in Warner or her nineteenth-century audience, since that position (so far) has been buttressed primarily by readings of horsemanship that are not consistent with contemporary equestrian discourses. The education John gives Ellen bears little resemblance to the overtly physical riding valued in the Renaissance. There are certainly strong connections between Ellen and the Brownie because of their affective relationship and similarly disciplined natures, but Ellen and the Black Prince, in contrast, have little in common. By the time John's encounter with this disobedient horse is described in the novel Ellen has more than passed the turning point in her development. She neither identifies nor is identified with the misbehaving Black Prince.

Moreover, reading John as a "horse-beater," either in general or at the time of his first encounter with the Black Prince, exceeds the limits of nineteenth-century beliefs about equine abuse. In the brief passage that has received so much critical attention, Miss Sophia tells Ellen a story about John's use of whips after Ellen says that she does not want to use a whip and "should be afraid to besides" (376). This scene serves a function in the novel similar to the one in which Ellen discovers Mr. Van Brunt slaughtering a hog. Her shock shows her sentimentality, yet the novel's point is to teach her that some forms of "physicality" with animals are acceptable. As Alice Hayes, author of *The Horsewoman* (1893), explains, a "judicious application of the whip," while recommended for all riders, was essential for a woman riding sidesaddle: "A lady has no leg at all on the right side, and the movements of her left leg are a good deal obstructed by the comparative shortness of her stirrup and by the presence of her skirt. She can, however, make up, to a certain extent, for these disadvantages by the use of her whip or cane."[49] In her 1857 *The Habit and the Horse,* Clarke claims that the whip "undoubtedly forms part of the fair rider's equipment, and, by a novice, is not unfrequently the first article obtained. The whip must be regarded as a requisite aid in riding, and not as mere ornament."[50] By one means or another, Ellen must be persuaded to use a whip (judiciously) in order to ride effectively.

The story that Sophia relates is the novel's only account of John's use of the whip: "Do you remember, Alice, the chastising [John] gave that fine black horse of ours we called the 'Black Prince'?—a beautiful creature he was,—more than a year ago?—My conscience! he frightened me to death" (376). Alice's response, however, quickly reveals the level of exaggeration in Sophia's account, and she explains that the "chastising" was both "necessary" and "perfectly right":[51] "My dear Ellen . . . it was no such terrible matter as Sophia's words have made you believe. It was a clear case of obstinacy. The horse was resolved to have his own way and not do what his rider required of him; it was necessary that either the horse or the man should give up; and as John has no fancy for giving up, he carried his point,—partly by management, partly, I confess, by *a judicious use of the whip and spur;* but there was no such furious flagellation as Sophia seems to mean, and which a good horseman would scarce be guilty of" (377, emphasis added).

John's "judicious use of the whip and spur" (note the similarity between Alice's description and Hayes's recommendation cited above) completely accords with nineteenth-century standards; neither equestrians nor animal welfare advocates of the day would have defined John's behavior as abusive. Groups that deploy strategies of discipline rather than punishment to exert power over subjects select the "gentler way of punishment" because it is more effective and initiates less resistance. As Lora Romero has aptly pointed out, regimes of punishment continue to be used alongside those of discipline when a dominant group realizes the greater efficacy of punishment for any given problem. (And hence the same middle-class Americans who sought to control their children through love and not the rod had no qualms about controlling Native Americans through extermination.)[52] In her *Godey's* articles Clarke repeatedly praises the superior results of riders who overcome fiery equines with gentleness instead of force, yet she also acknowledges the appropriateness of more forceful measures: "There is, of course, no rule without an exception; and, as in human nature, we meet with many unruly tempers, we must not be astonished to find them sometimes in the brute creation; therefore, when a horse requires correction, it ought not to be withheld, but it should be given with judgment, coolness, and, above all, without ill temper on the part of the rider" (169).

It is this kind of cool composure that John demonstrates not only in his chastening of the Black Prince but also in his dispensing of Saunders. John orders Saunders away from Ellen with "a command . . . calmly given," while "not put[ting] himself in a passion" (400). To deal with Saunders and his horse John does only what is necessary to remedy the problem—each time, as Clarke recommends, "with judgment, coolness, and, above all, without ill temper." His decision to use force does not align him with the novel's worst character; rather, it shows him an effective evaluator of appropriate means. (John, after all, is training a horse so wild that "no one on the place would ride him" [377], while Saunders is merely terrorizing a very well-behaved horse and his young rider.) As Alice explains, the Black Prince "was resolved to have his own way and not do what his rider required of him"; instead of a docile equine, this horse was "as obstinate as a mule" (377). Some beings—cats, mules, and Saunders—are simply not candidates for control through disciplinary intimacy. While the Black Prince's recalcitrance was temporary, Saunders' mule-like obstinacy seems to be more permanent. As historical evidence shows, even contemporary animal-welfare advocates would have smiled upon the kind of "judicious use of the whip and spur" that John practices here. For example, in Anna Sewell's *Black Beauty* (1877)—the nineteenth century's most famous and enduring argument for equine welfare (both in England and the United States)—horse handlers earn condemnation not by using a whip but by using a whip inappropriately. There are those today who argue that any use of whip or spur constitutes abuse, but regardless of our sympathy with this position we must recognize it as a product of the twentieth—and not the nineteenth—century. Virtually all critics who find subtextual resistance to domestic ideology in *The Wide, Wide World* place John's "propensity for horse-beating" as the keystone of their argument. We may view John as an overbearing and unlikable character, but I think we have yet to discover convincing evidence that Warner or her contemporaries thought the same.

Reading *The Wide, Wide World* in the context of the nineteenth-century discourse on affect-based horsewomanship shows Ellen successfully and actively mastering a project of subject formation in which class figures as critically as gender. Through her educational program that includes and is figured by riding, Ellen successfully turns herself into a model middle-class woman and achieves certain types of cultural power. What her behavior on horseback, and everywhere in Europe, shows is that, contrary to Goshgarian's claims, Ellen *is* able to keep herself right (though she is certainly miserable without like-minded company).[53]

On two additional occasions after receiving the Brownie, Ellen receives a horse as a reward for her successful self-discipline. Although Ellen initially becomes enraged when Mr. Lindsay confiscates her beloved copy of *Pilgrim's Progress,* she masters her passion and apologizes wholeheartedly. Two paragraphs later we learn that she receives another present of "a fine horse" (555). And in the final chapter of the novel, she again shows that her delight in fine things rests in her private, interior enjoyment of their spiritual meaning, rather than a desire for ostentation or aristocratic display. John fills her private room with beautiful and expensive artwork, and Ellen (correctly) responds that she would never wish such things to be downstairs where they would be subject to "other people's envy and admiration." John answers: "A wife that would have wished them there, Ellie, I would never have married. With splendours we have no concern. Whatever has to do with the highest perfection of body and mind I will seek and have, both for you and myself. Accordingly I have desired a friend in whose judgement I can trust, to send me out as good a riding-horse for you as can be had" (577). Ellen is not (as Goshgarian would have her be) the passion-driven horse of the Renaissance who yields only to bit and spur. Through her equestrian education she becomes the right kind of horsewoman—that is, the right kind of horse and the right kind of woman. If figured as a horse, Ellen is a docile equine body—like one of A. H. Rockwell's self-regulating, reinless horses. As a woman and rider, she knows how to manage through gentleness and love.

Although she remains less powerful than some characters in the novel, Ellen also gains power as she forms herself into the ideal of the desirable middle-class woman. Since the process of defining Ellen as desirable depends upon defining other women (specifically aristocratic and working women) as less so, analyses of "women's" power in the novel are ill-equipped for detailing the complex web of power relations in Ellen's world. And while Alice, John, and other characters certainly exert strong influences on her development, their actions do not negate the active role that Ellen plays in the construction of herself. My point is not just that there is some degree of volition in "renounc[ing] self-determination completely" or "learn[ing] selfless passivity."[54] As Foucault explains, "The subject constitutes himself in an active fashion, by the practices of self, [yet] these practices are nevertheless not something that the individual invents by himself. They are patterns that he finds in his culture and which are proposed, suggested and imposed on him by his culture, his society and his social group."[55] Simultaneously physical and mental, prescribed and chosen, a strategy that controls her and one through which she controls—Ellen's riding evidences her socially channeled yet active construction of the self.

The monetary difficulties that had prompted Warner to write *The Wide, Wide World* also made her own riding at that time dependent upon the goodwill of the friends her family had formed before its financial ruin. The journal entry excerpted in the epigraph to this chapter records not only the elation Warner experienced as a result of her ride, but also her "feverish . . . desire" to continue her riding and her fear that her second lesson with her neighbor W. T. Sprole might be her last. Because Sprole "said nothing about my coming again," Warner felt "*as if I should like to cry.*" Even when *The Wide, Wide*

World began to earn money, fiscal discipline remained imperative. However, by the winter of 1851–52, Warner was able to reward herself in the way Ellen Montgomery was so often rewarded. As Anna Warner reported in her 1909 biography of her sister Susan, "two or three absolute luxuries stole in" at that time, among them "riding lessons." "Shall I ever forget the glee," Anna Warner wrote, "with which we cut and made some of the most inexpensive grey riding habits; and then on certain days marched up Fifth Avenue to the old Dickel School, to take our lesson! Feet might be orderly, but spirits danced." In the spring, Susan and Anna purchased a little brown horse, which they took with them back to Constitution Island and rode "every fair day."[56] The Warner sisters continued to write their family out of debt, eventually producing "more than eighty-five novels, short stories, essays, biographies, and religious tracts."[57] Creating this literary output while keeping house was demanding. In a journal entry dated October 7, 1860, Susan Warner wrote, after listing the work to be done that day, "And strength is so insufficient." Then she added, "Only when I ride, it is tripled."[58]

In an 1869 article in *Our Dumb Animals,* Harriet Beecher Stowe recommended a knowledge of horsemanship for women that extended beyond what one did in the saddle. "A woman who lives in the country," she suggested, "may sometimes be able to save a life by knowing how to harness or drive a horse. It is, of course, not a proper feminine employment." Reader Grace Greenwood took offense to Stowe's qualification and wrote an article for the same publication in protest. "I would harness and drive, saddle, bridle, ride, and be much with horses because *I love them,*" Greenwood wrote. "In my honest opinion no woman is more out of her place in the stable than in the garden. Horticulture may be a daintier employment than horsiculture (if I may be allowed to coin a word) but it contributes less to, because drawing less on the sympathetic, affectional nature of a woman. I truly believe that the love for and care of a fine horse would have a strengthening and ennobling influence on the character of any true woman. On this extreme ground I take my stand, against a world of proprieties."[59] Greenwood's argument that all aspects of horsemanship could develop a woman's moral nature reflected a development well underway at this time in discourses relating to human-animal interaction more generally. As the next several chapters demonstrate, in addition to the highly structured practice of riding horses, a wide range of people's everyday interactions with animals came to be seen as activities with important moral dimensions as well as an important source of information about both the nature of human beings and our place in the animal world.

Animal Transformations

Sagacious Dogs, Disgusting Apes, Evolutionary Theory, and Nathaniel Hawthorne's *The Marble Faun*

I think I could turn and live with animals, they are so placid and self-contain'd,
I stand and look at them long and long.

They do not sweat and whine about their condition,
They do not lie awake in the dark and weep for their sins,
They do not make me sick discussing their duty to God,
Not one is dissatisfied, not one is demented with the mania of owning things,
Not one kneels to another, nor to his kind that lived thousands of years ago,
Not one is respectable or unhappy over the whole earth. (684–91)

WALT WHITMAN, "Song of Myself"

OF ALL the traditionally canonized male authors of mid-nineteenth century American literature, Nathaniel Hawthorne has long been considered the least interested in nature. In his influential 1941 study *The American Renaissance,* F. O. Mattheissen attributes Hawthorne's failure to embrace a transcendentalist interest in the nonhuman world to his insistence on clinging to the human one. Mattheissen contends that Hawthorne maintained throughout his life the position he expressed in the brief essay "On Solitude" that he wrote at age sixteen: "Man is naturally a social being. . . . It is only in society that the full energy of his mind is aroused." "He did not," Mattheissen continues, "share Thoreau's unswerving confidence that man could find himself by studying nature; indeed, in no respect is his difference from all the transcendental writers more fundamental than in this."[1] Subsequent scholars have, for the most part, followed Mattheissen's lead, assuming that Hawthorne took little interest in the natural world and that he held the rearguard and not the vanguard of American thought on the subject.[2] Thus the few critics who have addressed the subject of animals in Hawthorne's work have also assumed that since Hawthorne elevated culture over nature, his comparisons between people and animals must necessarily be pejorative. Recently, scholars have suggested that Hawthorne linked people to animals for the purpose of depicting the former's boorishness, dependency, or genetic inferiority.[3]

Such readings reveal no common ground between Hawthorne's thoughts on animal-human connections and Whitman's fantasy of "turn[ing]" to "live with animals," whose existence he imagined to be so much happier than ours. But as I argued in the introduction, living among animals did not require a turn away from civilized life. In this chapter, I will show that Hawthorne did engage seriously and passionately with the issue of humans' relationship to nonhuman creatures. Like Whitman and Thoreau, Hawthorne looked long at animals and longed. But for him connection with the animal world entailed no "turn" from the human one. Instead, Hawthorne's interest in animals and humans' affinities with them was constructed—not thwarted— by his attachment to the institutions of human society and by the human-animal encounters that were attendant with antebellum urban and suburban existence: the keeping of companion animals and exposure to zoos, menageries, and trained animal exhibitions.

While my analysis does reveal unrecognized continuities between Hawthorne and the canonical white, male, antebellum writers with whom he is traditionally associated, it also shows that Hawthorne's thinking about animals actually corresponded much more closely to views presented in the domestic and sentimental fiction against which Hawthorne's writing has been typically—insistently—opposed. Rather than the wild animals long thought to be the object of fantasies of identification for all mid-nineteenth-century white men, it was the nonhuman denizens of Hawthorne's home—animals who demonstrated an aptitude for and not an aversion to domestic life—that figured most prominently in his imagination. And instead of signaling his attachment to an outmoded view of the natural world, Hawthorne's encounters with and preference for civilized creatures propelled his thinking about human-animal connections along a trajectory that was in many ways far more radical than that traveled by his wilderness-loving peers. For Hawthorne as well as many of his contemporaries, affection for companion animals generated receptiveness to scientific and popular discourses that (however dissimilar their outward forms) were unified by their rejection of the long-standing assumptions that humans were both separated from animals by a wide and impassible gulf and incontestably superior to them. As my analysis of *The Marble Faun* (1860) and pre-Darwinian evolutionary debates will reveal, in the nineteenth century beliefs about dogs and other companion animals did as much if not more than studies of nonhuman primates to facilitate acceptance of the theory of evolution.[4]

Living with Animals

> If I have written anything well, it should be this Romance; for I have never thought or felt more deeply, or taken more pains. . . . If you should happen to hear of a puppy-dog, of a large and good breed, I should like to get such a one.
>
> NATHANIEL HAWTHORNE, in a letter to his publisher William Ticknor written shortly after the publication of *The Marble Faun*[5]

Two passages in Hawthorne's writing provide particularly clear illustrations of the differences between his and Thoreau's orientations toward the animal world. The first appears in a journal entry for August 5, 1842, which is the opening entry in the journal Hawthorne began at the Old Manse shortly after his marriage to Sophia. The theme of the entry is the "Paradise" (he uses the word five times) of his new, married home. Near the end of the entry, Hawthorne lists the two things with which he would ask Providence to improve his "sacred precincts": a more convenient water supply and "a kitten." After this wish, the passage concludes: "Animals (except, perhaps, a pig) seem never out of place, even in the most paradisaical spheres. And, by the bye, a young colt comes up our avenue, now and then, to crop the seldom trodden herbage; and so do a company of cows, whose sweet breath well repays us for the food which they obtain. There are likewise a few hens, whose quiet cluck is heard pleasantly about the house. A black dog sometimes stands at the farther extremity of the avenue, and looks wistfully towards the house; but when I whistle to him, he puts his tail between his legs, and trots away. Foolish dog!—if he had more faith, he should have bones enough" (*CE* 8:317). Like the sections from "Little Annie's Rambles" quoted in the introduction, this passage testifies to the presence animals had in mid-nineteenth-century suburban communities. Even though Hawthorne (at this point) owns no animals himself, he encounters a horse, cows, hens, and a dog without even leaving his yard. These domesticated animals do not, as they did for Thoreau, inspire a kind of panic at the possibility of his own enervation and domestic immurement.[6] Rather, they seem fitting accoutrements to what he considers an ideal life. But the most remarkable aspect of this passage (for my purposes) is the final part, in which Hawthorne, standing in his yard or perhaps his doorway, calls out to a passing dog, and then curses the dog's lack of "faith" when he fails to come to his call. In many ways, this passage represents the inverse of Thoreau's exhilarated pursuit of the loon across Walden Pond. As I discussed in the introduction, Thoreau's pleasure in that chase lies in his secure knowledge that he will never succeed because the loon is a self-reliant, wild creature who does not need him and whose resources (physical as well as mental) always enable him to evade human contact. For Hawthorne, in contrast, interest terminates with the dog's retreat.

The second passage, also written at the Old Manse, appears in the autobiographical essay written as the preface to *Mosses from an Old Manse* (1846). In it, Hawthorne recounts a restorative excursion with Ellery Channing into the woods and streams surrounding his Concord home. Hawthorne's loving descriptions of their boat ride up the Concord and Assabeth rivers seem initially to celebrate wild nature as enthusiastically as Thoreau would have. (Indeed, he cites Thoreau in this passage, noting that it was he who told him that the pond-lilies along the shore blossom when "kissed" by the day's first sunlight.) But the passage concludes with a decidedly un-Thoreauvian tribute to domestic life. As Hawthorne and Channing turn their boat homeward, Hawthorne's thoughts turn to "how sweet it was to return within the system of human society" (*CE* 10:25). Indeed, it seems as though the greatest benefit of the excursion into the wilderness is that it enables him to perceive even more fully the pleasures of living in a house. Reaching the riverbank nearest the Old Manse, Hawthorne observes "a cloud in the shape of an immensely gigantic figure of a hound, couched above the house, as if keeping guard over it. Gazing at this symbol, I prayed that the upper influences might long protect the institutions [i.e., domestic life] that had grown out of the heart of mankind" (*CE* 10:25–26). Here as in *Walden,* the dog symbolizes domestic life, and the difference between each man's attitude toward this creature correlate precisely with their attitude toward domesticity: the sight of the dog or the sound of his bark inspires loathing in Thoreau, while this same image moves Hawthorne to prayer.[7]

But for Hawthorne and a large percentage of his contemporaries, the connection between companion animals like the dog and domestic life was more properly metonymic than symbolic, for in nineteenth-century America, middle-class domesticity was linked both in theory and in practice to the keeping of household pets.[8] Biographers of Hawthorne have had little to say about his animal companions, but his letters and journals reveal that throughout his life Hawthorne engaged in the highly affective mode of pet keeping characteristic of contemporary sentimental and domestic culture. One of the earliest mentions of pets in family papers appears in the *Spectator,* a sort of family newspaper which Hawthorne and his sisters wrote the summer he was sixteen. In one number, announcements of feline and human births receive equal attention: "Births. The Lady of Dr Winthrop Brown a SON and HEIR. Mrs. Hathorne's[9] cat SEVEN KITTENS. We hear that both of the above ladies are in a state of convalescence" (*CE* 23:47). That same summer, Hawthorne wrote to his mother regarding the transportation via boat of the family dog Watch from Salem (where Hawthorne was living with his uncle Robert Manning) to his mother's residence in Raymond, Maine. In a letter dated August 15, 1820, Hawthorne, who appears to be superintending Watch's transportation, worries about the dog's difficulty in breathing (which he attributes to a neighbor's excessive feeding of him). A few weeks later, he requests more information about the dog's condition, wanting to know if he "arrived safe" (*CE* 15: 128–29). When Hawthorne hears the news that Watch, the following spring, has strayed or has been stolen from home, he writes to his mother that he is "very much afflicted" by the dog's disappearance. A week later, he writes that his uncle "is in great affliction" over the dog's loss and that he and his sister Louisa "are in the like dolorous condition," and then urges his mother to advertise for the lost dog in the local paper (*CE* 15:38).

Hawthorne's bachelor correspondence with his sisters is sprinkled with lines about Beelzebub, the Hathornes' cat; "Pull Beelzebub's tail for me," he playfully closes an 1836 letter to Elizabeth (*CE* 15:230). The day after his wedding to Sophia, Hawthorne interrupted his honeymoon just long enough to dash off a short letter to Louisa to let her know that the wedding had been performed and that they had arrived safely at the Old Manse. In the postscript, Hawthorne writes: "We have not got a kitten—yet" (*CE* 15:639)—as though setting up house required obtaining a cat. In an 1843 letter to her sister-in-law Louisa, Sophia Hawthorne writes that their cat Pigwiggen (which they acquired soon after moving into the Old Manse)[10] "desires her love [be sent] to her venerable relative Beelzebub & to young Mite" (*CE* 15:668).

As her letter suggests, Sophia Hawthorne shared her spouse's fondness for animals and, like him, treated animals as members of the family. The letters Nathaniel wrote to her during her absences from him testify to the centrality of animals to their domestic life. During Sophia's 1844 visit to her family in Boston, Nathaniel wrote that, though he was lonely, he found "an excellent companion" in their Newfoundland dog Leo: "Thou canst not imagine how much the presence of Leo relieves the feeling of perfect loneliness. He insists upon being in the room with me all the time, (except at night, when he sleeps in the shed) and I do not find myself severe enough to drive him out. He accompanies me, likewise, on all my walks, to the village and elsewhere; and, in short, keeps at my heels all the time, except when I go down cellar. Then he stands at the head of the stairs and howls, as if he never expected to see me again." In return for Leo's attentions, Hawthorne goes to no small trouble to make him happy. He feeds Leo with the same food he eats himself, and even goes out of his way to prepare a special meal to suit Leo's tastes. His letter recounts how he procured "some pouts and eels" for Leo and then proceeded to fry them "for he does not like raw fish." Although Hawthorne shares this meal with the dog, he confesses that it was done "on purpose for him. . . . I should hardly have taken the trouble on my own account" (*CE* 16:43–44).

Even more suggestive of the centrality of interactions with animals in the Hawthornes' home is Nathaniel's detailed record of July 28 to August 16, 1851, when Sophia left him home alone with Julian and took Una and newly born Rose to see their maternal relatives in Boston. After Sophia's departure, Nathaniel wrote to her that, instead of reporting his and Julian's activities in letters, he would "keep a regular chronicle of all our doings" in his journal, which she should read upon her return (*CE* 16:468). This chronicle of domestic life Hawthorne titled "Twenty Days with Julian and Little Bunny, By Pappa"—Bunny being the family's pet rabbit, who enjoyed free roam of the house. Finding himself, in Sophia's absence, saddled with the care of both boy and rabbit, Hawthorne at first seems to resent his obligations to the latter. "Bunny," he writes, "does not turn out to be a very interesting companion, and makes me more trouble than he is worth. . . . Julian pays him very little attention now, and leaves me to take the whole labor of gathering leaves for him; else the poor little beast would be likely to starve. I am strongly tempted of the Evil One to murder him privately; and I wish with all my heart that Mrs. Peters would drown him" (*CE* 8:437).[11] Hawthorne's boastful indifference, however, is promptly revealed to be a sham, and it becomes clear that if Bunny fails to interest Julian, Hawthorne himself finds him fascinating. In fact during these twenty days nothing—save Julian—seems to interest Hawthorne so consistently or so strongly as Bunny, and the chronicle becomes filled with Hawthorne's ruminations on Bunny's inner life:

> Sometimes, indeed, he is seized with a little impulse of friskiness; but it does not appear to be sportive, but nervous. Bunny has a singular countenance—like somebody's I have seen, but whose I forget. It is rather imposing and aristocratic, on a cursory glance, but examining it more closely, it is found to be laughably vague. (*CE* 8:437)

> His most interesting trait is the apprehensiveness of his nature; it is as quick, and as continually in movement, as an aspen leaf. The least noise startles him; and you may see his emotion in the movement of his ears; he starts, and scrambles into his

> little house, but, in a moment, peeps forth again, and begins nibbling the grass and weeds;—again to be startled, and as quickly re-assured. Sometimes he sets out on a nimble little run, for no reason, but just as a dry leaf is blown along by a puff of wind. I do not think that these fears are any considerable torment to Bunny; it is his nature to live in the midst of them, and to intermingle them, as a sort of piquant sauce, with every morsel he eats. It is what redeems his life from dulness [*sic*] and stagnation. Bunny appears to be uneasy in broad and open sunshine; it is his impulse to seek shadow—the shadow of a tuft of bushes, or Julian's shadow, or mine. He seemed to think himself in rather too much peril, so important a personage as he is, in the breadth of the yard, and took various opportunities to creep into Julian's lap. (*CE* 8:439)

> It makes me smile to see how he invariably comes galloping to meet me, whenever I open the door, making sure that there is something in store for him, and smelling eagerly to find out what it is. . . . He is naturally so full of little alarms, that it is pleasant to find him free of these, as to Julian and myself. (*CE* 8:446).

As these passages suggest, the transformation in Hawthorne's interest in Bunny to a large degree rested in this creature's willingness to do exactly what the black dog passing the Old Manse did not—seek him out, show him confidence, and enter into his domestic world. "One finds himself getting rather attached to this gentle beast," Hawthorne writes, "especially when he shows confidence, and *makes himself at home*" (*CE* 8:442, emphasis added).

There is a very conspicuous link between Hawthorne's characteristic preference for animals willing to seek *him* out and his attribution, in *The Marble Faun,* to Donatello of "gifts by which he could associate himself with the wild things of the forests, and with the fowls of the air."[12] While reveling with Miriam in the Borghese gardens, "A bird happening to sing cheerily, Donatello gave a peculiar call, and the little feathered creature came fluttering about his head, as if it had known him through many summers" (83). The peasants around Donatello's ancestral estate tell Kenyon that he "grew up . . . the playmate not only of all mortal kind, but of creatures of the woods; although, when Kenyon pressed them for some particulars of this latter mode of companionship, they could remember little more than a few anecdotes of a pet-fox, which used to growl and snap at everybody save Donatello himself" (237). And the description, in the opening chapter of the novel, of the appeal of Praxiteles' sculpture of the faun strongly recalls the language with which Hawthorne described his fascination with Bunny. Of Bunny Hawthorne wrote, "The mystery that broods about him—the lack of any method of communicating with this voiceless creature—heightens the interest" (*CE* 8:446). In similar terms, *The Marble Faun* explains that "Praxiteles has subtly diffused, throughout his work, that mute mystery which so hopelessly perplexes us, whenever we attempt to gain an intellectual or sympathetic knowledge of the lower orders of creation" (10).

But the significance of Hawthorne's animal encounters to a reading of *The Marble Faun* extends well beyond these superficial congruencies. As I argue in the following sections, the relationship of Donatello and humankind more generally to "the lower orders of creation" constitutes a central concern of the novel, and we can read this concern only if we first understand the ways in which Hawthorne's and his contemporaries' beliefs about their affinities with animals were shaped both by encounters with animals in the built environment and by a preference for those creatures who readily adapted themselves to civilization.

"A Delightful Link Betwixt Human and Brute Life"

Donatello's uncanny resemblance to the statue of the faun (a mythological creature part man and part animal) and the novel's insistence that he may actually be one form the basis for the novel's plot. Despite this and the novel's declaration that "the animal nature, indeed, is a most essential part of the Faun's composition" (9), few modern readers have taken Donatello's animal status seriously. The majority of the twentieth-century readings of the novel can be divided, roughly, into two camps, neither of which has paid much attention to Donatello's animality. The first reads Donatello as a symbol for prelapsarian man and the novel as an allegory of the biblical story of the Fall. According to this interpretation, Donatello, the young Count of Monte Beni, exchanges his innocent, joyous, and carefree life for a life of guilt, suffering, and repentance when, out of love for Miriam, he murders the mysterious man who has been stalking and tormenting her. For much of the twentieth century, critics had little doubt that the Fall was the central concern of the novel; hence, readers in this camp primarily debated whether Hawthorne did or did not support the theory that humankind's fall from grace and ensuing expulsion from the Garden of Eden was in fact fortunate—or whether, as Richard Harter Fogle contends, Hawthorne deliberately "leaves the question in suspension."[13]

The same fact that readers in the first camp regard as irrefutable proof of their reading—that the novel repeatedly points out the parallels between Donatello's story and the biblical Adam's—has caused other critics to doubt this reading. Evan Carton, for one, observes that "the novel's ceaseless effort to dictate its own interpretation might itself be cause to question the confidence or honesty of its claim that the theme of the Fall lies at its heart."[14] Critics in the second camp have no single explanation of Donatello's role in the novel, and some pay little attention to him at all. Many, though, insist that Hawthorne's use of the "timeless" theme of the Fall—or alternately critics' focus on it—has obscured the novel's real concerns, which have been identified as anti-Catholic sentiment, racial mixing, nineteenth-century aesthetics, pursuit of an artistic career, or some other aspect of antebellum culture.[15] As critics in this camp are quick to point out, there are a number of problems with identifying the Fall as the novel's central theme. Among them is the unlikelihood that Hawthorne—who "did not attend church and showed little sign of religious devotion"—would find the theological question of the Fall sufficiently engaging to make it the "life-principle" (to use Fogle's term) of his novel.[16] What's more, the idea that man's Fall from grace ultimately raised him to a higher state of development was, as Richard Brodhead explains, "already well established long before Milton" and, by the nineteenth century, held the status of "a humanistic truism." The real "curiosity of *The Marble Faun,*" Brodhead points out, "is that Hilda finds the doctrine of the *felix culpa* new and inexpressibly shocking."[17]

I argue both that *The Marble Faun*'s central concerns are specific to antebellum culture and that Hawthorne's handling of those historically specific concerns depended on his ability to convince his readers of the parallel between his story and the story of the Fall. That is, though the issue of the Fall itself may be "timeless," Hawthorne's reasons for using it were not. Hawthorne's resurrection of the then-defunct *felix culpa* controversy enabled him (and forced his readers) to grapple with the question of whether humans were "the pinnacle of creation," set absolutely apart from and above nonhuman animals by virtue of their unique, God-given qualities of mind, or whether the qualities taken as markers of unique human status—intellect and a soul—could in fact be produced in animals through the nondivine forces of this world. Far from a return to a theme of his earlier fiction (as some readers have suggested), Hawthorne's use of the Fall in *The Marble Faun* evinces a development in his thinking about the relative positions of animals and humans in the cosmological order, and it demonstrates a serious reconsideration of the teleological view of history (natural and social) present in his previous work.

Thus, rather than adopting either of the positions outlined above, my reading identifies a common link between these two ostensibly opposed camps. One interpretation of the novel my reading does not assimilate, however, is Nancy Bentley's influential argument that *The Marble Faun* draws on contemporary ethnological discourse and participates in its project of translating nonwhite people's cultural differences into permanent racial or genetic inferiority. In Bentley's view, Hawthorne's decision to cast Italian Donatello as a mythological faun—along with his comparison of a group of fugitive slaves to fauns in "Chiefly about War Matters" (1862)—reflected his belief that non-white peoples trailed hopelessly behind whites on the timeline of human cultural development. But if the depiction of Donatello depicts a belief in fixed racial qualities, how are we to make sense of his subsequent transformation? This is precisely the question that recent studies have raised but not answered.[18] Donatello's genetics indeed prove not to be a limiting factor. Whatever sets him apart from the other fully human characters at the beginning of the novel is overcome through experience; the human capabilities he possesses at the end of the novel existed within him, latent, all the time. I am not proposing that contemporary racial theories don't factor into Hawthorne's decision to associate fauns with an Italian family in his 1860 novel and a group of African Americans in his 1862 essay. But I do insist that if we want to understand how Hawthorne uses animality to construct an argument about race, we must first understand what he is saying about animality. Rather than dramatizing emerging ideas about the genetic distance between national or racial groups of people, the depiction of Donatello as a faun and his subsequent transformation into a fully human man dramatizes a constellation of discourses centered on new ideas about the proximities between people and animals: cross-species hybridization, the development of animals' latent mental abilities, and the transformation or evolution of one species into another.

Recent readers' reluctance to take Donatello's animal status seriously may follow in part from his connection to a fabulous animal-human hybrid. For us, the mythical faun and the kind of fantastical hybridization he embodies exist on a register completely separate from that of bona fide natural history. In antebellum America, however, the faun's cross-species hybridity resonated strongly with both popular and scientific belief. Mid-nineteenth-century scientists had by no means ruled out the possibility that members of radically different species could produce viable offspring. In *On the Origin of Species* (1859), Darwin noted that the theory "that most of our domestic animals have descended from two or more aboriginal species" was "largely accepted by modern naturalists."[19] And when Linnaeus "at last conceded the necessity for an element of temporal change in nature, he chose to stress not adaptation to new conditions but hybridization as the source of new species."[20]

Moreover, in the first half of the nineteenth century menageries and impresarios regularly exhibited anomalous animals and humans as crosses between very different species. Among the most famous of these was Julia Pastrana, a very hairy woman exhibited throughout the United States, Europe, and Russia as a genuine orangutan-human hybrid. From her "discovery" in 1854 until her death from childbirth complications in 1860, Pastrana sang, danced, and even performed "acrobatic tricks on the back of a horse" before the large audiences that paid to see her. Late-twentieth-century researchers have been able to diagnose Pastrana's condition retroactively as "congenital, generalized hypertrichosis terminalis with gingival hyperplasia," but nineteenth-century scientists were unable to discredit authoritatively the claims about Pastrana's hybridity. Existing scientific literature on orangutans and nonhuman primates did not contradict the assertions of Pastrana's impresario. In *An Account of the Regular Gradation in Man, and in Different Animals and Vegetables, and from the Former to the Latter* (1799), Charles White reported that orangutans "have been known to carry off negro-boys, girls and even women . . . as objects of brutal passion" and that there were rumors that "women have had offspring from such connection."[21] Reports of apes' and especially orangutans' lascivious tendencies continued to circulate in scientific journals, spawning widespread if prurient interest. In 1859, Emmanuel Frémiet (who is most famous for his equestrian statue *Joan of Arc*) submitted to the Salon a sculpture of a male gorilla absconding with a naked woman.[22] In this context, it is no wonder that many people found the claims of Pastrana's impresario compelling. When Pastrana appeared in New York in 1854, Alexander B. Mott, MD, examined her and "declared her to be a hybrid between human and orangutan, and therefore 'one of the most extraordinary beings of the present day.'"[23]

Pastrana had toured England in 1857, the final year of Hawthorne's consulship at Liverpool, and when Hawthorne saw Praxiteles' marble faun in Rome the following year, he immediately connected the mythological faun with the present-day Pastrana. After his visit to the Villa Borghese in April of 1858, Hawthorne wrote of the fauns in his journal: "I like these strange, sweet, playful rustic creatures, almost entirely human as they are, yet linked so prettily, without monstrosity, to the lower tribes by the long, furry ears, or by a modest tail. . . . In my mind, they connect themselves with that ugly, bearded woman, who was lately exhibited in England, and by some supposed to have been engendered betwixt a human mother and an orang-outang; but she was a wretched monster—the faun, a natural and delightful link betwixt human and brute life, and with something of a divine character intermingled" (*CE* 14:173–74). Although Hawthorne renounces the connection between the "delightful" faun and the "wretched monster" Pastrana immediately after he observes it, the possibility of this association seems to linger, for when he wrote *The Marble Faun* Hawthorne took pains to distinguish both fauns and Donatello from Pastrana-like monstrosity. In the opening chapter of the novel, we are told that Praxiteles' faun is "neither man nor animal, *and yet no monster,* but a being in whom both races meet, on friendly ground!" (10, emphasis added). Donatello, the narrator insists, was "linked (*and by no monstrous chain*) with what we call the inferiour tribes of being" (71, emphasis added). And the ancient "progenitor" of the Monte Beni family is described as "a being not altogether human, yet partaking so largely of the gentlest human qualities, as to be neither awful nor shocking to the imagination" (233).

What about Pastrana did Hawthorne find so repulsive? And why was he so insistent on disrupting his own (and preventing his readers') associations between Donatello and Pastrana? It was not, it seems, the idea of human-animal coupling that repulsed him. In *The Marble Faun,* Hawthorne invites us to imagine that Donatello's family originated with the same kind of violent abduction presented in White's text and Frémiet's sculpture. According to a family legend (which Kenyon finds "wild, and perhaps grotesque, yet not unfascinating," 232), the "progenitor" of the "lineage of Monte Beni" was "a being not altogether human." This "sylvan creature" fell in love with a woman and "won her to his haunts" "perhaps by kindness, and the subtle courtesies which love might teach to his simplicity, or possibly by a ruder wooing" (233). Four days after he wrote the remarks about Pastrana's monstrosity in his journal, Hawthorne recorded his "admiration" for Paul Veronese's painting of the rape of Europa: "The bull has all Jupiter in him, so tender and gentle, yet so hot and passionate with desire that you feel it indecorous to look at him; and Europa, under her thick, rich stuffs and embroideries, is as much a woman as if she were naked" (*CE* 14:178).[24] (Another discussion of the *Faun* of Praxiteles, perhaps not coincidentally, immediately follows the discussion of this painting.)

What prompted both Hawthorne's repulsion toward Pastrana and his efforts to dissociate the faun from her was Pastrana's ostensible linking of humans to orangutans.[25] That is, as fascinated as he was with animals, Hawthorne was—like the majority of people at this time—loathe to believe that the animals to whom we were most closely connected were wild simians. The most convenient illustration of Hawthorne's and his contemporaries' shared thoughts on the matter can be found in the *American Magazine of Useful and Entertaining Knowledge,* which Hawthorne edited for six months, beginning with the March 1836 issue. As Arlin Turner has explained, Hawthorne was the sole contributor to this low-budget periodical during his tenure as editor. (Hawthorne was poorly or perhaps never paid, which prompted his early abdication of the post.) Turner estimates that one-quarter of its contents were original pieces written by Hawthorne; the remaining three-quarters he cobbled together from various sources—sometimes blending his own prose seamlessly into borrowed material, sometimes reprinting sources published elsewhere in their entirety. Hawthorne's sister Louisa assisted him by sending clippings of material she thought would be useful, and may have written (in part or in full) some of the pieces that appeared in the magazine. The murky status of the authorship of these pieces has factored, no doubt, into Hawthorne scholars' neglect of them, but this same quality makes them more useful for my purposes. As editor and sole contributor Hawthorne necessarily had knowledge of and control over the magazine's content; at the same time, his selections also represent the current state of knowledge about and interest in history, biography, geography, science, and natural history. And if Hawthorne and Alden Bradford (the editor whom Hawthorne succeeded and who resumed editorship after Hawthorne left) were any judge of public opinion, one subject Americans wanted to read about in that last category was orangutans. Volume 2 of the magazine (of which Hawthorne and Bradford each edited half the numbers) features three articles on orangutans, and volume 3 contains two more. We can be reasonably sure that Hawthorne read the issues published shortly before he took over, since, in his first issue he printed a short notice that announced the change of editors and stated: "And for ourself, the success that we can anticipate must be won by following out the principles which have guided our predecessor."[26]

The first of volume 2's orangutan articles, "The Female Orang Outang" (which appeared in December 1835 under Bradford's editorship), states in its opening that the orangutan "is truly the most disgusting animal." This creature "merits notice" for its "peculiarity" and because "it is considered also as a link between man and the mere animal or brute creation . . . yet we cannot be much flattered by being said to have any resemblance or relation to such ugliness." This acknowledgment of the anatomical similarities between orangutans and humans is followed by an insistence that the resemblance is merely physical: while the orangutan may be "in its form approaching nearer to the human species than any of the other" members of "the ape or monkey tribes," "we are not aware that it has given any indication of reason; or that it has more shrewd and cunning than some other animals."[27] Ten issues later, in August 1836, Hawthorne published "Species of Men," which replicates the former article's rhetorical moves. It begins: "Linnaeus, in his classification of the natural world, divided the genus Homo, or man, into two species. The first was the *Homo Sapiens,* or Man endowed with intellect. . . . The second species was the *Homo Troglodytes,*—or Orang Outang!" Like Bradford's piece, Hawthorne's insists that simians' similarities to humans are both disturbing and decidedly limited: "The pride of the *Homo Sapiens* certainly revolts at the idea of being placed so nearly on a level with these great monkeys." He acknowledges that "we might almost allow them to be our cousins," but hastily adds, "we deny them the name of brethren." Hawthorne concludes the piece by asserting the distance between humans and these animals: "However close upon our heels the inferior tribes of creation may seem to tread, there is one great and invariable mark of distinction between the Man with a soul, and the Animal without one."[28]

On the page preceding this article, Hawthorne placed a piece titled "Conformation of Man" (identified as an excerpt from "Cuvier's Animal Kingdom") that details explicitly the differences between human and primate anatomy.[29] This same issue also contains a very unflattering piece titled "Mischievousness of Monkeys," which describes how a "troop of monkeys" rolled "several great stones" down a hill on a scientist in the field "with a settled design to crush him. One of the stones, in fact, hit him on the head, fracturing his skull in so terrible a manner that a portion of the brain protruded, and was removed by the knife of a surgeon."[30] The orangutan articles that Bradford published in volume 3 continued to emphasize apes' differences from humans. "Orang Outang, Or Wild Man of the Woods" concludes with: "It is in their external form only, that [orangutans] have been classed as the next below the human family." Another piece proclaims, "Campen has proved by dissection, that [the orangutan] is not capable either of speech, or of walking naturally in an upright position."[31]

Hawthorne's loathing for nonhuman primates and his distress over our resemblances to them punctuate his fiction and nonfiction writing from the 1830s to the 1850s. In "Little Annie's Rambles" (1835, 1837), the narrator and the eponymous little girl delight in all the sights of the menagerie except the monkeys: "But, oh, those unsentimental monkeys! the ugly, grinning, aping, chattering, ill-natured, mischievous and queer little brutes. Annie does not love the monkeys. Their ugliness shocks her pure, instinctive delicacy of taste, and makes her mind unquiet, *because it bears a wild and dark resemblance to humanity*" (*CE* 9:127, emphasis added). In *The House of the Seven Gables* (1851), Clifford looks out the window at a passing organ grinder's monkey and "was so shocked by his horrible ugliness, spiritual as well as physical, that he actually began to shed tears." Like Annie, Clifford finds monkeys "shocking" precisely because—though ugly and wild—they nonetheless bear an uncanny resemblance to humans. As the organ grinder plays his tunes, the monkey, who had a "mean and low, yet strangely man-like expression," begs for money from "every passer-by," sometimes making a "personal application to individuals, holding out his small black palm, and otherwise plainly signifying his excessive desire for whatever filthy lucre might happen to be in anybody's pocket." When Phoebe tosses him down a handful of pennies, he "picked [them] up with joyless eagerness . . . and immediately re-commenced a series of pantomimic petitions for more." "Take this monkey just as he was," Hawthorne writes, "and you could desire no better image of the Mammon of copper-coin, symbolizing the grossest form of the love of money" (*CE* 2:164). As these examples suggest, Hawthorne rejected the idea that monkeys or apes were our closest animal relatives not because the theory seemed unlikely, but because it seemed unflattering.[32]

But for people like Hawthorne—who remained intrigued by affinities between humans and animals even as they recoiled from contemplation of our similarities to simians—there was another way of imagining humans' link to the animal world: the dog. In the world of pre-Darwinian science, it was by no means agreed upon that apes' physical resemblance to us gave them the distinction of being our closest relatives. As I explained in the introduction, even as eighteenth- and nineteenth-century natural historians began employing taxonomical models that organized flora and fauna into branches instead of "a single order of excellence"[33] (or Great Chain of Being), many of them continued (as adherents of the "chain" model did) to hold internal, psychological excellences more significant than physical traits in determining the proximities between and relative positions among animate beings. This logic enabled the celebrated French naturalist Buffon to argue that the dog was much closer to humans than the ape because, while the ape resembles humans only in form, the dog "possesses every internal excellence that can attract the regard of man."[34] This claim receives ten pages of elaboration in Buffon's *Natural History, General and Particular* (1749–89), which remained one of the best-selling scientific books well into the nineteenth century. Buffon's views on the dog were frequently cited in the popular press and informed virtually all nineteenth-century writing on the subject.

Contributing to the reception of Buffon's argument about the nature and significance of dog's virtues was also the fact that it fortified conventional beliefs against growing speculation about species transformation. As Buffon and other opponents of evolution well knew, the Great Chain of Being's principle of continuous gradation was less easily translated into a theory of evolution if dogs rather than primates occupied the link closest to humans. In addition, Buffon's argument gratified human vanity. Apes were widely regarded as wild and disgusting; to dogs Buffon attributed all human virtues but none of our vices. Thus, only pages after the *American Magazine*'s angst-ridden article on orangutans of December 1835, we find an article on dogs blithely proclaiming their closeness to humans: "All kinds of Dogs have powerful instincts, which places them near the rational creation [i.e., humans]. The elephant and the horse have similar powers and capacities. The Dog is sagacious; and discriminates by intuition, or instinct, with accuracy and promptness."[35]

There is no doubt that Hawthorne was familiar with Buffon's celebrated account of the canine mind; during his editorship of the *American Magazine,* Hawthorne published an article on dogs that begins by quoting it: "Buffon says of the Dog: 'Without enjoying, like man, the light of intellect, the Dog has all the warmth of sentiment; he possesses, in a higher degree than man, fidelity and constancy in his affections; he is all zeal, all ardour, and all obedience. He is more mindful of benefits than of injuries; he is not repelled by bad treatment. If a wrong be offered him, he bears it patiently, and forgets it; or only remembers it as a motive to stronger attachment.' "[36] As an examination of *The Marble Faun* reveals, this is a precise description of Donatello's character. Donatello's physical body, certainly, is patterned on Praxiteles' sculpture of the "wild" faun (10), but it would be difficult to find a more accurate description of Donatello's psychological traits than those that antebellum Americans—following Buffon—ascribed to the dog. Like the dog, Donatello is a "simpleton" (7) and "anything but intellectually brilliant" (22). In his attachment to Miriam, he displays zeal, ardor, and obedience in the extreme. When Miriam urges him to "cast [her] off" lest he be tainted with her sin, Donatello replies: "I will never quit you. . . . You cannot drive me from you!" (158). He even expresses his willingness to die for Miriam, if she should "desire it, or need it" (157). In fact, Hawthorne not only attributes to Donatello all of the qualities that Buffon attributes to the dog; he compares Donatello to a dog explicitly and repeatedly throughout the first seventeen chapters of the novel. Donatello's "faithful watch" over Miriam "was no more to be eluded than that of a hound" (157); "like a pet spaniel, he followed his beloved mistress wherever he could gain admittance" (131). Donatello "was as gentle and docile as a pet spaniel; as playful, too, in his general disposition, or saddening with his mistress's variable mood, like that, or any other kindly animal, which has the faculty of bestowing its sympathies more completely than man or woman can ever do" (43). Consistent with Buffon's description, Donatello is not repelled by Miriam's bad treatment; her displeasure only increases his desire to stand in her good graces. When Miriam takes offense at Donatello's refusal to let her touch his ears, he responds with a "mute, helpless gesture of entreaty [that] had something pathetic in it, and yet might well enough excite a laugh; so like it was to what you may see in the aspect of a hound, when he thinks himself in fault or disgrace" (14). Not yet winning her favor, Donatello kisses her hand and then gazes "into her cyes without saying a word," and in response Miriam "bestowed on him a little, careless caress, singularly like what one would give to a pet dog, when he puts himself in the way to receive it" (14).

The fact that Donatello incarnated the contemporary profile of the canine personality did not escape the notice of nineteenth-century readers. In an 1879 essay on Hawthorne, Anthony Trollope writes that Donatello "attaches himself to Miriam, as a dog does to a man, not with an expressed human love in which there is a longing for kisses and a hope for marriage, but with a devotion half doglike as I have said. . . . He scampers round her in his joy. . . . He is happy, except when the intruder comes, and then his jealousy is that as of a dog against an intruding hound."[37] It was, then, Hawthorne's success in distancing Donatello from wild apes and connecting him instead to the domestic dog that made this character (both for him and his readers) neither monstrous nor threatening but "delightful" instead.

The Transformation of the Faun

In the introduction to *The Great Chain of Being,* Arthur O. Lovejoy writes: "A term, a phrase, a formula, which gains currency or acceptance because one of its meanings, or of the thoughts which it suggests, is congenial to the prevalent beliefs, the standards of value, the tastes of a certain age, may help to alter beliefs, standards of value, and tastes, because other meanings or suggested implications, not clearly distinguished by those who employ it, gradually become the dominant elements of its signification" (14). This is exactly what happened with the idea that dogs stood closer than apes to human beings. Nineteenth-century developments in beliefs about dogs' closeness to humans—generated in part from the increasingly affective nature of people's relationships with companion animals and by the popularity of trained animal exhibitions as public entertainment—eventually shifted the effects of assertions about dogs' mental abilities so that the very discourse Buffon had used as resistance to evolutionary thinking came, in the end, to facilitate its acceptance. The case of Hawthorne and *The Marble Faun* provides one illustration of how and why this was so. Through the 1850s and well after that, thinking about wild simians' similarities to humans continued to elicit—as it did in the 1835–36 *American Magazine* articles—insistence on the insurmountable barriers between them and us. But as the closeness between the canine and human mind reminded us only of what we liked best in ourselves, people became increasingly willing to believe that the minds of dogs and humans were fundamentally the same—or could be made so through education.

Dogs are discussed in only two paragraphs of Lamarck's *Zoological Philosophy* (1809)—the first text to offer a fully elaborated theory of species transformation—but this brief discussion had lasting reverberations. Lamarck boldly argued that the earth's plant and animal species were neither unchanging nor the result of an original act of miraculous creation. As he succinctly explains in chapter 7 of part 1 of *Zoological Philosophy,* his argument that species of plants and animals underwent transmutation over time as a result of natural (rather than supernatural) forces departed radically from existing views:

> *Conclusion adopted hitherto:* Nature (or her Author) in creating animals, foresaw all the possible kinds of environment in which they would have to live, and endowed each species with a fixed organisation and with a definite and invariable shape, which compel each species to live in the places and climates where we actually find them, and there to maintain the habits which we know in them.
>
> *My individual conclusion:* Nature has produced all the species of animals in succession, beginning with the most imperfect or simplest, and ending her work with the most perfect, so as to create a gradually increasing complexity in their organisation; these animals have spread at large throughout all the habitable regions of the globe, and every species has derived from its environment the habits that we find in it and the structural modifications which observation shows us.[38]

Zoological Philosophy encompassed far more than biology; it attempted to synthesize geological, biological, and psychological phenomena. Lamarck began by pointing out that the belief in species fixity did not hold up when we considered that (1) each species is perfectly matched to its physical environment and (2) geological investigation revealed that the earth's environments had undergone repeated, radical alterations. As he explains, the existing theory was premised on the belief that environments did not vary, "for if they were to vary, the same animals could no longer survive" (126–27). Lamarck reasoned that since the environment had been—and continued to be—transformed, then the same must be true of living creatures. He proposed that when animals were confronted with alterations in their environment they changed their behavior accordingly: "great alterations in the environment of animals lead to great alterations in their needs, and these alterations in their needs necessarily lead to others in their activities" (107). According to the principle of use and disuse, new habits "long kept up" (114) could strengthen existing organs or even develop entirely new ones. If new habits resulted in the disuse of an organ, they could cause that organ to atrophy or even disappear. Subsequently, "all the acquisitions or losses wrought by nature on individuals, through the influence of the environment . . . are preserved by reproduction to the new individuals which arise" (113).[39]

The most radical aspect of Lamarck's theory was not its contradiction of the biblical story of creation. (Other scientists including Cuvier had, in response to fossil evidence, already suggested that there was not one creation, but a series of special creations that took place over great spans of time.) Rather, Lamarck's greatest affront to orthodox belief lay in the notion of non-miraculous creation—the creation of humans and other species by natural instead of supernatural forces. Lamarck's mentor Buffon had categorized humans as mammals, yet he maintained that humans, who possessed an immortal soul, were quite distinct from the rest of creation. *Zoological Philosophy* clearly delineates the development of humans from the "lower animals" (170–73). Even more shockingly, it "applied transformism to all aspects of human existence."[40] Lamarck's ultimate aim was to understand humans, which he believed he could do only by examining them in the context of the rest of the animal world. Thus, *Zoological Philosophy* culminates, in part 3, in an investigation of the biological development of human psychology. In this section—entitled "An enquiry into the physical causes of feeling, into the force which produces actions, and lastly into the origin of the acts of intelligence observed in various animals"—Lamarck argues that "the psychological capacities of human beings were grounded in the physiological faculties of the nervous system, itself a product of transformism." Lamarck saw human intelligence as "a product of the habit of thought" and "found the human brain to be the organ most responsive to constant use and development."[41]

Among many pieces of evidence Lamarck offers to support his argument is the existence of so many different "races of dogs." Lamarck theorized that all dog breeds had descended from "a single, original race, closely resembling the wolf, if indeed it was not actually the wolf." When humans domesticated this creature and carried it "into different countries and climates . . . the influences of their environment and of the various habits which had been forced upon them in each country" (presumably, by humans' different requirements of them) caused each population to undergo "remarkable alterations." The subsequent crossing of dogs from different regions of the world (effected when humans traveled for trade or other reasons) produced the diversity of dog breeds (110–11). Thus, for Lamarck, the forces that created new breeds of dogs (and, significantly, dog breeds were often afforded the status of species in nineteenth-century taxonomies)[42] were identical to those that created new species, including humans: changes in habits brought on by changes in environments.

As late as 1831, the opponents of the theory of species transformation still thought that discussions of canine sagacity supported their side. When Charles Lyell crafted, in *Principles of Geology* (1831–33), his meticulous recapitulation and refutation of Lamarck (an effort that succeeded, contrary to Lyell's purposes, in making Lamarck's theory exceedingly well known), he allotted much more attention to the subject of dogs than Lamarck did in *Zoological Philosophy.* Lyell acknowledges that "the modifications produced in the different races of dogs, exhibit the influence of man in the most striking point of view." Dogs "have been made . . . the servant, the companion, the guardian, and the intimate friend of man, and the power of a superior genius [i.e., that of humans] has had a wonderful influence, not only on their forms, but on their manners and intelligence."[43] However, Lyell insists (following Cuvier) that, as the changes wrought upon the dog in the material or human world did not constitute "essential changes" involving "the growth of new organs and the gradual obliteration of others," this example did not support a theory of species transformation (27). Later, he qualifies his earlier acknowledgment of humans' effect on the dog: "When such remarkable habits" as retrieving, pointing, and herding "appear in races of this species, we may reasonably conjecture that they were given [by the deity] with no other view than for the use of man and the preservation of the dog which thus obtains protection" (41). Lyell concludes, "As a general rule, we fully agree with M. F. Cuvier" that the traits of domesticated animals represent "modifications of instincts which are implanted in them in a state of nature" rather than "the influence of education alone" (41).

Lyell's rather contradictory account of the relative influence of God and man on the creation of the dog reflects growing popular belief that education by humans could in fact effect dramatic changes on the natural condition of dogs and other domesticated animals.[44] In chapter 1 I discussed the exhibitions of horses' self-regulatory capacities through which nineteenth-century "horse whisperers" generated revenue and attracted new clients. Although *The Wide, Wide World* attributes the capacity for education through disciplinary intimacy to equines only (among nonhumans), horses were just one of many animals argued to be capable of improvement through "education" and whose mastery of supposedly human mental operations was exhibited to the public in nineteenth-century America. Exhibitions of trained animals (along with exhibitions of wild animals or physiologically unusual farm animals) were "the earliest and most sustained source of public diversion in the New England region and the one least subject to regulation."[45] From the mid-eighteenth century onward, an increasing number of itinerant exhibitors of "sagacious," "learned," or "educated" animals clamored for the attention and surplus income of the citizens of New England's urban centers. These impresarios employed a wide variety of domesticated animals. In the 1790s, William F. Pinchbeck's "Pig of Knowledge" (also known as "The Learned Pig") impressed audiences throughout New England with his ability to read, spell (by moving letters with his snout), perform simple arithmetic, and tell the time, date, and year. In 1830, Isaac W. Merrill wrote in his diary that he saw a "learned goat" in Haverhill, Massachusetts, whose erudition made human children of her age seem "novices" by comparison.[46] However, the animals most frequently exhibited as "educated" were dogs and horses. Like most Americans, Hawthorne had repeated exposure to the "dog and pony shows" that were, by the early 1800s, ubiquitous in the northeastern United States. In 1835, Hawthorne saw a circus that featured "excellent horsemanship" and "a small white dog, of divers accomplishments" (*CE* 23:123–24). In 1836, he wrote about a "poodle-dog, trained by Prof. Blumenbach at Gottingen" that "hatched hen's eggs, and took motherly care of the chickens, attending on them and providing them food" (*CE* 23:150).

As dogs became an increasingly important part of the middle-class American domestic scene, their feats of loyalty and heroism began to convince many that their latent qualities were not just intellectual but moral as well. Hawthorne's writings from the 1830s to 1850s reflect increasing receptivity to contemporary arguments about animals' and in particular dogs' latent qualities—a trajectory that parallels attitudes of the general public. In the 1836 *American Magazine* article on the dog quoted above, Hawthorne seems undecided. After beginning with Buffon's encomium for the canine mind, the article continues: "Can this beautiful character belong to a creature without a soul?—to one of the brutes that perish, and whose virtues perish with them? How high, then, should be the excellence of beings endowed with immortal souls, and whose virtues might also be immortal!"[47] At first, the questions that begin the excerpt seem to be rhetorical: given dogs' virtues, shouldn't we assume that they, too, possess an immortal soul? Having tentatively ventured thus far into heresy, the article then scrambles back to safer ground with a banal and unobjectionable message about human excellence. But if this redirection fails to support the idea posited in the first sentence, it does not exactly erase it either, for the issue of canine immortality is not so much negated as left hanging in the air.

Eight years later, the issue of dogs' moral qualities reappears in Hawthorne's writing, in a context that is both more playful and more personal. In one of the letters written to Sophia during her 1844 absence, Hawthorne reports that he is feeding Leo "what is fit for Christians" (i.e., "people food") and then adds, "though, for that matter, he appears to be as good a Christian as most laymen, or even as some of the clergy" (*CE* 16:43). A letter written a week later offers a more extended though less positive consideration of Leo's moral standing:

> Leo, I regret to say, has fallen under suspicion of a very grave crime—nothing less than murder—a fowl crime it may well be called—for it is the slaughter of one of Mr. Hayward's hens. He has been seen to chase the hens, several times, and the other day one of them was found dead. Possibly he may be innocent; and as there is nothing but circumstantial evidence, it must be left with his own conscience. . . . I am afraid, too, that he is an incorrigible thief. Ellery Channing says he saw him coming up the avenue with a whole calf's head in his mouth. How he came by it, is best known to Leo himself. If he were a dog of fair character, it would be no more than charity to conclude that he had either bought it or had it given to him; but, with the other charges against him, it inclines me to great distrust of his moral principles. (*CE* 16:50–51)

Hawthorne's worries about Leo's "moral principles" here are clearly more sportive than serious, but, its humorous tone notwithstanding, the passage further illustrates the connection between the human-animal encounters concomitant with antebellum domestic life and a willingness to think about animals' minds in terms that violated the tenet Hawthorne himself recited at the end of his 1836 article on orangutans: "There is one great and invariable mark of distinction between the Man with a soul, and the Animal without one."[48] In a notebook entry dated December 9, 1850, (which, like many of the entries recorded around this time, stands alone and presumably represents an idea that Hawthorne hoped to use in the future in his fiction) Hawthorne clearly rejects this notion:

> If we consider the lives of the lower animals, we shall see in them a close parallelism to those of mortals;—toil, struggle, danger, privation, mingled with glimpses of peace and ease; enmity, affection, a continual hope of bettering themselves, although their objects lie at less distance before them than our own do. Thus, no argument from the imperfect character of our own existence, and its delusory promises, and its injustice, can be drawn in reference to our immortality, without, in a degree, being applicable to our brute brethren. (*CE* 8:300)

To the extent that the animals Hawthorne most often observed were the domesticated creatures in his home and surroundings, this passage may be glossed as saying observations of feelings and desires of those animals makes it difficult if not impossible to argue that we may be transformed from sinful, mortal beings into ones granted eternal life unless we also allow that the same transformations may happen to animals.

Hawthorne was far from alone in this belief. In 1856 as mainstream a publication as *Putnam's Monthly Magazine* printed "Have Animals Souls?" and from midcentury onward this question (which the *Putnam's* piece answered in the affirmative) came before the public with increasing frequency and intensity.[49] It was in this context that arguments about canine minds began to promote rather than suppress consideration of evolution. Discussions of dogs' manifest and latent mental abilities figure prominently in Robert Chambers' pro-evolution *Vestiges of the Natural History of Creation,* which he published anonymously (out of fear of reprisals) in 1844. Citing similarities between humans and canines, Chambers argued that the differences between human and animal minds were not absolute differences but "mere stages of development."[50] "The actions of children," he contends, "bear a resemblance to those of certain familiar animals. . . . A pampered lap-dog, living where there is another of its own species, will hide any nice morsel which it cannot eat, under a rug, or in some other by-place, designing to enjoy it afterwards. I have seen children do the same thing" (346–47). Chambers even goes so far as to argue that canines could—under proper conditions—develop advanced, ostensibly human levels of intelligence, citing the example of the dogs trained by M. Leonard as "remarkable examples of what the animal intellect may be trained to. When four pieces of card are laid down before them, each having a number pronounced *once* in connexion with it, they will, after a re-arrangement of the pieces, select any one named by its number. They also play at dominoes, and with so much skill as to triumph over biped opponents, whining if the adversary place a wrong piece, or if they themselves be deficient in a right one. Of extensive combinations of thought we have no reason to believe that any animal is capable—and yet most of us must feel the force of Walter Scott's remark, that there was scarcely anything which he would not believe of a dog" (338).

Passages such as these made opponents of evolutionary thinking realize that arguments for the closeness of canine and human minds were no longer helping their cause. Thus Chambers' claims about canine sagacity and educability became a point of early and particularly scurrilous attack in the scathing eighty-five-page denouncement of *Vestiges* written by Adam Sedgwick and published by the *Edinburgh Review.* "His credulity," Sedgwick wrote of *Vestiges'* anonymous author, "is quite on a level with his rashness. . . . He believes

. . . that dogs can play admirably at dominoes. . . . Under his celestial teaching we may live to see a grizzly dowager, a wheezing bachelor, and a withered maid, sitting down to a quiet game of whist with a new-fashioned dummy in the form of a solemn poodle; while a lively spitz, or fawning spaniel, is raised on its hind-quarters at the corner of the sofa table, and teaching the knight's move to the younger ladies of the household!"[51] But Sedgwick's satire deflated neither popular beliefs in canine potentiality nor the sales of *Vestiges.* Between 1844 and the year *The Marble Faun* was published, *Vestiges* went through eleven editions and sold 23,350 copies.[52] As historian Peter J. Bowler explains, the publication of *Vestiges* and its aftermath "brought the basic idea of evolution up to man to public attention fifteen years before Darwin's *Origin of Species* appeared."[53]

Hawthorne delivered the final manuscript for *The Marble Faun* to his publishers on November 9, 1859; *On the Origin of Species* was published twelve days later on November 24. Thus, Darwin's theory of natural selection could not have influenced Hawthorne's writing of *The Marble Faun.* And as Chambers believed that species transformation happened *in utero* (by a prolongation of the gestational period) his theory was hardly suitable for fictional dramatization. Instead, *The Marble Faun*'s transformation of Donatello from a dog-like character into a fully human one draws on what was, at that time, the most credible account of the evolutionary process: the theory of *transformisme* Lamarck advanced in *Zoological Philosophy.*[54] Significantly, Lamarck's term *transformisme* was translated into English as the doctrine of transformism or transformation, and Hawthorne's English publishers printed the novel there under the title *The Transformation.* Kenyon succinctly explains Donatello's development in Lamarckian terms at the end of the novel. When Hilda asks, "Was Donatello really a Faun?" Kenyon answers: "Faun or not, he had a genial nature, which, had the rest of mankind been in accordance with it, would have made earth a Paradise to our poor friend. It seems the moral of his story, that human beings, of Donatello's character, compounded especially for happiness, have no longer any business on earth, or elsewhere. Life has grown so sadly serious, that such men *must change their natures, or else perish, like the antediluvian creatures that required, as the condition of their existence, a more summer-like atmosphere* than ours" (459–60, emphasis added). Kenyon's answer illustrates the essential components of Lamarck's theory: (1) since every organism is perfectly suited to its environment, and since environments do change, organisms must either undergo change or perish; (2) that environmental factors (and not miraculous intervention) catalyzed transspecific transformation; and (3) that the same processes that shaped physiological traits (the bodies of "antediluvian creatures") also formed qualities of the human mind ("Donatello's character").

Though this passage offers the most succinct interpretation of Donatello's transformation in Lamarckian terms, we can see that these ideas are in fact carefully introduced in the first chapter of the novel and that Donatello's entire transformation proceeds according to the principles of Lamarckian transformation. In chapter 1, Kenyon observes the resemblance between Donatello and Praxiteles' sculpture, and Hilda promptly responds: "If there is any difference between the two faces, the reason may be, I suppose, that the Faun dwelt in woods and fields, and consorted with his like; whereas, Donatello has known cities a little, and such people as ourselves" (7). Hilda's response introduces Lamarck's idea that environmental changes produce changes in organisms, and it alerts us to the fact that Donatello's time in Rome has already set changes in him in motion, for the Donatello of chapters 1 through 17 (i.e., prior to the murder that most critics regard as the sole cause of his transformation) is not identical with the "easy, mirthful" faun described in the opening chapter, who was always "apt for jollity" but "endowed with no principle of virtue" and lacking "any high and heroic ingredient" (9). In chapter 16, Miriam observes an uncharacteristic "melancholy" in Donatello and urges him to remove himself from the pernicious effects of Rome: "You are getting spoilt, in this dreary Rome, and will be as wise and wretched as all the rest of mankind, unless you go back to your Tuscan vineyards" (143). A few pages later, Donatello asks Miriam: "Signorina, do I look as when you first knew me? . . . Methinks there has been a change upon me, these many months; and more and more, these last few days. The joy is gone out of my life; all gone!—all gone!" (148–49). Miriam responds by again attributing this change to his change of environment: "My poor Donatello . . . this melancholy and sickly Rome is stealing away the rich, joyous life that belongs to you. Go back, my dear friend, to your home among the hills, where . . . your days were filled with simple and blameless delights" (149). During their visit to the Church of the Capuchins, Kenyon makes a nearly identical observation: "You seem out of spirits, my dear friend. . . . This languid Roman atmosphere is not the airy wine that you were accustomed to breathe at home" (180). Miriam agrees that "this old, dreamy, and dreary Rome" cannot "sustain the life of such a creature" as Donatello (181).

The novel further emphasizes the environment's power to activate organic change by reminding us that the changes that befall Donatello are overriding or modifying his "essential" nature or genetic inheritance. Donatello's butler

Tomaso insists that "there had not been a single Count in the family, these hundred years and more, who was so true a Monte Beni, of the antique stamp, as this poor Signorino" (238). The causes for Donatello's changes are as clear to Tomaso as they were to Miriam and Kenyon. "The world has grown either too evil, or else too wise and sad, for such men as the old Counts of Monte Beni used to be," Tomaso laments. "His very first taste of it, as you see, has changed and spoilt my poor young lord" (238). Similarly, Kenyon is "affected . . . with infinite pity" when he "see[s] this young man, who had been born to gladness as an assured heritage, now involved in a misty bewilderment of grievous thoughts" (261). What Kenyon and the reader discover is the central component of Lamarck's thesis: that there is no such thing as "assured heritage," since the characteristics of organisms are not fixed, but constantly changing as the environment changes.

Consistent with Lamarckian theory, *The Marble Faun* presents environmental change as a necessary but not sufficient factor in Donatello's transformation. Lamarck theorized that "great alterations in the environment of animals lead to great alterations in their needs, and these alterations in needs necessarily lead to others in their activities" (107). Thus, while environmental changes precipitate transformations in organisms, it is the internal activity of the organism, rather than the environment per se, that is the mechanism of organic change.[55] According to the principle of use and disuse, new habits "long kept up" could strengthen existing organs or even develop entirely new ones. Close examination of Hawthorne's novel will show that Donatello's changes do not, as critics frequently insist, happen immediately after he commits murder. Well *before* Donatello hurls Miriam's persecutor over the cliff, "A higher sentiment brightened upon Donatello's face, than had hitherto seemed to belong to its simple expression and sensuous beauty" (158). In the moments after the murder, Donatello is described as having a sudden illumination. His face "had taken a higher, almost an heroic aspect from the strength of passion" (175). His eyes "blazed with the fierce energy that had suddenly inspired him. It had kindled him into a man; it had developed within him an intelligence which was no native characteristic of the Donatello whom we have heretofore known" (172).

However, the rest of the novel stresses that Donatello's is a gradual transformation, realized through his own internal activities—the result not of a single act of murder but rather of a prolonged and active struggle on his part or, in Lamarck's terms, from "new habits that are long kept up" (114). Although Donatello may not appear to be doing anything during Kenyon's visit to his ancestral home, he is quite actively exercising his powers of thought and remorse. Kenyon tells Miriam that "a wonderful *process* is going forward in Donatello's mind. . . . The germs of faculties, that have heretofore slept, are fast springing into *activity*" (282, emphasis added). Donatello gains increased control over his emotions, but only "after a struggle more or less fierce" (250). He acquires his "spiritual instruction . . . through sorrow and remorse" (320). He develops a "more definite and nobler individuality . . . out of grief and pain" (262). Though he may have fortuitously "found a soul" "in the black depths," he actively, and through his own volition, "was struggling with it towards the light of Heaven" (268). When Donatello comes close to losing his way, Kenyon is there to exhort him: "Not despondency, not slothful anguish, is what you now require—but effort!" (273). "There was an interval," Kenyon tells Miriam, "when the horrour of some calamity . . . threw Donatello into a stupour of misery. . . . But, as his mind roused itself . . . [and] rose to a higher life than he had hitherto experienced" (281).

The final result of Donatello's conscious, prolonged efforts to adapt to his changing circumstances is the acquisition of two properties of mind that, according to conventional wisdom, separated humans from animals: "intellect" and "a soul" (282). No comparisons between Donatello and dogs appear after chapter 17. When Donatello meets Miriam under the statue of Pope Julius in Perugia, "the change that had long been taking place in his interiour self" (323) had produced "a vivified intellect," "an altered and deepened character" (320). Rather than a "thing of sportive, animal nature, the sylvan Faun," Donatello was "now the man of feeling and intelligence" (320).

While Donatello's successful transformation from faun to human depends on the novel's ability to establish his connection with the dog and foreclose the connection between him and Pastrana, the threat that Pastrana represents is not entirely erased from the novel. Indeed, this threat haunts *The Marble Faun* in the form of the mysterious character who stalks Miriam and whom Donatello kills. This enigmatic figure (often referred to as the Model, since he serves in this capacity for Miriam and other artists), as Evan Carton has observed, is twice identified with satyrs, mythological part-human, part-animal creatures often depicted in the company of fauns. When the Model emerges from the catacombs, he is wearing "a pair of those goat-skin breeches, with the hair outward" which made the wearers look "like antique Satyrs" (30). Later, Miriam jokingly asks Donatello to summon the fantastical creatures known to be "kindred" to fauns, insisting that she would not shrink "even if one of your rough cousins, a hairy Satyr, should come capering on his goat-legs out of the haunts of far antiquity, and propose to dance with me among these laws" (78); this is precisely what the Model does later in the chapter.[56]

However, although the Model's connection to satyrs links him to Donatello to a certain extent, Hawthorne's choices also mark important differences between Donatello and the Model and their respective connections to contemporary evolutionary thinking. Unlike the handsome, amiable fauns, satyrs were depicted as rude, aggressive, lecherous, and ugly. And, in the first half of the nineteenth century, satyrs (but not fauns) were also associated with orangutans and other simians.[57] *Simia satyrus, Satyrus troglodytis,* and *Pitheus satyrus* were three of the scientific names ascribed to orangutans in Hawthorne's lifetime. Three of the articles on orangutans that appeared in the *American Magazine* under Bradford's editorship (all of which appeared shortly before or shortly after Hawthorne's tenure as editor) prominently feature the name "*Satyrus*" in their title. The full headline for the orangutan article that appeared in the December 1835 number, for example, is: "The Female Orang Outang.—[Simia Satyrus, vel Satyrus Troglodytis]." The text of this piece claims that orangutans are "generally less mischievous and ill-natured, than common monkeys and satyrs."[58] Hawthorne himself connects monkeys and satyrs in his 1853 retelling of the story of Proserpina's abduction by Pluto; when Ceres is searching for her daughter, she encounters "a rude gang of satyrs, who had faces like monkeys . . . and who were generally dancing in a very boisterous manner, with shouts of noisy laughter. When she stopt to question them, they would only laugh the louder, and make new merriment out of the lone woman's distress. How unkind of those ugly satyrs!" (*CE* 7:310).[59] Even later, the association between "satyr" and simian remained strong enough for one political cartoonist to lampoon post-Darwinian evolutionary debates by presenting an ape who asks, "Am I satyr or man?"

Moreover, the Model, as we discover after his death, had been moonlighting as "Brother Antonio" of the Capuchin monks. Then as now, "Capuchin" meant both monk and monkey: the term applies equally to a Franciscan friar and to the South American primate *Cebus capucinus,* whose most remarkable feature was a cowl-like head of hair. As capuchin monkeys were the species most commonly kept as pets and used by organ-grinders,[60] the monkey that elicits Clifford's revulsion in *Seven Gables* was probably a capuchin. Hawthorne's own personal association of monkeys with the devil and the priesthood with gross sensuality[61] further solidifies this connection, as what brings Kenyon, Miriam, and Donatello to the Church of the Capuchins in the first place is their observation that the Model's face bears an uncanny resemblance to the demon in Guido Reni's painting *St. Michael Trampling the Devil.*

Finally, this Capuchin is also connected to antebellum anxiety about humans' links to simians in his threat to Miriam and in his occupation as an

From *Punch* magazine, May 18, 1861. As this cartoon illustrates, the term "satyr" was used interchangeably with "ape" and "monkey" in the nineteenth century. Image courtesy of Hulton Archive / Getty Images.

artist's model. The "influence of this ill-omened person over Miriam" we are told "was such as beasts and reptiles, of subtle and evil nature, sometimes exercise upon their victims" (93). Rather than physical harm, however, what the Model/monk threatens to do is expose the shocking nature of their relationship and of Miriam's history. What that past is, Hawthorne resolutely (or perversely, some readers say) refuses to reveal. But the repeated connections between Miriam and Beatrice Cenci suggest that he might be her brother, an interpretation supported by his claim that he has known her since her "girlhood" (94). If that is the case, however, Miriam's unwillingness to recognize this man as a brother echoes Hawthorne's unwillingness—in his 1836 "Species of Men" article—to bestow "the name of brethren" on orangutans. Indeed, even without his goat-hair trousers, the Model/monk resembles a wild man if not an orangutan: he is "dark, bushy bearded, wild of aspect and attire" (19). These facts offer compelling evidence that the anxiety surrounding the Model in the novel was at some level connected to the anxiety Hawthorne and his contemporaries experienced when they considered the possibility that nature might have formed humans out of monkeys just as easily as artists "convert[ed]" their models "into Saints or assassins, according as their pictorial purposes demand" (19).

But as the novel cryptically admits this possibility, it also insists on killing it off. Carton observes that the "most uncanny role" of the Model "is that of a double for Donatello," for after Donatello kills the Model he assumes a bond of guilt with Miriam that is in many ways identical to the relationship between Miriam and the Model that he sought to end.[62] What is even more uncanny still about the relationship between these two figures is the way in which Donatello's killing of the Model and his subsequent assumption of the function he sought to abolish dramatizes the way in which ideas about the closeness between human and canine minds—which Buffon sanctioned when he advanced them in an attempt to kill off speculation about human evolution—ended up facilitating exactly what Buffon sought to annihilate: popular acceptance of evolutionary theory.

Eventually, ideas about the closeness of dogs' minds to humans' came to be used by Darwin himself. The rhetorical strategies Darwin adopts in *The Descent of Man* (1871) and *The Expression of the Emotions in Man and Animals* (1872) reflects his knowledge that people felt exactly as Hawthorne did about closeness to civilized as opposed to savage animals. For the first image of *Descent of Man* (in chapter 1's discussion of the correspondences between human and animal bodily structure), Darwin chose an illustration of the similarities between a human embryo and a dog embryo. The comparison (in chapters 2 and 3) of animals' and humans' "mental powers" proceeds, more often than not, by first establishing the presence of emotion, memory, imagination, reason, and moral sense in the dog (or, less commonly, the cat or the horse) and then presenting evidence showing that monkeys and apes also possess such capacities.[63] Similarly, *Expression*'s argument about parallels between the physiological manifestations of emotional states in animals and humans does not, as we might expect, begin with data on nonhuman primates. Instead, Darwin introduces his theory by comparing the emotions of humans to those of the dog, the cat, and the horse. Only after his argument is well underway does he introduce examples or illustrations relating to primates. For example, chapter 5, "Special Expressions of Animals," moves (as its headnote summarizes) from "The dog, various expressive movements of—Cats—Horses—Ruminants—Monkeys, their expressions of joy and affection—Of pain—Anger—Astonishment and terror."[64] Like any skillful rhetorician, Darwin establishes his least controversial points before moving to claims likely to alienate his readers. The organization he selected for this chapter corresponds to the esteem in which people held these animals—and hence the reader's willingness to admit these creatures' resemblance to themselves.

Doubting God's Providence

> "Hilda!—my religious Hilda!" whispered Miriam, suddenly drawing the girl close to her, "do you know how it is with me? I would give all I have or hope—my life, Oh, how freely!—for one instant of your trust in God! You little guess my need of it. You really think, then, that He sees and cares for us?"
>
> "Miriam, you frighten me!"
>
> ". . . Am I strange? Is there anything wild in my behaviour?"
>
> "Only for that moment," replied Hilda, "because you seemed to doubt God's Providence." (166–67)

Given nineteenth-century reaction to other texts proposing that humans' ostensibly unique mental qualities had developed—by natural, not divine, forces—out of an animal state, it is easy to understand why "the events and language of *The Marble Faun*" so "insistently recall the story of the Fall."[65] In Hawthorne's lifetime, as Peter J. Bowler explains, any theory that challenged the belief that humankind was a distinct creation "was automatically the enemy of true religion." After the publication of Chambers' *Vestiges*, "Many journals published reviews condemning the crude materialism of the book as a force that should be stopped before it undermined the foundations of religion and the social order." But Bowler also argues convincingly that our customary habit of opposing theological and evolutionary thinking does not reflect the nineteenth-century cogitation on these issues. "Religious debates," he explains, "constituted a framework within which all scientists at the time had to function." Erasmus Darwin—"a deist who believed that God had designed living things to be self-improving through time"—"claimed to have developed his idea of transmutation not from natural history but from David Hartley's account (1749) of how the soul is affected by the habits of life." *Vestiges,* too, seamlessly integrates scientific and religious concerns; that opponents objected to its theology does not mean that its framework was not theological.[66]

As biblical language *was* the lexicon of evolutionary debate in the 1850s, Hawthorne was following contemporary rhetorical conventions when he decided to structure his engagement with evolutionary thinking in terms of the story of the Fall. While the Fortunate Fall theory was neither new nor inexpressibly shocking in the 1850s, the issue of evolution for many Americans was both. Moreover, contemporary objections to evolutionary theory were rooted in the same principle that drove theologians centuries before to oppose the idea of the Fortunate Fall. Most opposition to the theory of evolution (then as now) can be traced back to "the traditional view [that] assumes that there *cannot* be any change [in the organic world] because the forces of nature can only maintain the original forms created by God—they are not by themselves creative."[67] Similarly, the original stumbling block to acceptance of the Fall as fortunate, was that such a view required belief that "man's" actions (actions expressly forbidden by God) could have brought him to a higher state of development than the actions of God himself. Both theories insisted that natural, nondivine forces could be creative, while, according to orthodox views, only God was. Furthermore, the most extensive critique of Chambers' *Vestiges,* Sedgwick's eighty-five-page "review" published in the *Edinburgh Review* (a publication that, as we know from Marion L. Kesselring's study, Hawthorne regularly read),[68] dramatized the public's receptivity to the book as a replay of the story of the Fall of Man. Sedgwick insisted that the ideas of *Vestiges* were "seductions" that would "poison the springs of joyous thought and modest feeling" of "our glorious maidens and matrons." The author, he claimed, "comes before them with a bright, polished and many-coloured surface, and the serpent coils of a false philosophy, and asks them again to stretch out their hands and pluck forbidden fruit . . . that their Bible is a fable when it teaches them that they were made in the image of God—that they are the children of apes and the breeders of monsters . . . and that all the phenomena of the universe . . . are to be put before the mind . . . as the progression and development of a rank, unbending, and degrading materialism" (3).

But there is another reason why *The Marble Faun*'s "glorious maiden" Hilda finds Kenyon's explanation of Donatello's transformation "shock[ing] . . . beyond words" (460): in terms of questioning cornerstones of contemporary belief, the novel actually goes well beyond *Zoological Philosophy* and *Vestiges.* Lamarck and Chambers challenged the notion that species were fixed in nature, but they both interpreted the development of new species as the protracted unfolding of a divine plan and thus fully supported a teleological view of natural history that—like the account of creation recorded in Genesis—held humankind to be the pinnacle of creation. Thus, while Lamarck and Chambers argued that divine intervention was not required for the creation of each new species, they maintained the relative positions of humans and animals in the cosmic hierarchy. "Behold, then, the wonderful unity of the whole system," Chambers wrote in *Vestiges.* "The grades of mind, like the forms of being, are mere stages of development. . . . In man the system has arrived at its highest condition" (347).

The Marble Faun, by contrast, exudes no such confidence about this placement of humans at the apex of creation. Miriam, Kenyon, and Hilda all begin the novel certain of their superiority to their faun-like companion: Donatello's "many agreeable characteristics . . . won him the kindly and half-contemptuous regard of Miriam and her two friends" (22). Thus, initially the group's (and especially Miriam's) attitude toward Donatello parallels that attitude toward animals that characterized Hawthorne's early thinking and which had been—up until the nineteenth century—an axiom of Western civilization: animals were clearly inferior to humans, and though they could serve or amuse us, as beings beneath us on the *scala naturae,* they did not merit our esteem. In the opening scene of the novel, Miriam declares, within Donatello's hearing, that "no Faun in Arcadia was ever a greater simpleton than Donatello. He has hardly a man's share of wit" (7). Hilda promptly chides her "ungrateful" behavior: "Hush, naughty one! . . . he has wit enough to worship you, at all events" (8). But Miriam's rudeness persists, as when she abruptly breaks off Donatello's visit to her studio with: "leave me now, for, to speak plainly, my good friend, you grow a little wearisome" (50). Hilda never questions her original view of the natural order and, consequently, she sees Donatello's transformation as an unqualified improvement. Of the bust of Donatello that Kenyon sculpted of him some time after "the fine, fresh glow of animal spirits had departed out of his face" (180), she remarks: "It gives the impression of a growing intellectual power and moral sense. Donatello's face used to evince little more than a genial, pleasurable sort of vivacity, and capability of enjoyment. But, here, a soul is being breathed into him; it is the Faun, *but advancing towards a state of higher development*" (380, emphasis added).

But whether the state of human development was in all respects "higher" than that of nonhuman animals is precisely what the novel calls into question. In one of the many passages that invite us to believe that Donatello might indeed possess pointed ears, the narrator proposes that this morphological trait would link him "with *what we call the inferiour* tribes of being, whose simplicity, mingled with his human intelligence, *might partly restore what man has lost of the divine!*" (71, emphasis added). According to the traditional view, one cannot move down the chain, toward the animal side of creation, in order to move up, toward the Godhead. The chain is absolutely unidirectional: each being possesses a little less divine infusion than the one above it. Hawthorne's resistance to this logic appears as early as his first notebook entry on the faun sculptures he saw in Italy: "the faun," he writes, was "a natural and delightful link betwixt human and brute life, and with something of a *divine* character intermingled" (*CE* 14:174, emphasis added).

True—Miriam and Kenyon draw parallels between Donatello's transformation and the Fall of Man, so far as they admit that his experiences have educed mental and moral qualities that before were only latent. But what both Miriam and Kenyon grapple with over the course of the novel is the question of whether attaining those traditional markers of human status—intellect and a soul—can rightly or simply be interpreted as moving "up." As Miriam spends more time with the faun-like Donatello, her opinion of him begins to waiver, so that "alternately, she almost admired, or wholly scorned him, and knew not which estimate resulted from the deeper appreciation" (80). Miriam's inability to identify her feelings arises from the fact that, in his animal state, Donatello seems simultaneously more and less developed than humankind—and thus confounds traditional notions of human ascendancy. Donatello seems to Miriam "not precisely man, nor yet a child, but, in a *high* and beautiful sense, an animal; a creature in a state of development less than what mankind has attained, yet the more perfect within itself for that very deficiency" (78, emphasis added). Significantly, Miriam's reconsideration of her dismissal of Donatello as an inferior "simpleton" remains coupled with the decidedly animal (and specifically canine) aspects of his nature. When Donatello states, in Borghese Gardens, his belief that his ecstasy from being in love with her will last "Forever!—forever!—forever!" Miriam thinks to herself: "But, is he a simpleton indeed? Here, in those few, natural words, he has expressed that deep sense, that profound conviction of its own immortality, which genuine love never fails to bring. He perplexes me—yes, and bewitches me—wild, gentle, beautiful creature that he is! It is like playing with a young greyhound!" (81–82).

If the novel as a whole refuses to take a position on whether Donatello's transformation was "fortunate," it steadfastly maintains that Donatello was, if nothing else, a great deal happier in his pretransformation, part-animal state. (Once his transformation into a fully human being is underway, Donatello begins to do all the things that Whitman says animals do not do: "sweat and whine about their condition, . . . lie awake in the dark and weep for their sins, . . . make me [or Kenyon and Miriam, in this case] sick discussing their duty to God.") Had Donatello been able to preserve his original "nature," Kenyon insists, it "would have made earth a Paradise to our poor friend" (459). At the end of the novel, Donatello is not in paradise but prison. Miriam comes to look back on Donatello's earlier state with awe instead of scorn, and she curses her own role in the change of his animal self into a fully human one: "Alas! and it was I that brought it ['strange horrour and gloom'] on you. . . . What repentance, what self-sacrifice, can atone for that infinite wrong? There was something sacred in the innocent and joyous life which you were leading!" (320). For his part, Kenyon concludes that "the growth of a soul, which [he] half imagined that he had witnessed in [Donatello], seemed hardly worth the heavy price that it had cost, in the sacrifice of those simple enjoyments that were gone forever" (393). Seeing "the glad Faun of his imagination and memory, now transformed into a gloomy penitent . . . deepen[ed] the cloud that had fallen over [his] spirits" and "caused him to fancy . . . that the whole world was saddening around him" (393–94).

As Hawthorne was well aware, the consequences of interrogating belief in a simple hierarchical relation between humans and animals were profound, for questioning humankind's position at the pinnacle of creation necessarily undermined belief in the *telos* of natural phenomena. If the status of humans, who were created last, was not unequivocally superior to that of all other creatures, then how could natural history represent the unfolding of a design? Thus, rather than the novel's consideration of evolutionary theory per se, it is its serious consideration of a nonteleological view of the universe that constitutes its most heretical and shocking aspect and drives its heavy-handed and almost nervous insistence on the parallels between Donatello's transformation and the biblical story of the Fall. The full effects of the novel's imposition of an evolutionary narrative onto a biblical one are not revealed, however, until the final chapter, which dramatizes the relationships among the radical ideas with which the novel engages: the development of "human" intellectual and moral qualities in an "animal" mind via natural rather than divine forces; the inability of a linear hierarchy to account for the relative positions of animals and humans; and the difficulties in sustaining either a progressive view of natural history or a belief in divine Providence.

In the concluding scene of the novel, Kenyon and Hilda decide, while they are walking about the Pantheon, that the effect of the magnificent building comes primarily from the opening in the dome—"that great Eye, gazing heavenward"—which, by providing a view to the natural sky, makes the structure "so unlike all the snugness of our modern civilization!" (457). Hilda adds that she likes looking at the "bright, blue sky, roofing the edifice where the builders left it open" better than the paving stones beneath. She then continues to associate this element of nature (as opposed to architecture and shrines beneath it) with the divine: "it is very delightful, in a breezy day, to see the masses of white cloud float over the opening, and then the sunshine fall through it again, fitfully, as it does now. Would it be any wonder if we were to see angels hovering there, partly in and partly out, with genial, heavenly faces?" (457). But just moments later, Hilda reveals the limits of her willingness to elevate the nonhuman above the human. She and Kenyon decide to examine a "dusky picture" hanging over one of the altars set up inside. "Approaching the shrine, they . . . could not forbear smiling, to see that a very plump and comfortable tabby-cat (whom we ourselves have often observed haunting the Pantheon) had established herself on the altar, in the genial sunbeam, and was fast asleep among the holy tapers. Their footsteps disturbing her, she awoke, raised herself, and sat blinking in the sun, yet with a certain dignity and self-possession, as if conscious of representing a Saint" (458). Kenyon finds the cat pleasing and ventures that there may truly be something saintly about her. "I presume," he remarks, "that this is the first of the feline race that has ever set herself up as an object of worship, in the Pantheon or elsewhere, since the days of ancient Egypt. See; there is a peasant from the neighboring market, actually kneeling to her! She seems a gracious and benignant Saint enough." Hilda, however, finds this tableau horrifying. Specifically, she objects to the elevation of animal above human and the positioning of the animal between man and God. Hilda responds "reproachfully": "help me to drive the creature away. It distresses me to see that poor man, or any human being, directing his prayers so much amiss" (458). Despite her transcendentalist talk about the spirituality of nature, Hilda can't abandon traditional notions of human ascendancy.[69]

Moments after this exchange, Hilda suddenly asks Kenyon, "Was Donatello really a Faun?" Of his three successive answers to her question, she accepts none of them. First, Kenyon explains Donatello's transformation in Lamarckian, biological terms:

> It seems the moral of his story, that human beings, of Donatello's character, compounded especially for happiness, have no longer any business on earth, or elsewhere. Life has grown so sadly serious, that such men must change their natures, or else perish, like the antediluvian creatures that required, as the condition of their existence, a more summer-like atmosphere than ours. (459–60)

When "the hopeful and happy-natured Hilda" replies, "I will not accept your moral," Kenyon translates the issue of organic transformation, as Chambers did, into more specifically religious terms: the eduction of latent intellectual and moral qualities:

> Then, here is another; take your choice. . . . He perpetrated a great crime; and his remorse, gnawing into his soul, has awakened it; developing a thousand high capabilities, moral and intellectual, which we never should have dreamed of asking for, within the scanty compass of the Donatello whom we knew. (460)

Here, Hilda exhibits momentary confusion, returning, "I know not whether this is so," until Kenyon proceeds to connect these previous explanations to the theological issue of the Fall:

> "Here comes my perplexity," continued Kenyon. "Sin has educated Donatello, and elevated him. Is Sin, then—which we deem such a dreadful blackness in the Universe—is it, like Sorrow, merely an element of human education, through which we struggle to a higher and purer state than we could otherwise have attained? Did Adam fall, that we might ultimately rise to a loftier Paradise than his?"
>
> "Oh, hush!" cried Hilda, shrinking from him with an expression of horrour which wounded the poor, speculative sculptor to the soul. "This is terrible; and I could weep for you, if you indeed believe it. Do not you perceive what a mockery your creed makes, not only of all religious sentiment, but of moral law, and how it annuls and obliterates whatever precepts of Heaven are written deepest within us? You have shocked me beyond words!" (460)

Hilda's objection—that the explanation is not compatible with the belief that "Heaven" (as opposed to natural phenomena) has written precepts "within us"—applies equally to the *felix culpa* and evolutionary controversies. However, the real reason why Hawthorne resurrects the now-defunct Fall of Man controversy here and stages Hilda's staunch refusal to view the Fall as fortunate is that Hilda—in refusing to believe that humans' current, fallen state was superior to their prelapsarian, Edenic one—advances a view of human history that, though theologically sanctioned, is not progressive. In an ingenious rhetorical move, Hawthorne positions his questioning of the progressive or teleological nature of natural history not as a rejection of theology but rather as a return to a much older and even more conservative theological position.

More than that, though, the question of whether or not Donatello's transformation was fortunate turns out to be a trick question, in that any answer to it will necessarily undermine some aspect of prevailing belief about the natural world. Viewing Donatello's transformation from faun to man as fortunate upholds humans' superiority over animals, but allows that natural forces produce improvements on original design. Refusing to view Donatello's transformation as fortunate preserves the belief that creative powers belong to the Deity alone, but forces the concession that either natural history is not progressive or we are not its indisputably best product. In short, Hawthorne suspected what Darwin illustrated in *Origin of Species* just fifteen days after Hawthorne delivered the final manuscript for *The Marble Faun* to his publishers: that an understanding of the natural processes by which species changed could not be reconciled with traditional understandings of God's Providence.

A Unifying Theory

Hawthorne's decision to cast his human-faun hybrid as an Italian reflects the belief universally held at that time by people of Anglo-Saxon descent: that they themselves had attained the ultimate level of civilization and all other ethnic groups were both less civilized and more animal-like than they. But as the novel, following Lamarck, argues that there is no such thing as "assured heritage" (since the characteristics of organisms are not fixed, but constantly changing as the environment changes), it can hardly be said to support the contemporary project of translating non-Anglo-Saxon people's cultural differences into permanent racial or genetic inferiority. Here—and in "Chiefly about War Matters"—aligning people with animals simultaneously marks their distance from norms of northeastern U.S. middle-class culture as well as their capacity to achieve them.[70] And rather than a celebration of Hawthorne's group's position at the top of the ladder, *The Marble Faun* is more concerned with the difficulties of sustaining belief in the progressive nature of civilization when one recognized that life at the "top" was so miserable. If what befalls Donatello is representative of any particular ethnic group's experience, it seems to be that of the Anglo-Saxons themselves, for the novel explicitly compares his experience to what "we" all have gone through. Donatello's plight makes Kenyon think how:

> The entire system of Man's affairs, as at present established, is built up purposely to exclude the careless and happy soul. The very children would upbraid the wretched individual who should endeavour to take life and the world as (what we might naturally suppose them meant for) a place and opportunity for enjoyment.
>
> It is the iron rule in our days, to require an object and a purpose in life. It makes us all parts of a complicated scheme of progress, which can only result in our arrival at a colder and drearier region than we were born in. It insists upon every-

> body's adding somewhat (a mite, perhaps, but earned by incessant effort) to an accumulated pile of usefulness, of which the only use will be, to burthen our posterity with even heavier thoughts and more inordinate labour than our own. No life now wanders like an unfettered stream; there is a mill-wheel for the tiniest rivulet to turn. We go all wrong, by too strenuous a resolution to go all right. (239)

The novel's anxiety about the progress of civilization is thus inextricably related to its concerns about the natural world. What Lamarck offered in *Zoological Philosophy* and Chambers offered in *Vestiges* were not mere explanations of the organic world. Rather, each man saw himself as articulating a theory that unified all geological, biological, psychological, and (in Chambers' case) theological knowledge. This aspect of pre-Darwinian evolutionary theory is most clearly illustrated in the 1850s publications of Herbert Spencer, who (like Chambers) became convinced of Lamarck's theory after reading Lyell's *Principles* and who subsequently championed Lamarck's ideas in his own writing. In his 1857 essay "Progress: Its Law and Cause," Spencer argues that laws governing the transformation of organisms were identical to those that governed all aspects of social development. The "law of organic progress," he writes, "is the law of all progress. Whether it be in the development of the Earth, in the development of Life upon its surface, in the development of Society, of Government, of Manufactures, of Commerce, of Language, Literature, Science, Art, this same evolution of the simple into the complex, through successive differentiations, holds throughout."[71] While this idea, no doubt, was comforting to those who shared Spencer's belief that natural history was progressive, the implications of the unification of natural and all other histories were far bleaker for those, like Hawthorne, who had begun to wonder about natural history's *telos.* Indeed, the idea that *The Marble Faun* is engaged with a question of *telos* appears repeatedly (though not always explicitly) throughout twentieth-century criticism on the novel. Uniting the members of the seemingly irreconcilable "timeless allegory" and "historically engaged novel" critical camps is their sense that *The Marble Faun* questions whether some development long held to be progressive was in fact a wholly fortunate evolution—whether that evolution was the change from humans' prelapsarian to fallen state, from childhood to adulthood, from Catholicism to Puritanism, from Old World authoritarian regimes to New World democracy, from art of antiquity and the Renaissance to the aesthetics of Protestant America.[72] The recurrence of this idea in the critical literature reflects Hawthorne's growing concern that all histories—natural, political, religious, artistic, individual—might not represent the unfolding of some ever-improving divine plan.[73]

While *The Marble Faun*'s concerns with natural history relate to and unify its political, religious, and artistic concerns, there is a particularly strong relationship between the latter and evolution. First, during Hawthorne's lifetime the most vocal opponents to species transformation linked their critiques of evolutionary thinking to a critique of the kind of imaginative creation that Hawthorne identified as the essence of his literary art. Cuvier's infamous "Biographical Memoir of M. de Lamarck" (which, like Lyell's more evenhanded refutation, assisted enormously in the promulgation of Lamarck's theory) was constructed as a warning to others who might entertain such "fanciful conceptions" as the theory of species transformation.[74] Cuvier frames his scurrilous "memoir" with the observation that biographies of men like Lamarck were useful primarily for demonstrating the disastrous results of "too great indulgence of a lively imagination" (435). Though he does not deny that Lamarck did make genuine contributions to science, he declares that his "real discoveries" have sadly been "mingled [with] many fanciful conceptions" (434). Cuvier faults Lamarck's ideas for being "conceived by the unaided power of his own mind" (443) and claims that he "laboriously constructed vast edifices on imaginary foundations, resembling the enchanted palaces of our old romances" (434). Similarly, Sedgwick's extended execration of *Vestiges* (which, like Cuvier's "Biographical Memoir," abounds with *ad hominem* attacks) complains, "The author is intensely hypothetical, and builds his castles in the air" (2). To explain how a book so bad can sell so well, Sedgwick claims that the people buying *Vestiges* are those incapable of evaluating it because they have been "fed on nothing better than the trash of literature" (2). Only those who have "soil[ed] their fingers with the dirty knife of the anatomist" (3), Sedgwick contends, may rightly judge *Vestiges'* argument. He points out the similarities between *Vestiges'* theory and that of Lamarck, which he calls "baseless as the fabric of a crazy dream" (7). He concludes, dramatically: "woe to the world if our knowledge is to be made up of idle speculations, like those we have been reviewing—'as endless as a spider's thread, and of no substance or profit' " (85).

The terms of Cuvier's and Sedgwick's texts are precisely those that Hawthorne uses to defend the aesthetic of romance. At the beginning of *The Marble Faun*'s final chapter, he explains his intention of *not* offering "one of those minute elucidations" to "[clear] up the romantic mysteries of a story." Invoking the metaphors of dissection and spider's threads that Sedgwick employed, Hawthorne expresses his hope that the reader will be "too wise to insist upon looking closely at the wrong side of the tapestry, after the right one has been sufficiently displayed to him"—that "kindly Readers" will accept the book "at its worth, without tearing the web apart, with the idle purpose of discovering how its threads have been knit together" (455). Readers, however, did not prove so kindly as he had hoped, and he addressed the public's demands for the kind of minute elucidation he did not wish to give in a "Postscript" that was added to the second American edition. Speaking of himself in the third person, he writes that he adds this explanation "reluctantly . . . because the necessity makes him sensible that he can have succeeded but imperfectly, at best, in throwing about this Romance the kind of atmosphere essential to the effect at which he aimed" (463). Though Hawthorne tosses his readers a few facts, the primary purpose of the "Postscript" seems to be to satirize these readers' untoward demands for clarification about Donatello's status as a faun and other hazy elements of the novel. He writes that he "had hoped to mystify this anomalous creature between the Real and the Fantastic, in such a manner that the reader's sympathies might be excited to a certain pleasurable degree, without impelling him to ask how Cuvier would have classified poor Donatello, or to insist upon being told, in so many words, whether he had furry ears or no. As respects all who ask such questions, the book is, to that extent, a failure" (463–64). As this remark reveals, Hawthorne recognizes Cuvier to be the enemy—as he was—both of fanciful speculation and of belief in the mutability of species.

This passage also reflects Hawthorne's understanding of the essential difference between Lamarck's and Cuvier's position on species transformation. As Cuvier writes in his "Biographical Memoir," Lamarck claimed that "it is not the organs, that is to say, the nature and form of the parts, which give rise to habits and faculties; but it is the latter which in process of time give birth to the organs" (446). Lamarck would not care what Donatello's ears looked like, because he did not believe an organism's nature to be determined by its anatomy. Cuvier, who held the opposite view, would have regarded full knowledge of Donatello's anatomy essential for an understanding of his character.[75]

Hawthorne's decision to articulate his aesthetic theory in terms of contemporary science also reflects a fundamental link between evolutionary thinking and the romantic conception of art. As Lovejoy has explained, the shift from an eighteenth-century aesthetic of neoclassicism to a nineteenth-century aesthetic of romanticism reflected a larger shift from a view in which no element of the created world (including humans in their capacities as artists) could improve on God's design to a view in which humans and other creatures could contribute to their own and the world's perfection. As Lovejoy explains: "If by 'God' you meant [as Westerners in the eighteenth-century generally did] . . . the Being who is, or eternally possesses, the good in the highest degree; and if 'the good' meant absolute self-sufficiency; and if all imperfect and finite and temporal beings are, as such, not to be identified with the divine essence—then it manifestly followed that *their* existence—that is, the existence of the entire sensible world in time, and of all conscious beings who are not in any sense genuinely self-sufficient—can bring no addition of excellence to reality. The fullness of good is attained once for all in God; and 'the creatures' add nothing to it."[76] Thus Hilda proves herself to be the "daughter of the Puritans" both in her rejection of evolutionary thinking and in her refusal to believe that she can improve on the work of the "Old Masters." As that most famous Puritan Jonathan Edwards wrote: "No notion of God's last end in creation of the world is agreeable to reason which would truly imply or infer any indigence, insufficiency and mutability in God; or any dependence of the Creator on the creature, for any part of his perfection or happiness. Because it is evident, by both Scripture and reason, that God is infinitely, eternally, unchangeably and independently glorious and perfect; that he stands in no need of, cannot be profited by, or receive anything from the creature, or be truly hurt, or be the subject of any suffering or impair of his glory and felicity from any other being."[77] From the neoclassical and Puritan perspectives, the artist's task was to hold a mirror up to an already perfected nature.

In contrast, both evolutionary theory and the romantic aesthetic were premised on the possibility of nondivine original creation. In scientific terms, this meant the creation of new species. In artistic terms, this meant the production of original art that improved on, rather than merely reflected, the created world. According to the romantic view of art, "Man's high calling was to add something of his own to the creation."[78] This, then, is why the aesthetic based on original creation—embodied in Miriam's belief that her art could improve both on objects in the real world and on the work of the Old Masters (a view which correlated to the belief that new species more complex than the old could be created through natural rather than divine forces)—is persistently identified in *The Marble Faun* with patricide.[79] Creativity is patricide, in that ascription to the aesthetic of romance requires killing off, if not God himself, then at least the view of him held by Hawthorne's Puritan forefathers.[80]

The evolution of Hawthorne's thinking about animal-human connections and his handling of this issue in *The Marble Faun* indicate the direction that thinking about humans and animals would take as the century progressed. The arguments that were made tentatively in the 1830s, '40s, and '50s about animals' intellectual and moral abilities became, by the '70s, '80s, and '90s, if not universally accepted at least thoroughly mainstream. As I demonstrate in the next two chapters, in the final third of the nineteenth century Americans became more and more willing to believe that the mental and moral qualities of "certain select" animals were fully manifest, rather than latent. And in these decades, speculation that animals living among us could become or actually had become as mentally and morally developed as people gave way to the growing belief that they were not just as good as us but were in many ways a great deal better.

The Domestic ~~Angel~~ Animal

Nature, Nurture, and Difference in the Work of Harriet Beecher Stowe

"A dog," [Bolton] added, fondling his ragged cur, "why, he's nothing but organized love—love on four feet, encased in fur, and looking piteously out at the eyes—love that would die for you, yet cannot speak—that's the touching part. Stumpy longs to speak; his poor dog's breast heaves with something he longs to tell me and can't. Don't it Stumpy?"

As if he understood his master, Stumpy wheezed a doleful whine, and actual tears stood in his eyes.

". . . Poor fellow, maybe on the other shore your rough bark will develop into speech; let's hope so. I confess I'm of the poor Indian's mind, and hope to meet my dog in the hereafter. Why should so much love go out in nothing? Yes, Stumpy, we'll meet in the resurrection, won't we?"

HARRIET BEECHER STOWE, *My Wife and I; Or, Harry Henderson's History* (1871)

WORKING FROM very different sets of assumptions, Arthur Riss and Elizabeth Barnes have both argued that one of Harriet Beecher Stowe's primary objectives was the creation of a nation that would—like the ideal family—be devoid of difference. Riss, who contends that Stowe attributed racial differences exclusively to biological factors, argues Stowe's belief that "substantive blood relations [were] the only determining sign of a family" made her unwilling to incorporate free blacks into the "national family" of the United States.[1] Barnes, in contrast, argues that psychological rather than biological homogeneity is Stowe's criterion for familial and hence national membership. According to Barnes, instead of emphasizing physiological differences, *Uncle Tom's Cabin* "claim[s] that individuals are all alike under the skin" and thus "makes diversity virtually unrepresentable, reinforcing the idea of humanity as dependent upon familiarity. One of the key strategies Stowe employs for creating a democratic readership is the subordination of physical difference to psychological and emotional sameness."[2] Thus, in Barnes's view, Stowe welcomed blacks into the national family, but only on the condition that they made themselves identical, psychologically, to whites: "By employing a familial model to construct a more liberal democratic state . . . personal differences are elided in favor of a homogenous family image. Sameness, rather than difference, offers the key to democratic equality and, hence, to national identity" (16); "Ironically, in order to effect the political union she envisions for her readers, Stowe must first elide the personal differences that constitute individuality" (92).

Riss and Barnes's disagreement over whether Stowe wanted to oust blacks from the nation or incorporate them into it hinges on what has become a central question in Stowe scholarship: did Stowe attribute differences between people to nature or to nurture? That question, along with the question of Stowe's exact position on difference, remains sharply contested. (In fact, the critique of Stowe's insistence on differences and the critique of Stowe's erasure of differences have proven equally enduring.)[3] Amid all this disagreement, scholars had long enjoyed one point of common ground: the assumption that the answers to the questions on race, embodiment, and difference are to be found in *Uncle Tom's Cabin* (1852). Only recently has *Uncle Tom*'s ability to yield up a complete picture of Stowe's racial politics been questioned. In the last five to ten years, *Dred* (1856) has gained attention as "Stowe's other antislavery novel"—as "a missing text in Stowe's canon."[4] But efforts at canon recovery have not yet ranged far. No one has yet suggested that we need look beyond 1856 to understand fully Stowe's ideas on race and difference.[5]

Drawing on texts that span her literary career, this chapter first unpacks Stowe's beliefs about the continuities between the ontological status of humans and other animals and then argues that this theory of humans' animality provides an essential yet previously uninvestigated context for understanding the issues of nature, nurture, embodiment, and difference that have figured so prominently in Stowe criticism and set the terms of the debate on the racial and gender politics of her work. Stowe's language of animality—informed by such diverse sources as natural history, animal welfare, and her own lifelong experiences with animals—enabled her to eschew any simple dichotomy between nature and nurture and to transform potentially oppressive comparisons between people and animals into a key component of her broadly aimed program of societal reform.

Nature and Nurture

In "The Rhetoric of Race," Susan Marie Neurnberg identifies two positions on race available to antebellum Americans: "Pre-Darwinian scientific theories of racial difference debated whether differences were innate or the product of environment. Environmentalism, the idea that all races were members of the same species and had a common remote ancestry (also known as 'monogenesis'), attributed differences in color, anatomy, intelligence, temperament, and morality to differing physical and social environments." The alternate theory of "polygenesis, or the separate creation of the races as distinct species" asserted "that racial differences were innate and not the product of environment." This position, Neurnberg contends "gave proslavery advocates a scientific basis for viewing blacks as members of separate and permanently inferior species."[6]

The work of Robert Young shows that nineteenth-century debates were substantially more complex than Neurnberg allows: there was no neat correspondence between monogenesis and environmentalism, on one hand, and polygenesis and racialism, on the other.[7] And several Stowe scholars, most notably Arthur Riss, have challenged Neurnberg's conflation of racialism and racism. Yet, despite his differences from Neurnberg, Riss also sees only two logical choices for Stowe: environmentalism or racialism. Consequently, his claim that Stowe espoused racialism is closely tied to the claim that she rejected environmentalism: "Personal characteristics, according to Stowe, are transmitted through biology rather than through culture and environment" (518). Working with the assumption that antebellum Americans had two mutually exclusive positions on race from which to choose, Stowe scholars have forwarded a total of three different theories of Stowe's views on race: (1) Stowe was a racialist, (2) Stowe was an environmentalist, or (3), as Neurnberg suggests, "Stowe's ideas are confused and contradictory."[8]

Among recent critics, Robert Levine offers the most sophisticated treatment of the complexity of Stowe's racial ideas. Levine offers a trenchant critique of critics' unwillingness "to deal with transformations in Stowe's complex and contradictory racial politics" and their disinclination "to [attend] to black influences on Stowe's texts, except when those influences 'expose' her mendacity and blindness." Yet even as he reads her nonalignment with either racialist or environmentalist positions as an understandable product of her persistent efforts to combat racism, Levine, like Neurnberg, still finds Stowe's ideas on race "provisional, inconsistent, and contradictory." "I will allow the unsurprising," he states, "that [Stowe], like her contemporaries, could at times be utterly confused and contradictory on questions of racial identity." He insists that

> one risks considerable reductionism in attempting any sort of precise anatomy of Stowe's racial views. This is not to deny that Stowe worked with racialist categories throughout her writing career. But Stowe continually tested those categories and the politics to which racialist thought could give rise, and it is simply unfair to isolate a particular statement from a particular text as evidence for her hidebound racial views. Invariably, any statement conveys Stowe's ideas at a precise textual/historical moment, conditioned by the language and conceptualizations available to her at that time. It is frequently contradicted by other statements in the Stowe corpus, sometimes on the very same page.[9]

The following passage from Stowe's essay "Sojourner Truth, the Libyan Sibyl," which was published in the *Atlantic Monthly* in April 1863, could easily be seen as an example of Levine's last claim:

> It is with a sad feeling that one contemplates noble minds and bodies, nobly and grandly formed human beings, that have come to us cramped, scarred, maimed, out of the prison-house of bondage. One longs to know what such beings might have become, if suffered to unfold and expand under the kindly developing influences of education.
>
> It is the theory of some writers, that to the African is reserved, in the later and palmier days of the earth, the full and harmonious development of the religious element in man. The African seems to seize on the tropical fervor and luxuriance of Scripture imagery as something native; he appears to feel himself to be of the same blood with those old burning, simple souls, the patriarchs, prophets, and seers, whose impassioned words seem only grafted as foreign plants on the cooler stock of the Occidental mind.[10]

In the rhetoric of environmentalism, the first paragraph attributes any seeming inferiority of blacks to the conditions imposed on them by slavery. If blacks seem "cramped, scarred, [and] maimed," it is because they have been raised in "the prison-house of bondage" and denied "the kindly developing influences of education." In the very next paragraph, however, is Stowe's racialist belief, reiterated throughout *Uncle Tom's Cabin,* that blacks have an innate emotional sensitivity that makes them suited to be Christians. There is something "native," or innate, in blacks that enables them to identify with the emotional intensity of biblical language.

Stowe's textual choices are produced, as Levine suggests, by her effort to "situate her ideas in a dialogical context" (148). The second paragraph offers support for Martin Delany's destabilizing claim that civilization originated not with white Greeks but with black peoples of Northern Africa. More directly, however, Stowe is fashioning her argument as a response to Hawthorne's "Chiefly about War Matters," which appeared in the same publication nine months before. There, Hawthorne expresses his hope that freedom and the mysterious workings of Providence will eventually bring about the development of the African American race, but he suggests that such development will not be realized in "the present generation of negroes."[11] To refute Hawthorne's position, Stowe contends that blacks already possess all the innate faculties required for moral and religious education.

But the presence of both racialist and environmentalist ideas "on the very same page" does not evince Stowe's confusion. Rather, it points us to a fundamental feature of Stowe's belief system: that humans, like all animals, are products of both nature and nurture. Stowe's more general theories of the relationship between nature and nurture constitute an important context for understanding the rhetoric of racial and gender essentialism that circulates in her fiction.

Human Animality and Animal Sensibility

The ineluctable forces of each individual's biology and embodiment came to occupy a central role in Stowe's work and thought. In Stowe's belief system, the inability to escape or transcend one's biological, essential, or "animal" nature was not the unfortunate plight of certain groups or individuals, but rather the divinely ordained, universal condition of all animate beings. Thus it becomes necessary to situate Stowe's theory of human nature in her larger framework of "animal" nature as it applies to humans and nonhumans alike. Stowe's beliefs about the ontological status of humans reflect her lifelong interest in animals as well as influences of natural history and the animal welfare movement. Drawing on and modifying these discourses, Stowe developed a language for articulating her views on the relationship between mind and body.

In the houses in which Stowe lived, animals had a regular and welcomed presence. In the 1860s she describes her household as "Cunopolis," the city of dogs. "We . . . are a dog-loving family," she writes. "We have a warm side towards everything that goes upon four paws."[12] In *My Wife and I; Or, Harry Henderson's History* (1871), Bolton proclaims that "a cat is a happiness-producing machine. . . . No family is complete without a cat."[13] In addition to canines and felines, squirrels, frogs, hummingbirds, and cardinals also assumed membership in the Stowe family. Stowe's adult pet-keeping habits extended from her childhood interest in and exposure to animals. *Poganuc People* (1879)—a semiautobiographical novel based on Stowe's childhood in Litchfield, Connecticut—describes the family dog Spring as the child heroine's "faithful attendant, the most loving and sympathetic of dogs, her friend and confidential counsellor in many a solitary ramble."[14] As a girl Stowe "used to spend many happy hours in Aunt Esther's parlor talking with her. Her favorite subject was always the habits and character of different animals, and their various ways and instincts, and she used to tell us so many wonderful, yet perfectly authentic, stories about all these things, that the hours passed away very quickly."[15]

Through these conversations about the "instincts," "habits, and character of different animals," Stowe was introduced as a very young child to a central tenet of natural history: that the unique habits, character, and instincts of each animal derived from its essential nature. Through natural history, animals became objects of scientific inquiry. In accordance with Enlightenment science's project of explaining all phenomena according to natural laws, natural historians attempted to understand animal behavior through the laws of each animal's being. By the late eighteenth century and early nineteenth century, books on natural history comprised a standard component of juvenile reading. Stowe herself contributed to this genre when she immortalized the stories told to her in her childhood in "Aunt Esther's Stories" of her juvenile volume *Queer Little People* (1867).[16]

Stowe's engagement with the new science of animal nature was mediated, however, by her commitment to the principles of animal welfare. The proper treatment of animals was also a recurrent topic of her childhood discussions with her aunt, and this issue—along with the treatment of animals' habits and instincts—is also a focus of *Queer Little People.* Adjacent to the chapter "Aunt Esther's Stories" is "Aunt Esther's Rules," which instructs readers in treating animals humanely. Although organizations committed to animal welfare reform did not appear in the United States until the late 1860s, many Americans were well aware of the animal activism taking place on the other side of the Atlantic. Thus in the course of recounting (in the mid-1860s) her family's rescue of a nearly drowned hummingbird, Stowe describes herself and her family as constituting their own humane society.[17] We see the influence of the animal welfare agenda also in Stowe's belief that animals—while possessing an essential, biological nature—nonetheless were shaped by their environment and responded to kind treatment. In "Dogs and Cats" Stowe narrates the story of the extraordinary feline Juno, who, "carefully trained by [her] mistress, was a standing example of the virtues which may be formed in a cat by careful education." She concludes by pointing out: "You see by this story the moral I wish to convey. It is, that watchfulness, kindness, and care will develop a nature in animals such as we little dream of. Love will beget love, regular care and attention will give regular habits, and thus domestic pets may be made more agreeable and interesting."[18]

In addition to allowing for the shaping influences of environment and kind treatment, Stowe also stridently rejected the views of scientists who maintained that animals did not experience rational thought or genuine consciousness (and hence had no claim to ethical consideration). In *Discourse on Method,* Descartes advanced his claim about the mechanical nature of animal life by comparing animals to the automated artificial birds produced by French engineer Salomon de Caus for the fountains of wealthy patrons. De Caus used hydraulic pressure to make his mechanical birds move and even sing, and in Descartes' view the actions of animals were similarly "strictly a matter of engineering."[19] Some supporters of Descartes' ideas went so far as to claim that animals lacked even the capacity to feel pain, insisting that "the cry of the beaten dog was no more evidence of the brute's suffering than was the sound of an organ proof that the instrument felt pain when struck."[20] In "A Talk about Birds," Stowe picks up Descartes' comparison of birds to machines and deploys it for different ends. After young Jamie's mother observes him throwing stones at birds for sport, she calls him into the house and shows him a music box. Jamie is fascinated with this intricate treasure, and even more fascinated to learn that birds possess far more complex, and far smaller, instruments in their throats through which they produce music more beautiful than that of any music box. Jamie's mother proceeds to describe a bird's optical, neurological, and skeletal structures as various kinds of intricate machinery wrought by God. In this story, however, the similarities between birds' bodies and complex machines highlight the immorality of a wanton disregard of avian life. "How should you feel," Jamie's mother asks him, "if you had contrived some curious and beautiful little plaything, and just as you had it all nicely finished off, some boy should come along with a great stick, and knock it all to pieces?" Jamie replies that he would "be mad enough!" and then realizes that God must feel much the same way about the stoning of his birds. After additional thought, Jamie remarks that killing birds is "a great deal worse" than breaking a toy or machine "because little birds can *feel,* you know."[21] Stowe both insists on birds' feelings and posits such feelings as the basis for their ethical consideration. (*Sentio ergo sum* would be her motto.) In her view, the similarity between animal bodies and highly wrought machinery only increases our duty to refrain from harming them.

Stowe's refusal to limit the capacity for suffering to human beings or champion rationality as the criterion for ethical consideration also appears in the long address on suffering in chapter 24 of *The Minister's Wooing* (1859): "What are the natures that cannot suffer? Who values them? From the fat oyster . . . to the hero who stands with quivering nerve parting with wife and child and home for country and God, all the way up is an ascending scale, marked by increasing power to suffer; and when we look to the Head of all being . . . to behold by what emblem the Infinite Sovereign chooses to reveal himself, we behold, in the midst of the throne, 'a lamb as it has been slain.'"[22] The final sentence reminds us not just that Jesus was one who suffered, but that our symbol for him is a suffering *animal.* Thus, at the apex of this ascending scale is a being whose form is divine and animal simultaneously.

As she rejects the traditional separation of humans from animals by a wide and impassible gulf, Stowe continues to talk about humans and animals in terms that violate the absolute elevation of humans over animals that was built into the Great Chain of Being and sustained by its successor, Enlightenment science. In *Dred* (1856), the eponymous hero tells a fellow runaway that he took to the swamp because he "found the alligators and the snakes better neighbors than Christians. They let those alone that let them alone; but Christians will hunt for the precious life."[23] "Our Country Neighbors" describes the animal "neighbors" the Stowe family encountered while living in a neighborless house in rural Maine. After narrating the exploits of animals who help themselves to the Stowe garden, infiltrate the Stowe house, and even eat their poor animal "brethren" alive, Stowe concludes the essay: "So you see how many neighbors we found by living in the woods, and, after all, no worse ones than are found in the great world."[24] And in "The Grand Tour Up River" (an essay describing an 1872 excursion on the St. John River in Florida) Stowe expatiates on her disgust with the senseless and distinctly human cruelty displayed by some of her fellow passengers:

> One annoyance on board the boat was the constant and pertinacious firing kept up by that class of men who think that the chief end of man is to shoot something. Now, we can put up with good earnest hunting or fishing done for the purpose of procuring for man food, or even the fur and feathers that hit his fancy and taste.
>
> But we detest indiscriminate and purposeless maiming and killing of happy animals, who have but one life to live, and for whom the agony of broken bones or torn flesh is a helpless, hopeless pain, unrelieved by any of the resources which enable us to endure. A parcel of hulking fellows sit on the deck of a boat, and pass through the sweetest paradise God ever made, without one idea of its loveliness, one gentle, sympathizing thought of the animal happiness with which the Creator

> has filled these recesses. All the way along is a constant fusillade upon every living thing that shows itself on the bank. Now a bird is hit . . . and a coarse laugh choruses the deed. Now an alligator is struck; and the applause is greater. We once saw a harmless young alligator, whose dying struggles, as he threw out his poor little black paws piteously like human hands, seemed to be vastly diverting to these cultivated individuals. They wanted nothing of him except to see how he would act when he was hit, dying agonies are so very amusing!
>
> . . . If the object were merely to show the skill of the marksman, why not practise upon inanimate objects? An old log looks much like an alligator: why not practise on an old log? It requires as much skill to hit a branch, as the bird singing on it: why not practise on the branch? But no: it must be something that *enjoys* and can suffer; something that loves life, and must lose it. Certainly this is an inherent savagery difficult to account for. Killing for killing's sake belongs not even to the tiger. The tiger kills for food; man, for amusement.[25]

Shooting at branches or logs fails to amuse the men because it is the animals' suffering that occasions their pleasure. The infliction of suffering is constitutive of, rather than merely incidental to, their "sport." Stowe remains at a loss to explain this disturbing spectacle of cruelty for its own sake.

In addition to giving witness to human behavior far more debased than that of any animal, Stowe frequently draws our attention to instances of "human" or superhuman virtue in animals. The "A" of animal is also the "A" of angel. One of the many signs of Dred's sanctification is his ability to communicate with the creatures of the woods. The birds, Dred tells Fanny, enjoy a special communion with God and the angels: "After the great judgement, the elect shall talk with the birds and beasts in the new earth. Every kind of bird has a different language, in which they show why men should magnify the Lord, and turn from their wickedness. But sinners cannot hear it, because their ear is waxed gross. . . . But the birds fly up near the heavens, wherefore they learn droppings of the speech of angels. I never kill the birds, because the Lord hath sent them between us and the angels for a sign."[26] Dred's speech, of course, is frequently fantastical, but we cannot dismiss his association between animals and angels, as it is repeated throughout Stowe's work. In *The Minister's Wooing* Mary looks out her window and sees "thousands of birds . . . answering to each other from apple-tree and meadow-grass, and top of jagged rock, or trooping in bands hither and thither, like angels on loving messages" (426).

Eventually, these rather conventional (in the Christian tradition) connections between birds and angels evolve into more radical assertions that animals are performing the work of God. To Stowe, and to many nineteenth-century Americans who brought animal companions into their homes, animals' behavior often stood out as much more selfless, generous, and loyal than that of the average person. Like her domestic angels, Stowe's domestic animals bestow affection without regard for an individual's social standing or net worth. In her fiction, animals frequently model the kind of benevolent behavior she wanted humans to adopt: they love lowly people whom society ignores and casts off. In *My Wife and I*, for example, the lonely bachelor Bolton finds companionship in his dog Stumpy. A dog, Bolton remarks, is "nothing but organized love—love on four feet, encased in fur, and looking piteously out at the eyes—love that would die for you" (322). *We and Our Neighbors* (1875) describes dogs as "the special comforters of neglected and forgotten people."[27] But the lively terrier Jack goes beyond comforting Miss Dorcas Vanderheyden and Mrs. Betsey Benthusen—two isolated and childless sisters (Dorcas never married; Betsey is widowed) who find that New York society no longer welcomes them now that they are old, unfashionable, and impoverished. Jack functions as a sort of assistant to Eva Van Arsdel in her work of reaching out to people society has discarded. It is through Jack that Eva is able to draw Dorcas and Betsey out of their isolation and save Maggie from a life of prostitution. By the end of her career, Stowe promoted angel-like animals from the supporting role to the starring role. Her 1884 novella *A Dog's Mission, or, The Story of Old Avery House* tells how a Scotch terrier named Trip saves the hardened and lonely Miss Zarviah Avery, who was "a human wreck . . . nobody came to see her, and she visited nobody."[28] Tripp succeeds not only in getting Miss Avery to return his affection; he also manages to reunite her with her brother from whom she had long been estranged.

What Stowe's writings about animals make plain is that there was no neat connection between animality, embodiment, and soullessness on one hand and humanness, the mind, and soulfulness on the other. Stowe remains invested in challenging the dichotomies between mind/body and human/animal in her writings that do not focus primarily on animals. Her 1868 essay "Bodily Religion: A Sermon on Good Health" radically overhauls the long-standing tradition in Christian theology of casting the body as the prison and enemy of the soul. "The hygienic bearings of the New Testament have never been sufficiently understood," Stowe contends.[29] Citing doctrine of the resurrection of the body and the body's role as "the temple of the Holy Spirit," she insists that the human body "cannot be intended to be a clog and a hindrance to spiritual advancement" (345). Instead, Stowe proposes viewing the relationship between body and soul as one of mutual cooperation toward a common goal, and she allows for the body to be the enabling partner in the voyage to heaven. Instead of the "soul's great enemy and hindrance," the body, properly cared for, is better understood as the soul's "best friend and most powerful help" (346). "The body," she declares, "if allowed the slightest degree of fair play, so far from being a contumacious infidel and opposer, becomes a very fair Christian helper, and, instead of throttling the soul, gives it wings to rise to celestial regions" (339).

The physical condition necessary for this ideal cooperation between body and soul is not mere freedom from disease. Stowe laments the fact that most consider themselves "well" merely "because they are not, at present, upon any particular doctor's list" (330). Instead, Stowe wants people to enjoy "that fullness of life, that vigorous tone, and that elastic cheerfulness, which make the mere fact of existence a luxury, that suppleness which carries one like a well-built boat over every wave of unfavorable chance" that we observe "in animals" (330). "Bodily Religion" offers recommendations on diet, exercise, ventilation designed to help adults restore what Stowe calls "animal vigor" (334): the "vitality," "buoyancy," and "superabundant vigor" associated with their animal nature (332).

The "Irritability" chapter from *Little Foxes* (1866) is another text from which we can easily mine Stowe's ideas about human embodiment. (The "little foxes" are the seven domestic sins which ruin domestic felicity, an allusion to the biblical foxes that spoil one's harvest.) As Stowe describes it, irritability is the sin of driving oneself to an irritable state of mind by failing to care for one's corporal needs. But while Stowe's concern for bodily health was typical of the age, her strategy for addressing it was not. At the beginning of the essay, she holds up for emulation not a practitioner of the newest craze in diet or exercise, but the family dog: "Look at Rover there. He is never nervous, never cross, never snaps or snarls, and is ready, the moment after the grossest affront, to wag the tail of forgiveness,—all because kind nature has put his dog's body together so that it always works harmoniously."[30] As Stowe elucidates, Rover's admirable state of mind results not only from being born healthy, but from living a life that maintains health. Dogs, unlike nineteenth-century Americans, did not stay up late into the night studying Latin, sewing dresses, writing sermons, or dancing at balls. They did not abstain from exercise, subsist on unwholesome food, drink, smoke, or confine themselves to poorly ventilated interiors. All of these human proclivities, Stowe contends, imperil jointly the human body, mind, and soul. In contrast to those who sought to distance not only humans from animals but also the intellect from the body (*cogito ergo sum)* Stowe maintains that "the foundation of all intellectual and moral worth must be laid in a good healthy animal" (353). Thus

Stowe's argument operates, in large part, by reminding her audience that humans are ruled by the same laws of mental and bodily health that regulate the rest of the animal world.

Stowe's interest in health may seem like just another manifestation of the preoccupation with health prominent in nineteenth-century America. But she is doing something far different from the majority of her male contemporaries who were writing about health: Stowe is neutralizing the misogynist force of the medicalized discourse used to justify patriarchal domination of women. In their 1973 essay "The Female Animal," Carroll Smith-Rosenberg and Charles Rosenberg detail the way in which "men hopeful of preserving existing social relationships . . . employed medical and biological arguments to rationalize traditional sex roles as rooted inevitably and irreversibly in the prescriptions of anatomy and physiology." Nineteenth-century medical men argued that "the female nervous system was finer, 'more irritable,' prone to overstimulation and resulting exhaustion. . . . Few if any questioned the assumption that in males the intellectual propensities of the brain dominated, while the female's nervous system and emotions prevailed over her conscious and rational faculties."[31] The essays in *Little Foxes* are calculated to disprove this reigning medical lore. Although she devotes a good deal of time to women's health, Stowe's arguments are rooted in a theory of not the *female* animal but the *human* animal. Women cannot escape their biological nature, but neither, she maintains, can anyone else. The psychological and physiological traits of all people and animals are rooted in and limited by each one's ineluctable and immutable nature. By generalizing the arguments her contemporaries applied to female biology, Stowe transforms a tool of patriarchal oppression into one of matriarchal empowerment.

Consistent with contemporary medical discourses, Stowe defines irritability as "a bodily state": "It is a state of nervous torture; and the attacks which the wretched victim makes on others are as much a result of disease as the snapping and biting of a patient convulsed with hydrophobia" (352). Yet in Stowe's theory gender does not determine the strength of one's nerves, and the female body is no more susceptible than the male body to the nervous exhaustion that produces irritability. While medical men traced all female irritability back to women's reproductive organs,[32] Stowe attributed most cases of human irritability to a combination of biological predilections not tied to gender and to courses of action that "overdraw and use up in advance [the] life-force" (358). Excessive stimulation from "too much business, too much care, or too much amusement" (357) can render anyone's body into a state of nervous irritability. Narrator Christopher Crowfield begins the essay with a description of his holiday celebrations. From Christmas Eve to New Years Day, he rises early and goes to bed late, romps with his grandchildren, and gorges himself on holiday delicacies. After a week of these exertions, the normally genial Crowfield finds himself cross, miserable, and unable to restrain himself from snapping at his wife and even kicking the family dog. This story segues into his sermon proper: that when the nerves are taxed, no one's rational or conscious faculties can prevail.

Stowe's arguments not only undermine male assertions that woman alone was ruled by her body; they are designed with an eye toward improving the quality of women's domestic lives. Like the example of Crowfield with which the chapter begins, the essay's subsequent examples tend to illustrate how men's overindulgence—in food, alcohol, tobacco, or work—ends up making the women in their lives miserable. "The Reverend Mr. X." overextends himself for two weeks "doing all the time twice or thrice as much as in his ordinary state he could, and sustaining himself by the stimulus of strong coffee" in order to deliver a passionately moving sermon at church. But "poor Mrs. X. knows, when she hears him preaching, that days of miserable reaction are before her" (358). She knows that by channeling too much energy into his (admittedly sacred) profession, Mr. X. has reduced himself to a physical state that renders him incapable of fulfilling his duties to his wife and family: "He who spoke so beautifully of the peace of a soul made perfect will not be able to bear the cry of his baby or the pattering feet of any of the poor little X.'s . . . and he who could so admiringly tell of the silence of Jesus under provocation will but too often speak unadvisedly with his lips. Poor Mr. X. will be morally insane for days or weeks, and absolutely incapable of preaching Christ in the way that is the most effective, by setting Him forth in his own daily example" (359). Throughout these lamentations for Mr. X., it is clear that "poor Mrs. X." will be the one to suffer most on account of her husband's exertions. Preaching the maintenance of bodily health becomes, for Stowe, a way of deploying medical and religious authority to regulate the despotic control men could exercise over their wives and children.

No Printless Tablets

Throughout her life, Stowe actively championed the expansion and improvement of education. She both taught and assumed administrative duties in her sister Catharine's Hartford Female Seminary and Western Female Institute. Her first publication was not a work of fiction, but a geography textbook.[33] *Dred, The Pearl of Orr's Island, Oldtown Folks, My Wife and I, Pink and White*

Tyranny, and *We and Our Neighbors* all criticize the inferiority of the education typically offered to girls, and several of these novels vociferously defend girls' right to the same rigorous education offered boys and women's right to pursue a college education. In "The Laborers of the South," Stowe urges her readers to improve the educational opportunities available to newly emancipated African Americans.[34]

The kinds of educational reform that Stowe championed are generally attributed to the spread of Locke's idea that humans are born tabula rasa. To characterize American attitudes toward child-rearing, Ann Douglas, in *The Feminization of American Culture,* quotes the following passage from Lydia Huntley Sigourney's well known *Letters to Mothers:* "How entire and perfect is this dominion over the unformed character of your infant. Write what you will upon the printless tablet with your wand of love. Hitherto your influence over your dearest friend, your most submissive servant, has known bounds and obstructions. Now you have over a new-born immortal almost that degree of power which the mind exercises over the body. . . . The period of this influence must indeed pass away; but while it lasts, make good use of it."[35] Sigourney's idea of the child as a "printless tablet" constituted entirely through nurture (not nature) follows directly from Locke. Because the doctrine of tabula rasa, which implies that all humans are fundamentally equal at birth, figured so vitally in the expansion of educational opportunities to people previously denied them because of socioeconomic, gender, or racial status, we tend to associate nineteenth-century rejections of Locke's theory with desperate attempts of affluent white men to retain their privilege. Any effort to repudiate tabula rasa must, we assume, equal a repudiation of the scholastic aptitude of women and people of color.

Integral to Stowe's educational theory, however, was a strident *rejection* of the idea that children were "printless tablets"; arguments against Locke's theory can be found in almost everything she wrote on the issue of education. In Stowe's mind, the strong environmentalist position on development (which allowed only for the influences of nurture and discounted those of nature) left women and children defenseless against the efforts of the powerful to reshape them. Drawing on a rhetoric of animal nature jointly indebted to the traditions of natural history, which emphasized animals' innate natures, and the humane movement, which emphasized animals' positive responses to proper treatment, Stowe refutes strong environmentalist positions of contemporary educational theorists and uses essentialism as a tool for defending children's and women's efforts at self-determination. In Stowe's view, humans (like animals) were neither merely products of their environment nor, conversely, merely the sum of their biological inheritance. By insisting that both nature and nurture made important contributions to each person's character (at a time when her contemporaries' thinking was generally circumscribed by binary views of environment and inheritance), Stowe offered a theory of education responsive to individual interests, needs, and desires, which held that any individual could succeed, if given the right kind of education.

Though these views appear in many of Stowe's texts, the essay "Intolerance" in *Little Foxes* serves as a good example, as it is devoted to arguing that "intolerance of other people's natures is one of the greatest causes of domestic unhappiness" (412). The happiest people in life, Stowe contends, are those who can follow the lead of Mother Nature, by "not wishing or asking of any human being more than that human being was made to give" (412). These wise people "have the portion in due season for all: a bone for the dog; catnip for the cat; cuttle-fish and hempseed for the bird; a book or review for their bashful literary visitor; lively gossip for thoughtless Miss Seventeen; knitting for Grandmamma; fishing-rods, boats, and gunpowder, for Young Restless, whose beard is just beginning to grow;—and they never fall into pets because the canary-bird won't relish the dog's bone, or the dog eat canary-seed, or young Miss Seventeen read old Mr. Sixty's review, or young Master Restless take delight in knitting-work, or old Grandmamma feel complacency in guns and gunpowder" (412). Here, and throughout the essay, Stowe strategically recasts individual desire as biological "nature" to provide "scientific" justification for relatively powerless individuals' attempts to resist conformity to social norms imposed on them by the more powerful. Stowe slyly draws her readers into her line of reasoning with conventional associations (between young girls and gossip, young boys and fishing), only to draw them along, ultimately, to conclusions that explode conventional notions about gender and education.

Stowe presents the tabula rasa theory as the cause of much misery for children, mothers, and new wives: "On no subject is there more intolerant judgment, and more suffering from such intolerance, than on the much mooted one of the education of children. . . . Parents have been talked to as if each child came to them a soft, pulpy mass, which they were to pinch and pull and pat and stroke into shape quite at their leisure,—and a good pattern being placed before them, they were to proceed immediately to set up and construct a good human being in conformity therewith" (423). This theory, Stowe argues, encouraged tyrannical child-rearing practices, in which children were driven toward life paths they detested and prevented from pursuing their own interests. Having no conception that their newborn infant "has perhaps folded up in it a character as positive as that of either parent," too many parents "seize on their first new child as a piece of special property which they are forthwith to turn to their own account" according to their own "arranged and predetermined" idea of what that child is to become (414). Stowe's examples include the female "dreamy scholar" who is scolded by her mother—"a bustling, pickling, preserving, stocking-knitting, universal-housekeeping woman"—for constantly peering into books on Greece, Rome, and Germany when she is ordered to knit stockings. She also describes "a very pretty, sensible, domestic girl" whose father, a literary man, "is disappointed and treats her coldly" because she prefers cross-stitch embroidery and sponge-cake making to the study of Milton (415). What the diversity of these examples and other examples in Stowe's fiction illustrates is that gender (and class) stereotypes turn out to be notoriously unreliable markers of an individual's "nature."[36]

In addition, Stowe's theory of education had as significant implications for women—in their roles as mothers and wives—as it did for children. If parents could, as Sigourney suggested, exercise complete control over their young children, then filial disobedience and filial failure indicated a mother's failure to make good use of her "wand of love." "Treatises on education," Stowe contends, "require altogether too much of parents, and impose burdens of responsibility on tender spirits which crush the life and strength out of them" (423). The "tender spirits" whose "life" is "crushed out of them" by the burdens of educational theory belong not to the children here, but to the mothers who were charged with doing the impossible: shaping their children like so many lumps of clay. Though she uses the gender-neutral word "parents" in this sentence, Stowe clearly realizes that women, the designated caretakers of children, suffered disproportionately to men. She writes, "Many a poor, feeble woman's health has been strained to breaking, and her life darkened, by the laying on her shoulders of a burden of responsibility that never ought to have been placed there" (209). Again, the rhetoric of animal nature underscores Stowe's claim that mothers cannot simply change their children's nature at will: "It . . . is as utter an impossibility to the woman's nature [for her to change that of her child's] as for a cow to scratch up worms for her calf, or a hen to suckle her chickens" (424). The impossibility lies on both sides. Cows don't have beaks and calves won't eat worms; hens don't have udders and chicks won't suckle milk. Similarly, women have no power of changing their children, and a child's nature won't be changed. Making children partial arbiters of their own destiny relieves women of the blame cast upon them by nineteenth-century culture.[37]

In addition to child-rearing, "Intolerance" spends considerable time addressing marriage, for while male children assumed control of their own destiny upon adulthood, women's capacity for self-determination remained compromised. (As Caroline remarks in *My Wife and I,* a male's "minority comes to an end at a certain period—mine, never" [114].) When a woman and man marry, Stowe advises, "Their first wisdom would be to find out each other's nature, and accommodate to it as a fixed fact" (413). Though, again, the argument seems gender-neutral in theory, it supports in practice a redistribution of domestic power in the favor of women and provides a biological justification against demanding heroic housekeeping from women who have no interest or inclination for it. It is not fair, Stowe argues, for a man to take "out of the bosom of an adoring family one of those delicate, petted singing-birds that seem to be created simply to adorn life and make it charming" and then expect her to run his household as one of those "strong-limbed, practical women, that have never thought of anything but housekeeping from the cradle" (413). "If a man wanted such a housekeeper," she asks, "why did he not get one? There were plenty of single women, who understood washing, ironing, clear-starching, cooking, and general housekeeping, better than the little canary-bird which he fell in love with, and wanted for her plumage and her song, for her merry tricks, for her bright eyes and pretty ways. Now he has got his bird, let him keep it as something fine and precious, to be cared for and watched over, and treated according to the laws of its frail and delicate nature" (414). Translating female desire into natural "laws," Stowe gives women a strategy for resisting a system in which female graces are valued before marriage, yet female economy after, and in which women are expected to transform themselves accordingly.

Animals, Family, Race, Nation

In addition to her allowance for the effects of nature *and* nurture, two important features distinguish Stowe's strategic use of essentialism from that of her contemporaries.[38] First, in Stowe's theory, the only real evidence of essence is an individual's expressed inclinations. Contentment is both a necessary and a sufficient condition of living in accordance with one's nature. For example, in *Oldtown Folks* the only evidence we have—and the only evidence we need—of the conflict between Tina's nature and Miss Asphyxia's training is that this training makes Tina utterly miserable. With biological nature aligned with individual preference and desire, the individual is the only one authorized to determine her or his own nature. Consequently, it would be quite difficult to use this particular version of essentialism to justify the oppression and disenfranchisement of others. In *Little Foxes,* Stowe takes pains to clarify the enabling purpose behind her design: "Each of these natures, under judicious training, might be made to complete itself by cultivation of that which it lacked. . . . But this must be done by tolerance of their nature,—by giving it play and room,—first recognizing its existence and its rights, and then seeking to add to it the properties it wants" (415–16). Stowe, in short, believes we must pay attention to nature (i.e., individual desire), so that we can provide each individual with the nurture best suited to occasion productive development. "Every human being," she insists, "has some handle by which he may be lifted, some groove in which he was meant to run; and the great work of life, as far as our relations with each other are concerned, is to lift each one by his own proper handle, and run each one in his own proper groove" (427).

Second, while an individual's nature is rooted in biology (children's natures are described as "the great physical facts of their being" [427]), neither race nor family determine one's nature absolutely. In fact, while Stowe never abandons the rhetoric of racialism completely, her fiction and prose repeatedly emphasize that people's essential natures frequently have little or no relation to their genetic inheritance. As she stresses in "Intolerance," the disparities between the parents' plans for their children and their children's desires results from the fact that natures are not always passed from parent to offspring: "As parents come together out of different families with ill-assorted peculiarities, so children are born to them with natures differing from their own and from each other" (414). In *The Minister's Wooing,* Stowe writes, "One sometimes sees launched into a family-circle a child of so different a nature from all the rest, that it might seem as if, like an aërolite, he had fallen out of another sphere" (107). The "aërolite" in that novel is James Marvyn. All previous Marvyn babies were "of that orderly, contented sort, who sleep till it is convenient to take them up, and while awake suck their thumbs contentedly and look up with large, round eyes at the ceiling when it is not convenient for their elders and betters that they should do anything else" (107). After their infancy, James's siblings all grew into "quiet and decorous children." James, in contrast, "was an infant of moods and tenses, and those not of any regular verb. He would cry of nights, and he would be taken up of mornings, and he would not suck his thumb." Unlike his well-mannered brothers and sisters, James "did not take to study,—yawned over books, and cut out moulds for running anchors when he should have been thinking of his columns of words in four syllables" (107–9). At age twenty-five James runs off to be a sailor, against his parents' wishes. Upon hearing this news, James's father declares angrily, "He went out from us because he was not of us" (114).

Eventually, Mr. Marvyn learns that affection, not homogeneity, constitutes a family, and he comes to value James not just in spite of but even because of his difference. As she reiterates this argument in other texts, Stowe draws again on, and manipulates, the rhetoric of animal nature from natural history. The chapter in *Queer Little People* entitled "Our Dogs" describes the Stowe family's experiences with the more than ten dogs who lived in their household from the late 1840s to mid-1860s. The subsequent chapter, "Dogs and Cats," offers a brief overview of the traits and temperaments of different breeds of dogs. "There are among dogs certain races or large divisions," Stowe writes, "and those belonging purely to any of those races are called blood-dogs. . . . and each has a strongly marked character" (103). The analogy that prefaces her discussion of canine genetics, however, compares the diversity in canine nature to the diversity in natures among Stowe's own children. Referring back to "Our Dogs," she explains, "In these stories you must have noticed that each dog had as much his own character as if he had been a human being. Carlo was not like Rover, nor Rover like Giglio, nor Giglio like Florence, nor Florence like Rag, nor Rag like Wix,—any more than Charley is like Fred, or Fred like Henry, or Henry like Eliza, or Eliza like Julia. Every animal has his own character, as marked and distinct as a human being" (102). The collective offspring of a single human pair—Harriet Beecher and Calvin Stowe—exhibits as much diversity as a collection of dogs whose breeding has been carefully calculated to produce diversity.[39] In the same volume, "The Hen Who Hatched Ducks" tells the story of a young hen whose eggs hatch into ducklings instead of chickens. Officious elders of the chicken community guess at what Mrs. Feathertop could have done wrong to produce such queer offspring, and they bombard her with advice for breaking her young ones' strange habit of getting into water. The young mother suffers miserably until she decides that she and her children just have different natures and that she must let them determine their own course in the world. The mother hen bears no genetic connection to her children (her eggs had been switched by the farmer's son), but the dissimilarities between hen and duck serve as an allegory for the differences that are possible between a mother and her children when all are genetically related.

This recurrent troping of differences between family members as differences between animal breeds or species also carries significant implications for nineteenth-century debates about the place of African Americans and other people of color in the United States. Stowe's argument about the discontinuities between essence and inheritance invokes and confounds—deliberately, I believe—contemporary antimiscegenation and antiassimilation arguments. From the 1860s onward, Stowe routinely describes *intra*racial marriage among white people as interracial miscegenation. Stowe's argument about respecting the fixed nature of marriage partners in *Little Foxes* begins: "A man and woman come together out of different families and races, often united by only one or two sympathies, with many differences" (413). In *My Wife and I,* Harry Henderson's uncle Jacob uses the rhetoric of racial difference to *justify* the possibility of marriage between Harry and his cousin Caroline, though both parties are of exclusively white, Puritan descent. Jacob explains: "The only objection to the intermarriage of cousins is one that depends entirely on similarity of race peculiarities. Sometimes cousins, inheriting each from different races, are physiologically as much of diverse blood as if their parents had not been related, and in that case there isn't the slightest objection to marriage. Now, Caroline, though her father is your mother's brother, inherits evidently the Selwyn blood. . . . Caroline is a Selwyn, every inch, and you are as free to marry her as any woman you can meet" (117). Here the mixing of "diverse blood" is unequivocally positive.

This collapsing of racial and familial differences undermines even more dramatically the logic behind contemporary campaigns for a racially homogenous nation when Stowe argues that if the differences between family members are like the differences between races then the reverse is also true: the differences between races are like the differences between family members, and hence no object to national unity. An important passage in *My Wife and I* reveals Stowe's awareness of and control over the racial implications of the confounding of familial and racial differences. Harry Henderson's description of his mother's skill in mediating between the different natures present in her household segues into an argument on diversity and nationalism. Mrs. Henderson

> read the character of each [family member], she mediated between opposing natures; she translated the dialect of different sorts of spirits, to each other. In a family of young children, there is a chance for every sort and variety of natures; and for natures whose modes of feeling are as foreign to each other as those of the French and the English. It needs a common interpreter, who understands every dialect of the soul, thus to translate differences of individuality into a common language of love. . . .
>
> The state, at this very day, needs an influence like what I remember our mother's to have been, in our great, vigorous, growing family, . . . it needs a divining power, by which different sections and different races can be interpreted to each other, and blended together in love. (35–36)

The comparison between family and nation naturalizes the vision of a racially diverse nation—for the ideal family, as Stowe has so sedulously articulated, tolerates difference. *Little Foxes* offers this description of the ideal family: "If I were to picture a perfect family, it should be a union of people of individual and marked character, who through love have come to a perfect appreciation of each other, and who so wisely understand themselves and one another that each may move freely along his or her own track without jar or jostle,—a family where affection is always sympathetic and receptive, but never inquisitive, where all personal delicacies are respected, and where there is a sense of privacy and seclusion in following one's own course, unchallenged by the watchfulness of others, yet withal a sense of society and support in a knowledge of the kind dispositions and interpretations of all around" (442–43). If the differences between races are like the differences between family members, there is no reason why the nation—guided by women—cannot also function as a family in which difference is not erased but embraced. Elizabeth Barnes's mistaken belief that Stowe's use of the "the family model . . . intensifies the psychological link between humanity and homogeneity" (97) rises from her reliance on a model of family very different from the one that Stowe advocated. While Barnes believes that "Stowe's novel reveals the sentimental necessity of sacrificing democratic difference to the cause of union" (98),[40] I argue that Stowe's fiction teaches that the survival of the union, like the survival of a family, depends on the recognition and respect of difference.

Race and Privilege

Because racialism and racism have so often been collapsed in studies of Stowe, it is important for me to point out that, for Stowe, recognizing difference does not equal an assertion of hierarchies based on those differences.[41] In contrast, Stowe not only argues in favor of a racially integrated society, she points out to whites the biases behind their own "objective" racial science. Even as she allows for both biological and environmental explanations of racial difference, Stowe argues unequivocally that racial hierarchies and social inequalities were produced by whites alone. Examination of "The Laborers of the South" should terminate critics' continuing speculation about Stowe's desire for an all-white America.[42] One of a series of essays that appeared in the *Christian Era* and were subsequently published as *Palmetto Leaves,* "Laborers" was written from Stowe's winter home in Mandarin, Florida, in 1872. Anticipating Booker T. Washington's famous Atlanta Convention address (with its call to "cast down your bucket where you are"), Stowe tells her Southern white audience that in order to achieve economic success, they must abandon schemes to import (white) foreign laborers and instead forge productive relationships with eminently qualified African Americans who already live there. To overturn whites' reservations about social and economic partnership with blacks, Stowe makes an argument that combines, as "Sojourner Truth, the Libyan Sibyl" does, racialist and environmentalist arguments. In response to contemporary racist arguments that nonwhite races were physically compromised and even dying out, Stowe cites blacks' physical strength and adaptability. The black laborer, Stowe suggests, is undeterred by summer heat and tropical diseases: "he thrives and flourishes physically under a temperature that exposes a white man to disease and death" (283). At the same time, Stowe counters the stereotypes—produced by slavery—of the black worker as lazy, shiftless, and dishonest, by stressing the importance of a properly nurturing environment: "Take any set of white men, and put them for two or three generations under the same system of work without wages, forbid them legal marriage and secure family ties, and we will venture to predict that they would come out of the ordeal a much worse set than the Southern laborers are" (287). "The untrained plantation hands and their children," Stowe writes later in the essay, "are and will be just what *education* may make them" (314–15, Stowe's emphasis). Black laborers' position at the bottom of the social hierarchy, far from being "ordained" by God, is presented as a direct result of white oppression. Given the same treatment, whites could just as easily occupy the rung of the ladder currently occupied by blacks.

"Miss Katy-Did and Miss Cricket," a beast fable from *Queer Little People,* offers an even fiercer attack on those who theorized the existence of a natural hierarchy among humans. At the beginning of the story, Miss Katy-Did solicits the help of her "gallant cousin," Colonel Katy-Did, in drawing up an invitation list for her upcoming insect ball (29). The colonel, finding something good in every proposed invitee, recommends each party to the list; Miss Katy frequently protests, but yields to the colonel on every case—until the he proposes inviting the Crickets. The colonel is confused as to why his cousin absolutely refuses to invite the Crickets, whom she admits are "perfectly nice and respectable,—very good people" (32). "My dear cousin," he says, "I am afraid you must explain."

> "Why, their *color,* to be sure. Don't you see?"
>
> "Oh!" said the Colonel. "That's it, is it? Excuse me, but I have been living in France, where these distinctions are wholly unknown, and I have not yet got myself in the train of fashionable ideas here."
>
> "Well, then, let me teach you," said Miss Katy. "You know we republicans go for no distinctions except those created by Nature herself, and we found our rank upon *color,* because that is clearly a thing that none has any hand in but our Maker. You see?"

> "Yes; but who decides what color shall be the reigning color?"
>
> "I'm surprised to hear the question! The only true color—the only proper one —is *our* color, to be sure. A lovely pea-green is the precise shade on which to found aristocratic distinction. But then we are liberal;—we associate with the Moths, who are gray; with the Butterflies, who are blue-and-gold-colored; with the Grass-hoppers, yellow and brown;—and society would become dreadfully mixed if it were not fortunately ordered that the Crickets are black as jet. The fact is, that a class to be looked down upon is necessary to all elegant society, and if the Crickets were not black, we could not keep them down, because, as everybody knows, they are often a great deal cleverer than we are. They have a vast talent for music and dancing; they are very quick at learning, and would be getting to the very top of the ladder if we once allowed them to climb." (33)

Through satire, this story exposes scientific justifications of racial hierarchies (supposedly based on "no distinctions except those created by nature herself") as the self-delusions of those who want to retain their position at the top of the social hierarchy. Taking aim at one of America's principal points of national pride, Stowe charges that racial hierarchies are nothing more than an American aristocracy in disguise. The existence of "elegant society," or a privileged social group, depends upon creating "a class to be looked down upon." Miss Katy's belief in the innate superiority of "lovely pea-green" mocks the self-interestedness and arbitrariness of white people's racist theories. The story repeats common racialist beliefs about African Americans—that they "have a vast talent for music and dancing." The presence of these talents, however, is clearly not meant to indicate the absence of others, for the text also says that the black Crickets "are very quick at learning" and would soon rise in socioeconomic power if the other insects didn't conspire to keep them down. (And in the context of this story, Miss Katy's admission that the Crickets dance and sing well makes their exclusion from her party seem only more unmerited.) The resolution of the story both confirms Miss Katy's suspicion of the black Crickets' intelligence and metes out divine retribution right there on earth. Miss Katy throws her ball, and attends an endless stream of parties, all held outdoors, until she, little protected by "her flimsy green satin," succumbs to cold and dies when summer turns to fall. Displaying superior judgment, the Crickets avoid such dissipation. Intelligently relocating their family "to the chimney-corner of a nice little cottage," the Crickets survive the winter in comfort and triumph in the end (34).

Like Susan Warner, Stowe successfully manipulated contemporary discourses relating to animals in order to expand the power of white, middle-class women. Yet, as we have seen here, Stowe's political designs were significantly more far-reaching, and her very different use of animality enabled her to talk about race as well as gender.[43] Stowe's use of human-animal comparisons on behalf of domestic women, their children, and African Americans stands out as exceedingly remarkable given that not just the language of animality in general, but some of the very same images she deployed—domestic women as hens or songbirds—were typically deployed to justify the oppression of these groups of people.

While Stowe's belief in the continuities between humans and other animals infuses her entire canon, these ideas do not manifest themselves with equal emphasis. Stowe's efforts to undo rationalizations for slavery required focus on the distinctions between slaves and animals. She was quite aware that many of her contemporaries, like St. Claire's father in *Uncle Tom's Cabin,* regarded African Americans "as an intermediate link between man and animals, and graded all [their] ideas of justice or generosity on this hypothesis."[44] To secure blacks the freedom enjoyed by other members of the human race, Stowe did what Frederick Douglass and other abolitionists did: she labored to assert African Americans' membership in the human community by emphasizing the distinctions between slaves and animals. Though such a strategy was at odds with Stowe's worldview, she recognized its exigency and employed it throughout her antislavery writings. When asked by the minister if she desires her freedom, Candace of the *The Minister's Wooing* responds: "Why look at me,—I a'n't a critter. I's neider huffs nor horns. I's a reasonable bein',—a woman,—as much a woman as anybody" (176).[45] But despite the use of such strategies in her abolitionist writings, Stowe's emphasis on human-animal connectedness became part of the literary legacy she left to subsequent writers, as we will see in more detail in the next chapter. In the final decades of the nineteenth century, increasing numbers of people came to question the hierarchy of species that had been asserted throughout Western civilization. In this context, assertions of particular humans' affinities with animals no longer necessarily equaled an assertion of those people's inferiority.

Animal Justice

Charles W. Chesnutt, Black Animality, and the Politics of Animal Welfare

> If you pick up a starving dog and make him prosperous, he will not bite you. This is the principal difference between a dog and a man.
>
> MARK TWAIN

> A strong characteristic of Mrs. Glover was a passion for justice. . . . Nor did her compassion stop at human beings. A man beating a horse, a boy torturing a dog or a bird or an insect, would stir her to vigorous expostulation. She came very near rendering life in Booneville impossible for herself and her family, when, one Fourth of July, she saw a white boy tie a pack of fire crackers to a dog's tale and strike a match to set it off. He wasn't much of a dog and would probably have been happier dead, and the world none the worse, but she had read in a Negro newspaper some months before an account of an incident in a small Southern town, where the white young men of the village, bored stiff by the lack of amusement, had found it in pouring kerosene oil on the hair of a half-witted Negro lad and setting fire to it. The sight of the firecrackers tied to the dog so enraged her that she pulled the boy away none too gently and expressed her opinion of him in terms which were not complimentary. The boy's mother, to whom the incident was reported, was righteously indignant that a Negro woman should have laid hands upon her son.
>
> CHARLES W. CHESNUTT, *The Quarry* (completed in 1928 but not published until 1999)

SCHOLARS IN LITERATURE and environment studies have been working diligently in recent years to remedy what Elizabeth Dodd has described as "the absence of black writers from existing ecocritical discussion."[1] These efforts have resulted in an increasing number of ecocritical readings of African American texts written in the twentieth century, but the progress with black literature of the nineteenth century has been quite meager in comparison. If anything, these labors have led primarily to a proliferation of explanations why "African American scholarship may never rediscover a neglected counterpart to Henry Thoreau."[2] However, even as they acknowledge the many reasons why African American authors were unlikely to engage in the forms of nature writing and wilderness appreciation embraced by white authors, ecocritical scholars have been careful to insist, as Dodd does, that "we should not inadvertently ghettoize black literature, as if it had nothing to contribute to our understanding of the vexed human relation to the nonhuman world. In fact, this work has much to tell us, if we pay close enough ecocritical attention."[3]

This chapter argues that the fiction of Charles W. Chesnutt does indeed have much to tell us about both the history of humans' relationship with the nonhuman world and the relationship between that history and the history of race. However, I do not see reading the nonhuman presence in Chesnutt's work as simply a matter of "pay[ing] close enough ecocritical attention"—at least not if that means working within the parameters of ecocritical scholarship as it is currently conceived. There are, of course, multiple definitions of ecocriticism, and ecocritics agree on nothing so much as the still evolving nature of this discipline. Yet the one factor common to all definitions proffered to date is ecocriticism's alignment with what may be broadly termed the environmental movement. As Michael Bennett explains, "If we separate the term 'ecocriticism' into its two components, its parameters seem clear: 'criticism,' engaging in analytical reading practices, and 'ecological,' focusing these practices on environmental concerns."[4] Recovering what Chesnutt had to say about the affinities between human and nonhuman beings requires turning our attention to an issue that has not only historically fallen outside the boundaries of environmental and ecological activism, but has also been scorned by a considerable number of environmentalists: the prevention of cruelty to the domesticated animals living within the built environment.

Admittedly, through the lens of existing critical apparatus, African American engagement with the nineteenth-century animal protection movement would seem, for many reasons, highly unlikely. There was, first of all, a seeming opposition between the rhetorical strategies of the crusades for animal and racial justice. Animal protection advocates placed strong emphasis on the kinship between humans and animals. One 1872 text on the subject bore the title *Our Poor Relations.*[5] Publications produced by the most prolific nineteenth-century animal protection organizations—the Massachusetts Society for the Prevention of Cruelty to Animals (MSPCA) and the American Humane Education Society (AHES)—frequently stressed the common animality of human and nonhuman creatures. These organizations' typical emphasis on the sameness of humans and the rest of animal creation is reflected in the title of the speech George Angell delivered at the 1887 national convention of the Women's Christian Temperance Union: "Relations of Animals that Can Speak to Those That Are Dumb." Both this address and the title of the MSPCA monthly periodical *Our Dumb Animals* reflect the sentiment that the only real difference between human and nonhuman animals was the ability of the former to articulate their thoughts in spoken language. It would, of course, be an understatement to say that, historically, ideas about connectedness between humans and animals have not worked to the advantage of people of color. As scholars have thoroughly documented, arguments about blacks' affinities with or status as animals were used to justify their enslavement before the Civil War as well as the denial of their civil and political rights after it. Consequently, nineteenth-century black writers necessarily took up the task of opposing Western civilization's long history of categorizing people of African descent as subhuman animals—a task that would seem (from our vantage point, at least) to entail distancing African Americans from the animal world in order to establish their status as full members of the human race. Accordingly, existing arguments for and about African American appreciation for nonhuman nature in this period focus on "the landscape" or flora, rather than fauna.[6]

As very little thought has been given to how the intense late-nineteenth-century interest in animal welfare affected the writings of traditionally canonized American writers, there has, not surprisingly, been even less discussion of its relevance to African American literature. The small amount of scholarship that does exist on the U.S. animal welfare movement has had little to say about African Americans; historians, however, have framed the issue in terms that suggest that blacks were, at best, indifferent to or, most likely, strongly alienated by the animal protection cause. Recent considerations of this topic have accepted the theory advanced by James Turner's 1980 *Reckoning With the Beast: Animals, Pain, and Humanity in the Victorian Mind.* There, Turner attributes the widespread popularity of the animal welfare movement in postbellum America to two causes. First, he proposes that anticruelty laws provided elite whites with yet another means of policing the violent propensities of America's increasingly non-Anglo-Saxon working class (since cruelty toward animals was believed to be a precursor to violent crime or even full-scale working-class rebellion). Second, Turner suggests that, having seen the battle for abolition nearly destroy the Union, post–Civil War Americans embraced the humane movement with enthusiasm because—in contrast to a continued fight for black civil rights or the rights of workers—that cause did not fundamentally threaten the status quo. Fighting to end cruelty to animals, Turner concludes, provided "a cathartic outlet" for reformist impulses that was "without social risk."[7]

In Britain and the United States, nineteenth-century supporters of the humane movement characterized this cause as both part of a broad program of social reform and a logical extension of the humane principles that drove abolition. The masthead of Angell's *Our Dumb Animals* borrowed the iconography of Garrison's *The Liberator,* substituting the figure of an enchained slave with that of a beaten horse.[8] Similarly, an 1879 *Scribner's Monthly* magazine article suggested that, by championing the rights of animals, Henry Bergh (president and founder of the New York–based ASPCA) was following in the footsteps of Abraham Lincoln and John Brown. Bergh's work, the article states, "was first rendered possible by the liberation of the slave, because a reasonable people could not have listened to the claims of dumb animals while human beings, held in more ignoble bondage, were subjected to greater cruelty and added outrage. [Bergh] took up the principles of humanity, for which two chief martyrs fell, crowned with human love, and is carrying them forward by teaching men to be noble and strong through pity and self restraint."[9] But as the progression from abolition to animal protection has been recorded as an illegitimate and unfortunate succession—as an attenuation rather than an extension of Americans' commitment to social justice—these translations of abolitionist politics into the politics of animal protection can easily be read as an unseemly capitalization on or even denigration of racial injustice.

In this context, it would not be hard to imagine that Charles Chesnutt had the century's most influential animal protection novel in mind—Anna Sewell's *Black Beauty: The Autobiography of a Horse* (1877)—when he wrote to his editors at Houghton Mifflin of his hope that his recently published novel *The Marrow of Tradition* (1901) would become "the legitimate successor of *Uncle Tom's Cabin.*"[10] By 1901, dozens of texts had been promoted as responses, companions, sequels, or successors to *Uncle Tom's Cabin;*[11] among these, only *Black Beauty* captured the public's attention on a scale approaching its antecedent. Sewell's novel borrowed, first of all, on the genre of the slave autobiography. The title page of the first edition identifies the book as "The Autobiography of a Horse / Translated from the Original Equine by Anna Sewell." Sewell's equine protagonist is literally black, and the names given to him by his successive owners—Black Beauty, Darkie, Ebony, Blackbird, Black Auster, and Blackie—emphasize his blackness. But in its character types, plot structure, and rhetorical strategies, *Black Beauty* mirrors Stowe's *Uncle Tom.*[12]

When MSPCA president George Angell discovered *Black Beauty* in 1890, he promptly printed (through the auspices of the AHES) 600,000 copies of the novel, heralding it on the title page as "The 'Uncle Tom's Cabin' of the Horse." By 1891, other publishers, according to Angell, had printed "probably not less than 400,000 copies more, making a total of something like a million copies, probably by far the largest number ever issued of any book in the world in the same length of time from publication." To reach immigrant populations, Angell had the novel translated into Italian, German, Dutch, Swedish, and Spanish. He distributed copies of the book to the editors of thousands of American newspapers and magazines. In return for these efforts "not less than a thousand American papers, including those of highest literary standing and largest circulation, have published articles in its praise."[13] Like *Uncle Tom's Cabin* before it, *Black Beauty* gave birth to sequels, imitations, collectable memorabilia, and even a stage production (which featured live horses and toured dozens of U.S. cities in 1908 and 1909).

I do not, however, believe it was Sewell's novel that prompted Chesnutt, in his 1899 letter, to modify "successor" with "legitimate," for Chesnutt's understanding of contemporary animal politics and their relation to issues of racial justice differ radically from what existing critical approaches lead us to expect. While I do not doubt that the theory advanced by Turner (and readily taken up by others) does in fact account for some Americans' attraction to the animal welfare cause, I do want to question the assumption that these factors can adequately account for nineteenth-century interest in animal protection as a whole. Quite simply, the problem with Turner's thesis is that, as it locates animal welfare in a view of history that sees white people controlling discourses of which everyone else was a victim, it leaves no room for imagining nonwhite, nonelite contributions to the conversation. Examination of Chesnutt's fiction reveals that the fantastic successes of the first wave of the American animal protection movement opened up new possibilities for intervention into the racist rhetoric of black animality. In his discussion of signifyin(g) as the trope of black literary revision, Henry Louis Gates cites the example of jazz and blues musicians' manipulation of established forms. "Because the form is self-evident to the musician," Gates explains, "both he and his well-trained audience are playing and listening with expectation. Signifyin(g) disappoints these expectations; caesuras, or breaks, achieve the same function. This form of disappointment creates a dialogue between what the listener expects and what the artist plays."[14] We cannot, I propose, comprehend fully the arguments Chesnutt makes about race—in "The Bouquet," "The Passing of Grandison," and *The Marrow of Tradition,* among other texts—without understanding how those texts assume an audience well trained in, and receptive to, the rhetoric of animal welfare.

"Better than [White] Men"

In existing studies, the connection between people and animals in Chesnutt's fiction has been treated as an extension of one of the central narrative conventions of antebellum African American literature: the juxtaposition of animals and slaves.[15] This strategy appears repeatedly, for example, in Frederick Douglass's 1845 *Narrative,* in which Douglass observes that "slaves know as little of their ages as horses know of theirs." When slave children are fed, he explains, food was placed in a wooden trough and "the children were then called, like so many pigs, and like so many pigs, they would come and devour the mush." Describing the appraisal and division of slaves following the death of one of his masters, Douglass writes: "Men and women, old and young, married and single, were ranked with horses, sheep, and swine. There were horses and men, cattle and women, pigs and children, all holding the same rank in the scale of being. . . . We had no more voice in that decision than the brutes among whom we were ranked."[16] The "scale of being" to which Douglass refers is, of course, the *scala naturae,* or Great Chain of Being, and logic of his argument rests on his and his readers' belief in this theory that all beings occupied different places in a linear, hierarchical scale of increasing perfection. As humans were, according to this worldview, superior to all other beings of the created world, any system that placed humans and animals on the same rank violated the natural order. Thus, to show that slaves were ranked with animals was to show that slavery was unnatural.[17]

Several of Chesnutt's stories employ a similar strategy, most notably the stories about conjure in the antebellum South, the earliest of which appeared in the *Atlantic Monthly* in 1887 (making Chesnutt the first black author whose fiction appeared in this prestigious literary magazine) and which culminated in his 1899 collection *The Conjure Woman.* Eric Sundquist has written perceptively about the way in which Chesnutt uses conjure-induced, human-to-animal metamorphosis—in tales such as "The Conjurer's Revenge" and "Tobe's Tribulations"—to "demonstrate the elision between human and animal . . . in the philosophy of chattelism." As Sundquist explains, Chesnutt's conjure tales extend the political reach of the slave-animal juxtaposition, making the metamorphosis of slave into animal critique—simultaneously—both slavery and "its post-Reconstruction aftermath."[18] For this reason, however, I will not discuss the human-animal metamorphoses of the conjure tales here.

My interest lies not in Chesnutt's extension to postbellum politics of this rhetorical strategy that abolitionists used to critique slavery, but in Chesnutt's subsequent departure from and modification of that rhetorical strategy.

From our twenty-first-century perspective, the argument of Chesnutt's short story "The Bouquet" (first published in 1899 but written by 1897) seems—like that of Douglass's texts—firmly rooted in the centuries-old belief in humans' ascendancy over the rest of creation. The plot of the tale, set in the postbellum South, is structured around a series of juxtapositions between a young black girl—Sophy Tucker—and an admirable white dog—Prince. Sophy develops an "intense devotion" for her teacher Miss Mary Myrover, a white woman who has taken a position in the colored school to ease her once-prosperous family's strained finances. From the beginning of the story, Chesnutt creates a parallel between Sophy's relationship with Miss Myrover and the latter's relationship with her dog. "Sophy," Chesnutt writes, "had a rival in her attachment to the teacher, but the rival was altogether friendly. Miss Myrover had a little dog, a white spaniel, answering to the name of Prince."[19] Prince, we learn, "was very fond of his mistress, and always, unless shut up at home, accompanied her to school, where he spent most of his time lying under the teacher's desk" (277–78). Though Sophy is able to perform for Miss Myrover "the numberless little services that can be rendered in a schoolroom" (276), her ability to exercise her devotion is—unlike Prince's—circumscribed by the color line: "At school Sophy and Prince vied with each other in their attentions to Miss Myrover. But when school was over, Prince went away with her, and Sophy stayed behind; . . . Miss Myrover taught the colored children, but she could not be seen with them in public" (278). On one occasion Sophy does accompany Miss Myrover home in order to carry her books. But while Prince can trot by the teacher's side, Sophy follows "at a respectable distance" (279). When they arrive at the Myrover home, Miss Myrover is informed by her mother that her black pupils are not welcome there. "I wish," Mrs. Myrover says, within Sophy's hearing, "you wouldn't let those little darkeys follow you to the house. I don't want them in the yard" (279).

The contrasts between Prince's and Sophy's treatment are illustrated most dramatically, however, by Sophy's thwarted attempts to place a bouquet of yellow roses on Miss Myrover's casket. Convinced that her daughter's untimely demise was precipitated by her labors at the colored school, Mrs. Myrover "gave strict orders that no colored people should be admitted to the house" on the day of the funeral (281). Determined that her bouquet reach the coffin even if she cannot, Sophy attempts to deliver her bouquet surreptitiously through the intercession of the Myrovers' cook, but Mrs. Myrover discovers

Sophy at the kitchen door and orders her to leave. At the church, the ushers, following Mrs. Myrover's injunction, turn all the black mourners away. Undeterred, Sophy creeps to the side of the church and watches the service through a crack in a stained glass window, and there she observes Prince inside the church lying stretched out underneath his mistress's casket. The same people who so calmly barred the black mourners from the service did not have "the heart to remove him" (286) after he had slipped in unnoticed. After the service, Sophy, still holding her bouquet, follows the funeral procession to the graveyard—only to discover a sign reading, "This cemetery is for white people only. Others please keep out" (287). Here, too, Prince is admitted and Sophy is not.

In presenting a series of incidents in which Sophy is treated worse than the dog, Chesnutt clearly draws on the slave narrative's conventional juxtaposition of slave and animal. However, in this story, he also significantly modifies this convention, for the logic of "The Bouquet" does not rest upon a firm belief in humans' natural and rightful superiority over all nonhuman creatures. Instead, this story's critique of racism relies primarily upon its readers' receptiveness toward the rhetorical strategies of the movement that explicitly challenged this position: the animal protection movement. In order to understand the political implications of the juxtaposition of human and animal in "The Bouquet," we have to understand this story's relationship to the contemporary and enormously popular animal welfare narratives that, first, characterized dogs as broadly virtuous and even more virtuous than humans, and, second, demanded that dogs be granted legal protection on account of those virtues.

Undoubtedly, the most widely disseminated of these was the closing argument delivered by George Graham Vest in the famous 1870 case of *Burden v. Hornsby.* The suit was Charles Burden's attempt to avenge the death of his beloved dog Old Drum, who had been shot by his neighbor Leonidas Hornsby after the dog had wandered onto his property. The speech Vest delivered in his capacity as counsel for Burden (which William Safire identified in 1999 as the best speech of the last millennium) bears quoting in full:

> Gentlemen of the jury, the best friend a man has in the world may turn against him and become his enemy. His son or daughter whom he has reared with loving care may prove ungrateful. Those who are nearest and dearest to us—those whom we trust with our happiness and our good name—may become traitors to their faith. The money that a man has he may lose. It flies away from him, perhaps when he needs it most. A man's reputation may be sacrificed in a moment of ill-

> considered action. The people who are prone to fall on their knees to do us honor when success is with us may be the first to throw the stone of malice when failure settles its cloud upon our heads. The one absolute, unselfish friend that man can have in this selfish world—the one that never deserts him, the one that never proves ungrateful or treacherous—is his dog.
>
> Gentlemen of the jury, a man's dog stands by him in prosperity and in poverty, in health and in sickness. He will sleep on the cold ground, where the wintry winds blow and the snow drives fiercely, if only he can be near his master's side. He will kiss the hand that has no food to offer, he will lick the wounds and sores that come in encounter with the roughness of the world. He guards the sleep of his pauper master as if he were a prince. When all other friends desert, he remains. When riches take wings and reputation falls to pieces he is as constant in his love as the sun in its journey through the heavens. If fortune drives the master forth an outcast in the world, friendless and homeless, the faithful dog asks no higher privilege than that of accompanying him to guard against danger, to fight against his enemies. And when the last scene of all comes, and death takes the master in its embrace, and his body is laid away in the cold ground, no matter if all other friends pursue their way, there by his graveside will the noble dog be found, his head between his paws, his eyes sad but open in alert watchfulness, faithful and true even in death.[20]

Although this closing argument mentions no details of the actual case, the jury was so moved by it that they not only sided with Vest's client, but they also fined Hornsby double the amount of damages sought. Subsequently, Vest's speech was reprinted in papers throughout the nation, transforming Vest into a national hero, and from the platform of this popularity, Vest launched a political career that culminated in a seat in the U.S. Senate.

The effectiveness of Vest's speech and the national interest it received reflect a significantly new understanding of the relationship between humans and dogs. Vest was not just reciting age-old beliefs about canine fidelity; instead, he captured, in a particularly eloquent form, emerging ideas about dogs and their relationship to humans. Before the mid-nineteenth century, even the most vehement supporters of the moral instructiveness of nature still imagined that the earth's species formed a linear and hierarchical gradation whose apex was man. In the 1830s (as I demonstrated in chapter 2) contentions that the dog and other animals might, like us, be moral creatures with eternal souls seemed shocking and new. But by the end of the century, a critical mass of Americans had become willing and even eager to believe that the dog, at least, stood above humans in the moral hierarchy. In newspaper articles, popular magazines, and books about animals, canine behavior was held up as worthy of human emulation. By driving this point home, Vest was able to convince the jurors that dogs deserved at least a measure of the legal consideration traditionally reserved for humans.

Evidence of the speech's popularity and the public's receptivity to the ideas it contained appears, conveniently, in a brief story Chesnutt composed in his journal in 1874 at the age of seventeen.[21] "Bruno" narrates the heroism of a "large jet-black Newfoundland dog," whose first master, a down-and-out, out-of-work theater hand suffering from consumption, collapses in the street. When the narrator (who, like the narrator of *The Marrow of Tradition,* is a doctor) arrives on the scene, the man had lain there "half on the pavement, and half in the gutter" in the sight of many onlookers, but "no one had stirred a finger" to help the unconscious man. In contrast to these indifferent humans, Bruno lay attentively by his master's side "whining dismally and snuffing at him and licking his face and hands." After the narrator places the sick man in a boarding house, his dog "sat by the bed side, looking wistfully at his face, and licking [his] hand." Bruno's owner soon dies, but not before remarking: "I am a lone man, without money or friends except my good Bruno. Poor Bruno! You have stuck to me through thick and thin. You have accompanied me in all my rambles, shared my fortunes and misfortunes." Thus "Bruno" dramatizes the claims made by Vest four years earlier in his famous speech. Chesnutt's story concludes, as *Burden v. Hornsby* did, with canine virtue rewarded. After the sick man's death, the narrator adopts Bruno and cares for him the rest of his life. Bruno "became the pet of the family [and] the playmate of the children." "Dear old Bruno!" the narrator addresses his beloved dog, "Though you are old and blind, yet you are loved by me!"

As it connected virtue (and in particular devotion) with entitlement to protection under the law, Vest's rhetorical strategy resonated strongly with late-nineteenth-century white positions on the South's "race problem." During the 1880s and '90s, Southern whites regularly defended the increasingly violent measures used to suppress black civil rights by characterizing them as a necessary response to the freed black population's growing criminal and savage tendencies. If only blacks would serve whites in their free state with the same loyalty and devotion that they had during slavery, they argued, the "race problem" would cease to exist. It is precisely this assumption that Chesnutt addresses in "The Bouquet." By drawing on the animal welfare narratives in which canine fidelity receives its just reward, Chesnutt gives the lie to these claims that freed blacks would receive social justice if they continued to play the part of the white man's best friend. In this tale, the white community rewards only acts of devotion and fidelity performed by other whites. In addition to Prince (who is, we remember, a *white* dog), the Myrovers themselves have also benefited from the same principle that prevailed in the *Burden v. Hornsby* case. The white Myrover family (a pun, it seems, on "my rover") was renowned for its "pedigree" (270) and long history of selfless devotion. Colonel Myrover had sacrificed both his life and his wealth for the Confederate cause (the latter by investing the family fortune in Confederate bonds). On account of his altruism, "the name of Colonel Myrover was always used to illustrate the highest type of patriotic devotion and self-sacrifice" (271). Thus, "The Bouquet" argues that, while self-sacrifice and faithful devotion may earn white people and even a white dog respect and privilege, African Americans are not similarly compensated.

At the same time that Chesnutt capitalizes on the connection between devotion and rights proffered in animal welfare narratives, he also skillfully manipulates these tales' insistence that dogs were more virtuous than humans and therefore a model for human behavior. During the 1870s, '80s, and '90s these ideas were repeated not just in the publications of humane societies, but in a number of print formats not officially connected to them. Newspapers and popular magazines in this period published countless numbers of anecdotes illustrating dogs' virtues. The stories in Rush C. Hawkins' *Better than Men* (1896)—which the author offered as evidence that "a certain selected number of so-called lower animals are better, by nature and conduct in certain elemental virtues than men"—focused primarily on horses and dogs.[22] Mark Twain speculated in his notebooks that admission to heaven must go "by favor." "If it went by merit," he reasoned, "you would stay out and your dog would go in." In his 1887 *Harper's Bazaar* essay on pet keeping, Thomas Wentworth Higginson (editor of the *Atlantic Monthly* and famed correspondent of Emily Dickinson) argued, "A dog is of itself a liberal education, with its example of fidelity, unwearied activity, cheerful sympathy, and love stronger than death; nay love that is triumphant over shame and ignominy and sin—influences that so often wear out human love or make it change to hate."[23]

In "The Bouquet," Chesnutt invokes these contemporary ideas about canine superiority and then puts them in service of his antiracist agenda. Like the heroes of late-nineteenth-century dog stories, Prince is both idealized and heroic. His name, of course, connotes superior status; moreover, "He was a clever dog, and could fetch and carry, sit up on his haunches, extend his paw to shake hands, and possessed several other canine accomplishments" (277). It is, however, the story's end—which rewrites Vest's famous speech—that most clearly locates Prince within the animal welfare narrative about the superiority of dogs over humans. Standing outside the cemetery gate long after the other mourners had departed and still holding the bouquet she could not deliver, Sophy sees Prince "lying beside the new-made grave" (289). Her "eyes light[ing] up with a sudden glow," she calls to Prince, and he promptly "trotted down to the gate" where she stood. Sophy thrusts her bouquet through the bars and tells him, 'Take that ter Miss Ma'y, Prince, . . . that's a good doggie." In response, "the dog wagged his tail intelligently, took the bouquet carefully in his mouth, carried it to his mistress's grave, and laid it among the other flowers. When Prince had performed his mission he turned his eyes toward Sophy inquiringly, and when she gave him a nod of approval lay down and resumed his watch by the graveside" (290). True to Vest's speech, Prince has proven "faithful and true even in death." As Vest insisted, when "all other friends pursue their way, there by [the] graveside will the noble dog be found, his head between his paws, his eyes sad, but open in alert watchfulness." But as Chesnutt has Prince act out the ending of Vest's speech, he makes a significant modification. Here, the dog is not upstaging *human* virtue (for Sophy, has, throughout the story, demonstrated the same level of devotion). Rather, Prince is specifically upstaging the virtue of the white community. In bringing Sophy's bouquet to Miss Myrover's grave, Prince has done exactly what all the white characters in the story cruelly refused to do: recognize Sophy's rights of mourning. Thus, "The Bouquet" adds freedom from racism to the list of canine virtues humans would do well to emulate.

While "The Bouquet" provides a useful starting point for my discussion of animality in Chesnutt's writing, it does not represent the first instance in African American literature of a retreat from or rethinking of a natural rights theory premised on human superiority and uniqueness. The connection between the discourses of race and animality used in this tale has precedents both within Chesnutt's own work and within African American writing more generally. Although Douglass's writing affirms the traditional, hierarchical view of creation, it also contains passages that reject Enlightenment ideas about human uniqueness. "It should be the study of every farmer to make his horse his companion and friend," Douglass wrote, "and to do this, there is but one rule, and that is, uniform sympathy and kindness. All loud and boisterous commands, a brutal flogging should be banished from the field, and only words of cheer and encouragement should be tolerated. A horse is in many respects like a man. He has five senses, and has memory, affection, and reason."[24] Anticipating the strategy Chesnutt would adopt in "The Bouquet," Harriet Wilson's 1859 novel *Our Nig* emphasizes the dog's indifference to (what becomes cast as a purely human-constructed) racial hierarchy. In that novel, the companionship of her dog Fido provides the only happiness the protagonist Frado finds in her otherwise unrelentingly miserable childhood. "There were days," Wilson writes, "when Fido was the entire confidant of Frado. She told him her griefs as though he were human; and he sat so still, and listened so attentively, she really believed he knew her sorrows. All the leisure moments she could gain were used in teaching him some feat of dog-agility." Frado has no family from which to be separated, but the emotional trauma typically marked in slave narratives by the selling away of family members is registered in this novel by Mrs. Bellmont's selling of Frado's dog—an act which "remove[s] the last vestige of earthly joy" Frado possessed.[25]

For at least one man, experience of canine friendship during slavery translated directly into a desire to support the country's newly established animal welfare organizations. In 1869, a former slave (who identified himself only as J. G. T.) wrote to the editor of the MSPCA's *Our Dumb Animals* to express his pleasure with the new publication. He explains:

> I was a slave, was sold seventeen times, parted from my family four times, remained in bondage forty-three years. I made my escape by being a house servant for part of the time, and *learning to win the affections of the savage hounds.*
>
> I was seventeen days on my way to a land of freedom, without food except when I occasionally obtained fruit, nuts, and so forth. I was often pursued by the hounds, but could quell them immediately. They would quietly guide me on my journey some ways, then wagging their tails would seem to bid me good-bye. Thank Heaven, through the assistance of God and the fierce hounds I gained my freedom.
>
> It has been my fervent desire ever since I could remember that some means might be taken to protect the poor animals from cruel treatment. I treat my animals as I should desire to be treated, and hope every humane soul will pursue the same course. May God bless your efforts.[26]

The research that would allow us to say how many other nineteenth-century blacks joined SPCAs has yet to be performed.[27] After the Civil War relatively few African Americans were wealthy enough to donate to charities; those that could undoubtedly apportioned their contributions to the underfunded organizations serving African Americans. But just as official membership in or subscription to an antislavery society was not a necessary criterion for opposing slavery, neither should we assume that support for animal welfare was limited to or determined by SPCA membership. While organizations such as the AHES blanketed the country with pro-animal literature, endorsements of animal protection appear—throughout the 1870s, '80s, and '90s—in the nation's leading newspapers and literary magazines, in children's books and reading primers, and in books on natural history. For example, Nathaniel Southgate Shaler's *Domesticated Animals* (which I will discuss in more detail below) stresses humans' indebtedness to domesticates for their essential contributions to the development of civilization, and it contains a chapter titled "The Rights of Animals." Similarly, in the introduction to *Better than Men,* Hawkins states that the volume's stories about animals "are my plea for their greater civil rights."[28]

We have no record of Chesnutt's official membership in an SPCA, but in 1887 (ten years before he wrote "The Bouquet") he published a story critiquing animal abuse. Taking a tack Twain would later employ in "A Horse's Tale," "McDugald's Mule" uses regionalism and humor to critique animal cruelty, in this case the violent measures commonly used to compel cart animals to pull their loads. When McDugald begins driving his mule Beauregard home from the store, the animal plants his feet and refuses to budge. After McDugald's words of exhortation and application of the whip fail to produce any effect, officious onlookers recommend brutal (but, as SPCA records indicate, not uncommon) methods for combating the mule's recalcitrance: one urges a violent twisting of the tail and the other "that a fire be built under the mule." But to the crowd's astonishment, McDugald states he "hain't a-goin to do nothin' o' the sort" and then unhitches his animal and sets up camp for the night on that very spot. Later, McDugald explains his reason for letting the mule have his way. Six years ago the animal had refused to cross a bridge over a rushing river. Two passersby administer to Beauregard those violent remedies suggested earlier in the story, and the animal abusers get their just deserts. The man who twists Beauregard's tail receives a kick that sends him flying into a ditch. The man who starts a fire under Beauregard is punished when the mule stomps on the fire and sends a burning ember into his eye. The reason for Beauregard's balkiness is later revealed when the bridge collapses. (Horses and mules were known to have a preternatural ability to sense impending danger.) The way in which McDugald relates this event clarifies Chesnutt's position: "The pore feller with the cinder in his eye was right where the bridge broke, and him an' his hoss was drownded. It was a fine hoss, too; it was a shame to see a critter like that drownded."[29] The implication is that while the death of the horse is something to be regretted, the death of anyone willing to set fire to a living animal is not.

Like many of the other short stories Chesnutt published in magazines in the late 1880s, "McDugald's Mule" includes nothing to make readers doubt that the characters were—as most readers of *Family Fiction* (which published the piece) undoubtedly were—white. But while "McDugald's Mule" makes no explicit mention of race, the story effects a simultaneous critique of the systems of thought that place nonwhites as well as nonhumans beyond the boundaries of ethical consideration. "Mule," of course, is the etymon for "mulatto," and Beauregard's history has some striking parallels with the history of African Americans. McDugald reports that the mule first came into his possession in 1865 (the year the Civil War ended), having "found him down in the swamp on my place just after Sherman went through." Like blacks, Beauregard "served on both sides" in the war (which McDugald gathers from the fact that Beauregard has been branded with both "U.S.A." and "C.S.A."). On account of the services Beauregard has rendered him, McDugald considers himself "under obligations to that mule." "He saved my life once," McDugald insists, "and I ain't likely to forgit it soon."[30] But it is clear from the story that no one else in this Southern town shares McDugald's point of view. Similarly, the idea that the white community was under obligation to blacks (on account of their service before, during, and after the war) was also a minority opinion. Like the conjure tales Chesnutt would write over the next eleven years, "McDugald's Mule" exposes the limitations of its white narrator's perspective and validates other (in this case nonhuman) ways of knowing.

Despite the interest and ability Chesnutt shows in juxtaposing racial and animal politics here, it is not until the period between 1897 and 1901 that we see sustained engagement with this strategy. Several factors, I think, contributed to the timing of this turn. First, the initial wave of animal protectionism reached the height of its power in the mid-1890s.[31] Second, in 1895 the national convention of SPCAs took place in Chesnutt's hometown of Cleveland, Ohio, and—whatever effect it may have had on Chesnutt's personal views about animal protection—the convention certainly dramatized at close range the enormous power and popularity this cause enjoyed. As Chesnutt participated actively in local civic affairs, it is likely that he was acquainted with the humane reformers of Cleveland who hosted the convention. Such a connection is suggested by the fact that, in 1901, Chesnutt wrote a favorable review of an animal welfare novel written by fellow Cleveland resident Susanna Louise Patteson (an autobiography of a cat that was titled *Pussy Meow* and explicitly modeled on Sewell's *Black Beauty*). Chesnutt's review praises, in addition to the text itself, the "very pleasant introduction by Mrs. Sarah K. Bolton," another Cleveland-based social reformer, whom Chesnutt describes as "the well-known author, herself a devoted friend and champion of dumb animals."[32] As Bolton's introduction explains, *Pussy Meow* grew directly out of the activities of the 1895 Cleveland convention: "In the fall of 1895, while the National Convention of the S.P.C.A. was in session in Cleveland, a group of people stood in the assembly room one day discussing *Black Beauty* and *Beautiful Joe.* One expressed the hope that as the horse and dog had now secured a public hearing, some one would be willing to undertake the same for the cat. That same evening Pussy Meow began writing her story."[33] In his review, Chesnutt describes the book as "a welcome addition to the list of books which within the last few years have done so much to interpret animal life and bring it within the pale of human sympathy."[34]

But the most powerful factor influencing Chesnutt's engagement with animal welfare discourse in the late 1890s was the proliferation, from the early 1890s onward, of acts of violence against blacks that included but were not limited to lynching. As lynching and related crimes were being defended by whites' insistence that black men were "brute beasts," it is difficult to imagine how any discourse linking people (much less black people) and animals could help the matter. Among the factors that would make the adoption of such a strategy seem unlikely is a letter written by Chesnutt himself in which he not only spurns depictions of blacks as faithful dogs but vows to eschew such depictions in his own fiction. In a letter to George Washington Cable dated June 13, 1890, Chesnutt observed that all of the African Americans presented favorably in the magazine press "have been blacks, full-blooded, and their chief virtues have been their dog-like fidelity and devotion to their old masters. Such characters exist; not six months ago a negro in Raleigh, N.C., wrote to the Governor of the State offering to serve out the sentence in the penitentiary of seven years just imposed on his old master for some crime. But I don't care to write about these people." As the editors of Chesnutt's letters note, this uncharacteristically emotional letter was in fact a revision of an even more spirited draft completed on June 5. In that version, the passage quoted above concluded: "But I can't write about those people, or rather I won't write about them."[35] But if Chesnutt scholarship has shown us anything, it is that Chesnutt was a master of hijacking his opponents' discourses and redeploying them toward his own political ends.[36] By the end of the decade, Chesnutt had substituted a program of active intervention into the racist rhetoric of black animality for his earlier intention to refuse it outright. As I will argue in the next section, strategically (re)associating black men and dogs (vis-à-vis the rhetoric of welfare) is what enables "The Passing of Grandison" and *The Marrow of Tradition* to attack the animal-based stereotypes that informed both plantation fiction nostalgic for a slave-holding past and defenses of lynching inspired by the desire for an Anglo-Saxon future.

Grandison Comes Home; Or, White Supremacy and the Truth about Cats and Dogs

To twenty-first-century readers, "The Passing of Grandison" (1899) appears entirely consistent with Chesnutt's stated intentions to refuse depictions of blacks who display "dog-like fidelity." The story is currently read as both an ingenious trickster narrative and a masterful example of Chesnutt's signifyin(g), in which he deploys and then attacks the stereotype of the faithfully devoted slave.[37] Up until the final two paragraphs of the story, Chesnutt presents Grandison as a paragon of "the fidelity of the negro to his master."[38] The story opens with the narrative indirection for which Chesnutt is famous, concealing not just the nature of its hero, but also his identity, as "Grandison" initially appears to be a story about Dick Owens and his courtship travails. It begins, "When it is said that it was done to please a woman, there ought perhaps to be enough said to explain anything; for what a man will not do to please a woman is yet to be discovered" (168). We are then introduced to the plight of Dick Owens, the good-natured yet eminently underachieving only son and heir of a wealthy planter whose principal financial asset lay in human chattel. Dick's beloved, Charity Lomax, declares that she will never love him until he does something "harder than playing cards or fox-hunting" (172). As he had lately observed Charity's awe of the heroism and courage of an abolitionist who had helped a local slave escape his cruel master, Dick decides he could win Charity's love by adopting a similar course. However, to protect himself against recrimination (should the fugitive later be apprehended), Dick decides that he will help one of his own family's slaves run away and conceal his role in the escape from even the slave himself. Dick thus plans a trip to the Northern states, and, as Colonel Owen considers his loyal slave Grandison to be "abolitionist-proof," he agrees to let him accompany Dick as a manservant on this vacation. Much to Dick's dismay, the colonel initially seems to be right: Grandison refuses to run away, even after Dick leaves bags of money at his disposal, sends abolitionists to encourage him, and tells him (after taking him to the Canadian side of Niagara Falls), "If you wished, Grandison, you might walk away from me this very minute, and I could not lay my hand upon you to take you back" (191). Finally, Dick resorts to abandoning Grandison (while he is sleeping) in Canada, having exchanged words (to which we are not privy) and money with a free Canadian black. When Dick returns and tells Charity that he had facilitated Grandison's departure (omitting, of course, the part about Grandison's unwillingness to depart), she agrees to marry him, primarily, she states, because a man reckless enough to run off his own slaves clearly "needs someone to look after him" (196).

Three weeks later, when a very haggard and travel-worn Grandison returns to the plantation, Colonel Owens is overjoyed to be vindicated in his initial assessment of Grandison's character. "It's just as I thought from the beginning, Dick," the colonel beamed, "Grandison had no notion of running away; he knew when he was well off, and where his friends were." Repeating what Grandison had told him, the colonel explains to Dick that abolitionists had kidnapped their devoted servant because they "got the notion somehow that Grandison belonged to a nigger-catcher, and had been brought North as a spy to help capture ungrateful runaway servants." Grandison escaped his captors and "made his way, after suffering incredible hardships, back to the old plantation, back to his master, his friends, and his home" (198–99). A few weeks later, however, the colonel finds himself dispossessed of both his cherished "belief in the fidelity of the negro to his master" (200) and a sizeable portion of his property, when it is discovered that not only Grandison, but his new wife Betty, his mother, his father, his aunt, his uncle, his brothers, and his sister have all disappeared from the plantation. The colonel and his men pursue the fugitives to the Canadian border, only to catch a glimpse of one of the party "wav[ing] his hand derisively" from the deck of a ship sailing rapidly across Lake Erie (202).

Currently, readers agree that "The Passing of Grandison" upsets stereotypical, romanticized notions of slaves' dog-like fidelity by showing that behind his façade of "perfervid loyalty" (183) Grandison was all along a cunning, Br'er-Rabbit-like trickster. Indeed, the attributes of the animal trickster of African American folklore diametrically oppose those of the dog. Animal protection narratives such as Vest's present the dog as the one creature whose honesty is unflagging, whose motives are always transparent, whose signals always mean exactly what they seem. To use the words of a recent best seller, dogs "never lie about love."[39] In contrast, lying about love is the trickster's signature move. Self-seeking, duplicitous, canny, and vindictive, Br'er Rabbit frequently uses false friendship to conceal and accomplish his plans for revenge.[40] Grandison—who, in helping half a dozen other slaves escape, multiplies his master's financial loss—seems to be just such a figure. But setting the record straight about slavery is only one of the story's objectives. In "Grandison," Chesnutt is responding as much to the late-nineteenth-century trope of the black man as an undomesticatable brute beast as he is to the nostalgic romanticization of slaves' fidelity toward their masters that was promulgated in antiabolitionist rhetoric and postwar plantation fiction. As I will show, the story's refutation of both the faithful dog and the rapacious beast stereotypes is accomplished not so much by distancing Grandison from readers' ideas about dogs, but by strategically (re)associating him with them. Here, the employment of the tricksterism associated with animal heroes of African American folklore is both sustained and transformed by Chesnutt's use of the rhetoric of animal welfare.

To understand how a realignment of black man and dog could have been at all strategic, we must first examine the relationship between widely held ideas about natural history and late-nineteenth-century changes in the racist discourse of black animality. While the actual position of slaves on antebellum plantations most closely resembled—among animals—that of mules, horses, or oxen, it was comparisons with dogs, rather than these creatures, that played the most powerful role in antebellum defenses of slavery. Beasts of burden (and especially mules) were known for displays of passive resistance through which they registered their unwillingness to serve—hardly the image of the happy worker slaveholders desired. The dog, by contrast, was firmly associated with the qualities antiabolitionists wished to attribute to slaves. In a passage frequently quoted in antebellum U.S. books and periodicals, the famed naturalist Georges Cuvier described the dog as "the most complete, the most singular, and useful conquest ever made by man. . . . Each individual is devoted to its particular master, assumes his manners, knows and defends his property, and remains attached to him until death; and all this [proceeds] neither from constraint nor want, but solely from gratitude and pure friendship."[41] Thus, more than any other slave-animal comparison, portrayals of slaves as faithful dogs complemented the depiction of slavery as benevolent, masters as paternal, and slaves as content with their servitude. For the dog, separation from the master was traumatic rather than liberating. Just so, slave owners argued, would emancipation affect blacks.[42]

After the Civil War, images of slaves who loved their masters with dog-like fidelity continued to proliferate in nostalgic plantation fiction, and periodicals eagerly reported stories of blacks whose devotion to their former masters persisted after emancipation.[43] (It was this proliferation of which Chesnutt spoke in his 1890 letter to Cable.) By the late 1880s and early 1890s, however, the image of the black man as a faithful dog was rapidly being supplanted in racist discourse by the stereotype of the rapacious black beast. Though both stereotypes associated black men with animals, the move from the former to the latter redefined the black man as a wild animal rather than a domesticated one, and as the architects of the brute beast stereotype were keenly aware, this relocation on the other side of the domesticated/wild animal divide carried significant implications. As I discussed in the introduction, the differences between wild and domesticated animals were, in the nineteenth century, understood to be to a large degree God-given. While the qualities of particular breeds of dogs, cattle, or other livestock were attributed to generations of human effort, it was, according to reigning belief, the handiwork of the Creator that made those animals capable of being domesticated in the first place. Much like being herbivorous or carnivorous, the ability or inability (as one nineteenth-century naturalist put it) "to submit . . . cheerfully and willingly" to human control was considered an essential and unalterable quality.[44] Some species were serviceable to humans; other creatures were, by nature, not just undomesticated, but undomesticatable.

Although late-nineteenth-century Americans were becoming increasingly concerned with preserving the wilderness, such concerns did not extend to protecting wild animals that were harmful to human interests or dangerous to their persons. In this period, the necessity of destroying any individual animal or species of animals that posed a danger to humans was self-evident. One nineteenth-century naturalist, for example, suggested that "on procuring an Animal with which we are unacquainted, the first point . . . is to ascertain whether it is . . . applicable to the uses of Man . . . or should its habits be detrimental or obnoxious, what measures are pursued to destroy the species."[45] In the context of such beliefs, reclassification of the black man as a dangerous wild animal served as an axiomatic defense of lynching and the other violent measures whites employed to thwart blacks' acquisition of jobs, education, elected office, and property. An 1892 article in the Memphis *Daily Commercial,* for example, argued that lynching was justified because "nothing but the most prompt, speedy and extreme punishment can hold in check the horrible and beastial [*sic*] propensities of the Negro race."[46] But insisting, as Mississippi politician James K. Vardaman did in 1897, that the black man was "a lazy, lying, lustful animal which no conceivable amount of training can transform into a tolerable citizen" legitimated far more than the administration of summary justice for suspected offenders: it equaled a call for the extirpation of the black race from American soil. "We would be justified in slaughtering every Ethiop on the earth," Vardaman contended, "to preserve unsullied the honor of one Caucasian home. . . . We do not stop when we see a wolf to find if it will kill sheep before disposing of it, but assume that it will."[47]

Among men whose writings enabled whites to "reconcil[e] the traditional stereotype of black docility with the image of bold and violent offenders" was Nathaniel Southgate Shaler, a public intellectual and the dean of Harvard's Lawrence Scientific School.[48] In a series of articles that appeared, in the 1880s and '90s, in such popular magazines as the *Atlantic Monthly, Scribner's Magazine,* and *Popular Science Monthly,* Shaler offered scientific explanations for the inferiority of blacks. Drawing on his "cradle land theory," Shaler argued that the environmental conditions present during the early period of each race's development had lasting consequences for racial character. The harsh environment of Northern Europe had forced Aryan peoples, for example, to develop such admirable qualities as thrift, industry, and the ability to delay gratification while pursuing long-term goals. Tropical regions, by contrast, put little pressure on their inhabitants to develop these character traits, since there the wild sources of food were abundant year round and inhabitants required hardly any fuel or even clothing for survival. According to Shaler, then, the failure of African Americans to attain the same level of civilization as white Americans was a natural result of their ancestors not having had to face, during the crucial period in their race's development, a "struggle with a rude Nature." Unlike Vardaman, Shaler held blacks' continued progress toward a higher state of civilization to be possible. But he insisted that the pace of improvement would be slow and arduous and that unless whites continued their benevolent "training in civilization" which had been "begun in slavery," blacks would "revert to their ancestral conditions."[49]

Purportedly to prepare white Americans for their essential role in preventing blacks' reversion to savagery, Shaler's writings delineated the "inherited qualities" that dragged down blacks' continued progress toward standards of (white) civilization. Chief among the racial "defects" Shaler attributed to the black character is the "lack of a power of continuous will." It was the will, Shaler argued, that enabled men to eschew "the impulse of passion or excitement" in favor of long-term or abstract goals. "The gradations of this power," Shaler insisted, "mark the limits between savage and civilized man. In the negro the ability to maintain the will power beyond the stimulus of excitement is on the whole much lower than in the lowest whites. They are as a class incapable of firm resolve."[50] Another of the points where, according to Shaler, blacks "most need help" was "the monogamic motive" that enabled civilized men to become attached to and care for one woman, their spouse. As the nuclear family, it was thought, formed the building block of civilized society, the black man would never rise until his race had been "provided with these motives of the household . . . [and] made faithful to the marriage bond."[51] Regardless of his professed hope for the future of the black race, Shaler "[held] it to be clear" that in the present "the inherited qualities of the negroes to a great degree unfit them to carry the burden of our own civilization."[52] While Shaler himself did not characterize black men as undomesticatable savage animals, the traits his "scientific" writings ascribed to black men formed the foundation on which the brute beast stereotype was constructed. For if black men were deficient in "monogamic motive" and generally lacked the capacity for "firm resolve," what resources did they have to restrain sexual impulses elicited by the attractions of white women? White supremacists who did not share Shaler's paternalism had no trouble arguing that the kind of influence over blacks with which Shaler credits whites was possible only under the system of slavery and that, in the absence of this total control, the black man had already degenerated into a wild, dangerous sexual predator.[53]

This degeneration theory notwithstanding, the shifting of the black man from the category of docile dog to wild beast was complicated by the same concept that made that reclassification so useful: belief that wild and domesticated animals were separated by a wide and impassible gulf. If, according to contemporary belief, wild animals could not be reclaimed from nature, traffic did not flow in the other direction, either. There was, however, one animal regarded as an exception to this rule: the cat. The feline body and mind, unlike those of other domesticates, proved highly resistant to human modification. Breeders were unable to mold cats anatomically, and trainers had little success in getting cats to perform any useful functions other than their instinctive hunting of small prey (and this habit was, in many quarters, also a nuisance, as the title of one 1916 book on cats—*The Domestic Cat; Bird Killer, Mouser, and Destroyer of Wildlife; Means of Utilizing and Controlling It*—suggests).[54] Natural historians had long considered the cat to be imperfectly or spuriously domesticated. The eighteenth-century naturalist Buffon had declared that "as the cat may be considered as only half-domestic, he forms the shade between domestic and wild animals."[55] Throughout the nineteenth century, the cat's status as a domesticate was commonly held to be tenuous at best. Thus, in *Walden,* Thoreau remarks that "the most domestic cat, which has lain on a rug all her days, appears quite at home in the woods, and, by her sly and stealthy behavior, proves herself more native there than the regular inhabitants. Once, when berrying, I met with a cat with young kittens in the woods, quite wild, and they all, like their mother, had their backs up and were fiercely spitting at me."[56]

These popular beliefs about the cat's duplicitous or oppositional relationship to the civilized enjoyed, as much as they did in the eighteenth century, the support of the most respected scientists—including, as it would happen, the same scientist who used his authority to detail the defects of the black man. In addition to being one of the country's leading authorities on racial differences, Nathaniel Southgate Shaler also published a number of books and articles on animals similarly aimed at a popular audience. As with his writings on race, Shaler's publications on animals merit attention not because his ideas were particularly original, but because they extended to commonly held notions the legitimacy and authority of scientific "facts." In both its structure and its content, Shaler's *Domesticated Animals: Their Relation to Man and to His Advancement in Civilization* (1895) casts cats as animals without a legitimate place in human civilization. Though this 264-page text includes chapters on the dog, the horse, "Beasts for Burden, Food, and Raiment," "Domesticated Birds," and even "Useful Insects," it contains no chapter on cats. Instead, Shaler discusses the cat at the end of the chapter on dogs because the cat "afford[s] . . . a capital foil by which to set off the virtues of the dog." Cats, he declares, are "the least essential, and on the whole the least interesting, of domesticated animals" and "the only animal which has been tolerated, esteemed, and at times worshipped without having a single distinctly valuable quality." The qualities that Shaler does attribute to the cat are more or less identical to those his earlier writings had attributed to black men: an inability to form genuine attachments, inability to be trained to do useful work, and a tendency to revert to ancestral conditions. Shaler insists that he has "been unable to find any authentic instances which go to show the existence in cats of any real love for their masters." Though the cat "appears to indicate affection" by its "caresses," it cares "more indeed for its dwelling-place than it ever does for the inmates thereof." Cats, Shaler states, "often return to the wilderness" and become both "entirely wild" and "a serious menace to the birds and other weaker creatures of the country."[57]

Furthering the domestic cat's alliance with savagery was the long tradition (dating back to medieval bestiaries) that held wild felines such as the tiger and leopard to be the most utterly ferocious and untamable of animals.[58] An 1803 publication of the British Museum, for example, states that "no discipline can correct the savage nature of the tiger, not any degree of kind treatment can reclaim him." Similarly, the 1878 *Illustrated History of Wild Animals and Other Curiosities Contained in P. T. Barnum's New and Greatest Show on Earth* proclaims that the "great efforts . . . made to domesticate" wild cats have all been met "without success. You might as well attempt to change the spots of the leopard."[59] Along with beliefs in the domestic cat's specious domesticity, these ideas about the absolute savagery of wild felines enabled advocates of the brute beast stereotype to make reigning beliefs about the animal world complement rather than contradict the theory of a formerly docile black population's degeneration into savagery.

Thomas Dixon draws on such notions in his racist novels, the first of which, *The Leopard's Spots* (1902), opens with the epigraph: "Can the Ethiopian change his skin or the leopard his spots?" The novel goes on to argue, in effect, that the black race like the feline race had a nature on which no nurture would stick, as is apparent in the way the novel lampoons white Northerners' interest in black education. After Susan Walker (a white reformer from the North) describes her plans for establishing black schools and colleges as "an experiment of thrilling interest to me which will prove that their intellectual, moral, and social capacity is equal to any white man's," the Southern preacher to whom she is speaking offers an apparent non sequitur: "Is it true, Madam, that you once endowed a home for homeless cats before you became interested in the black people?" Walker replies that she did and was "proud of it. I love cats. There are more than a thousand in the home now, and they are well cared for. Whose business is it?" "I mean no offense by the question," the preacher disingenuously replies. "I love cats, too. But I wondered if you were collecting Negroes only now, or whether you were adding other specimens to your menagerie for experimental purposes?" The effect of this exchange is to suggest that training black men is as futile and idiotic as training cats. Dixon's equally infamous *The Clansman* (1905) continues in the same vein. There he contends that the black man's "passions, once aroused, are as the fury of the tiger." The climactic scene of the novel (the rape of a white woman by a black man) reads: "A single tiger spring, and the black claws of the beast sank into the soft white throat."[60]

But if, at the turn of the century, ideas about feline nature complemented racist arguments about black animality, the same could no longer be said of beliefs about dogs. This change resulted both from developments in white supremacists' agenda (which made comparisons to wild animals more useful than comparisons to domesticated ones) and from the developments in popular perceptions of canine nature that were concomitant with the rise of the animal protection movement. Dogs were now held by significant portions of the populace to be more virtuous than humans, and the qualities scientific and popular audiences attributed to dogs were precisely the qualities white supremacists argued to be absent in blacks as they defended their claims that blacks should be extirpated from rather than assimilated into civilization. That is, at the same time that whites were insisting that the black man was a brute beast who could not be civilized, the dog was being celebrated—in both popular and scientific writing—as a creature in whom civilization inevitably inhered.

In *The People's Natural History* (1903), discussion of the dog begins with the statement: "The dog, almost without exception, shows a marked liking for the society of human beings, and adapts itself to their ways more than any other animal."[61] Perhaps the most compelling evidence, however, of the association of dogs with civilization in late-nineteenth-century scientific and popular culture is the vehemence with which many authors—writing in their capacity as professional men of science—denied that the domestic dog had descended from or was in any way related to the wild animal it physically resembled: the wolf. As I explain in the conclusion, this idea came under heavy attack in the first decade of the twentieth century, especially after the publication of Jack London's *The Call of the Wild* in 1903. However, even as late as 1905, James Watson devoted the first ten pages of volume 1 of his 2-volume *The Dog Book* to arguing that dogs did not descend from wolves or other wild canids, but from some smarter, gentler, now extinct ancestor. If earlier writers devoted less space to the question of dogs' kinship with wolves, it seems to be because they considered the idea so easily refuted by common sense, for the differences of "character" between wolves and dogs appeared to them far more relevant than morphological similarities.[62] In *Domesticated Animals,* Shaler points out that wolves were "indomitably fierce and utterly self-regarding" (12). The dog, by contrast, possesses a "sense of property, a great part of human affections, [and] many of the attributes which constitute the gentleman" (48). Much like a gentleman, the dog was believed incapable, even under adverse conditions, of reverting to ancestral conditions. Dogs, Shaler insists, "show little or no tendency to revert to the form and habits of their brutal kindred. . . . When the stock [of domestic dogs] is allowed to go as nearly wild as they can be induced to become, we do not find that they thereby approach to any known wild form" (12–13). For Hawkins, the belief that dogs' civilized qualities were indelible formed an essential component of his argument that they were "better than men." Careful parental supervision was necessary, he argued, to bring about the "development of the higher and better qualities of our [that is, human] nature, either moral or intellectual" (4), but

> in the dog and horse, notably, their better qualities are inherent, born with them, grow stronger with time, and their almost perfect and complete development is natural, continues without aid, example, or instruction. Not more than one dog or horse in a thousand, if kindly treated and left to himself, would turn out vicious, and treat them as we may, no matter how unjustly or cruelly, we can never deprive them of their perfect integrity and splendid qualities of loyalty to master and friend.
>
> These most valuable of all moral qualities are natural to certain animals, and, no matter what man may do, they can never be extinguished. Although intangible, they are as much parts of the living organism of the horse and dog as are their eyes or other organs needed for physical purposes. (4–5)

On account of these changes, canine nature did not mean the same thing in the 1890s as it did in the 1830s, and neither, consequently, did being compared to a dog.

Returning to "The Passing of Grandison," we see how deeply imbedded this story is in the discourses of white supremacy and beliefs about canine ontology circulating at the time of its production. Even as Colonel Owens (until the very end) never doubts Grandison's docility, he attributes to him the qualities that, according to proponents of the black beast stereotype, predisposed the black man to lawlessness and rape. In explaining his selection of Grandison for Dick's servant on his trip to the North, the colonel cites not only his belief in Grandison's devotion to their family but also Grandison's lack of, to use Shaler's terms, the "power of continuous will" and capacity for "firm resolve." The colonel tells Dick that Grandison is "too fond of good eating"—too prone, that is, to indulging every momentary impulse "to risk losing his regular meals" by running away. To test Grandison's loyalty before giving his final assent to the trip, the colonel summons Grandison and asks him whether he thinks he is "a great deal better off than those poor free negroes . . . with no kind master to look after them and no mistress to give them medicine when they're sick" (177–78). Grandison's immediate, enthusiastic, and affirmative reply confirms the colonel's view (shared by Shaler et al.) that long-range planning for want or illness is beyond the scope of Grandison's inclinations and abilities.

Though it makes no explicit reference to dogs, "Grandison" nonetheless presents its eponymous hero in a way certain to recall the contemporary narratives of canine heroism with which the tale's early readers were familiar. After being taken off the plantation, Grandison behaves exactly like a dog accompanying his master on a trip. His constant, anxious concern is that he will become lost in an unfamiliar place, "an' den I won' hab no marster, an' won't nebber be able to git back home no mo' " (191). Grandison's mirroring of typical dog behavior is particularly apparent in the scene at Niagara Falls in which Dick—still hoping that Grandison will wander off on his own—instructs him to sit and stay outside while he dines in a restaurant. When Dick looks out the window, he sees (with disappointment) that Grandison "remained faithfully at his post, awaiting his master's return." Just as a dog would, Grandison was "turning his eyes away from the grand and awe-inspiring spectacle [of the falls] that lay close at hand" and "looking anxiously" toward the building his master had entered (192).

It is, however, Grandison's astonishing return that most closely aligns him with late-nineteenth-century narratives of canine fidelity—and which, in turn, enables Chesnutt to manipulate historical connections between blacks and dogs—for the lost or kidnapped dog's return home was one of the most common subjects of the late-nineteenth-century dog stories that, in the rising tide of sympathy for the animal welfare cause, flowed through newspapers, literary magazines, and widely distributed humane society publications. In an age of rail and steamboat travel, humans were separated from their canine traveling companions far more frequently than ever before. And as the pet-keeping craze created a booming market for dogs, dognapping became an organized and, according to contemporary accounts, exceedingly common crime. Bereft wealthy owners paid large sums to ransom their beloved companions; dogs who went unclaimed were killed or resold—sometimes for vivisection.[63] The numerous collections of dog anecdotes published in this period often devoted entire chapters to tales of dogs who made heroic journeys to return to their families. One such story contains many of the elements of Grandison's departure and return. A farmer in Gloucester, England, sends his favorite dog to accompany his brother as a traveling companion on a journey to Canada. After attending the brother safely to his Canadian destination, the dog disappears. Some time later, "the dog came back to the farm of his old master . . . and though at first it could hardly be believed that he was returned from Canada, yet he soon established his identity by taking his old place at the foot of his master's bed at night."[64] (Supposedly, the dog found his way to his port of entry to Canada, boarded a ship bound for England, and then, upon arriving on British soil, walked the rest of the way home.) It is impossible to determine whether this particular story is authentic or apocryphal. However, it was published in one widely circulated volume about three years before Chesnutt wrote "The Passing of Grandison." (The same story was also republished in 1901 in *Our Devoted Friend, the Dog,* an anthology of canine anecdotes edited by Sarah K. Bolton, the Cleveland-based social reformer whom Chesnutt praised in his review of Patteson's book.)[65] In any event, the connection between "The Passing of Grandison" and contemporary dog stories would have been readily apparent to the tale's early readers.

In his redeployment of the dog-come-home story, Chesnutt actually picks up on what would later become the central concern of the most famous tale of this type: Eric Knight's "Lassie Come-Home," which appeared in the *Saturday Evening Post* in 1938. Both "The Passing of Grandison" and "Lassie" explore the conflict between the laws of the marketplace and the laws of affection. In the original "Lassie," poverty forces the poor Carraclough family to sell their beloved collie to the Duke of Rudling. When Lassie runs away, Rudling thinks he has been tricked into buying a "come-home" dog—or one trained to return to the seller after each sale so that the seller may repeatedly resell the same dog. But as Rudling discovers—after Lassie travels several hundred miles from Scotland back to her beloved Timmy—love and not trickery is what motivates the Lassie's repeated returns. Having learned that the bonds of love can neither be formed nor broken through an economic transaction, Rudling corrects the disparity between the economic and affective orders by giving Lassie back to her family and employing Timmy's father on his estate. Similarly, the argument of "Grandison" is not so much that Grandison's devotion is spurious, but that it is directed toward his own fiancé and his own family rather than the (white) family that legally owns him. Grandison's return testifies as much to his dog-like fidelity as it does to his Br'er-Rabbit-like cunning.

Moreover, Grandison's dangerous and difficult retrieval of his family (for which he withstands hunger, fatigue, and bodily injury) demonstrates precisely those qualities—"family feeling," "monogamic motive," "firm resolve," and "power of continuous will"—that were, according to racial scientists, absent in black men and whose erasure the brute beast stereotype required. It seems likely, in fact, that Chesnutt conceived of the idea for "The Passing of Grandison" while reading an article by Shaler that appeared in the *Atlantic Monthly* in 1884. (Chesnutt published several of his own stories in the *Atlantic* between 1887 and 1904, and he "systematically surveyed the evidence in periodicals of the state of race relations in the United States" throughout his writing career.)[66] "The Negro Problem" contains one of Shaler's expositions on "the relatively feeble nature of all the ties that bind the family together among these African people." "The peculiar monogamic instinct which in our own race has been slowly, century by century, developing itself," Shaler contends, "has yet to be fixed in this people. In the negro this motive, more than any other the key to our society, is very weak, if indeed it exists at all as an indigenous impulse." At the conclusion of this sentence, *Atlantic* editor Thomas Wentworth Higginson (the same Higginson, coincidentally, who authored the article extolling dogs' virtues quoted above), inserted the following footnote, which appeared in the published version of the essay: "Is it not too soon after slavery to justify this statement? Slavery necessarily discouraged monogamy; but the multitude of cases in which slaves after escaping from slavery have gone back into danger to bring away their wives indicates an indigenous impulse."[67] In this context, then, we see that the tricksterly indirection of Chesnutt's narrative strategy involves more than temporarily directing the reader's attention to Dick's plight. The real trick turns out to be that the story's opening meditation on the boundlessness of masculine devotion

("When it is said that it was done to please a woman there ought perhaps to be enough said to explain anything; for what a man will not do to please a woman is yet to be discovered") applies less to Dick than it does to Grandison himself.

Why Nobody Likes a Dog-Killer: Making Racist Violence a Threat to Civilization

Published in the same year as Chesnutt's review of Patteson's animal welfare book, *The Marrow of Tradition* represents a culmination and extension of the strategies for juxtaposing the racial and animal politics that Chesnutt had practiced in his earlier short fiction. That Chesnutt would redeploy here the moves he had already formulated to undermine the racist rhetoric of black animality is not surprising, as Chesnutt wrote the novel in response to an event that dramatized both the urgency of refuting the black beast stereotype and the perils attendant with this process: the Wilmington, North Carolina, massacre of 1898. The initial catalyst in the chain of events that led to this riot was Rebecca Latimer Felton's attempt to use the black beast stereotype to justify (or, it seems, encourage) lynching. In an 1897 speech that was subsequently printed in multiple newspapers, Felton exhorted: "if it needs lynching to protect woman's dearest possession from the ravening human beasts—then I say lynch, a thousand times a week if necessary." In 1898, Alexander Manly published in Wilmington's black paper an editorial that attacked Felton's speech and the stereotype it invoked. "Every negro lynched," Manly wrote, "is called a Big Burly Black Brute, when, in fact, many of those who have been dealt with . . . were not only not black and burly, but were sufficiently attractive for white girls of culture and refinement to fall in love with them, as is very well known to all." Knowing that the white community would be outraged by Manly's contention that white women voluntarily entered romantic relationships with black men, Wilmington's white supremacists used the editorial to incite the riot in which mobs of armed white men roved through the city, brutalizing and killing black citizens, destroying or confiscating blacks' property, burning black-owned buildings, and driving thousands of blacks out of town.[68]

Like "The Bouquet," *Marrow* commandeers the contemporary discourse of dogs' moral superiority to recast segregation as yet another flaw of the existing human social order. Shortly after light-skinned Dr. Miller is ejected from the white train car in which he and some white colleagues were seated, Miller observes a dog enter the train with his white master: "He was a handsome dog, and Miller, who was fond of animals, would not have objected to the company of a dog, as a dog. He was nevertheless conscious of a queer sensation when he saw the porter take the dog by the collar and start in his own direction, and felt consciously relieved when the canine passenger was taken on past him to the baggage-car ahead. Miller's hand was hanging over the arm of his seat, and the dog, an intelligent shepherd, licked it as he passed. Miller was not entirely sure that he would not have liked the porter to leave the dog there; he was a friendly dog, and seemed inclined to be sociable."[69] Watching the dog being dragged from the white car, Miller initially sees a replay of his own expulsion from it and is struck with horror at the thought that his treatment should be equal to that of the dog. As his remark that he would not object to "the company of a dog, as a dog" reveals, Miller senses that this dog is about to function not "as a dog" but as a symbol of his own subhuman status. Chesnutt, however, is not content to let the dog lie here, and within a few sentences the dog comes to function not merely "as a dog," but as an emblem of the disinterested benevolence to which human beings should aspire. Miller's relief that the conductor does not leave the dog in the colored car quickly gives way to his awareness that in his initial reaction toward the dog (wanting the dog placed in a lower-ranked car than his own) he has—much like the white man who demanded Miller's removal from the white car—wished away a rather deserving passenger for the sake of asserting his superior status. By the end of the passage, the focus has shifted to the dog's unsolicited gesture of friendship, by which he has proven more sociable than anyone else on the train. George Vest had, in his famous "eulogy for the dog," observed that the dog will "kiss the hand that has no food to offer." Pointing out that the dog will also kiss a black hand as readily as a white one, Chesnutt once again positions racism as yet another of those temporal conditions (such as wealth, physical appearance, health, and popularity) that humans—in their state of moral imperfection—allow to govern their social relations.

But *Marrow* ultimately proves more like "Grandison" than "The Bouquet," in that it skillfully deploys contemporary beliefs about dogs in the absence of actual canine characters and does so specifically to address the subject of black masculinity. Sandy Campbell, Jerry Letlow, and Josh Green, who are—after Dr. Miller—the novel's most important black male characters, are all positioned, though in different ways, in relation to the discourse of black men's dog-like fidelity. The subplot of the novel that centers on Sandy Campbell is (perhaps not coincidentally) in many ways a retelling of the real-life case that had struck Chesnutt so forcibly in 1890: the man who (as he related in the letter to Cable quoted above) volunteered to serve out the seven-year prison term to which his former owner had been sentenced. Such men, Chesnutt had observed with much scorn, seemed "willing to sacrifice almost life itself" for the sake of their old masters.[70] In *Marrow,* Sandy takes this level of devotion one step further. He refuses to exonerate himself of the charge of robbing and murdering Polly Ochiltree—for which he is about to be lynched—because he knows he cannot do so without incriminating his old master's grandson, Tom Delamere, who brought about Polly's death in a bungled robbery and then framed Sandy for his crime. Thus, Sandy volunteers in effect to serve out no mere prison sentence but a death sentence (which he knows would be executed in the most gruesome manner) in order to save old Delamere's grandson, his equanimity (for Sandy surmises, correctly, that Delamere would be devastated by the discovery of Tom's nefarious nature), and his family name.

Chesnutt's dramatic reversal of his earlier refusal to write about this very type of character reflects his later recognition that he could (as he did in "Grandison") deploy such characterizations to his own ends. By making Sandy's dog-like fidelity to whites (unlike Grandison's) genuine and enduring, *Marrow* can, as "The Bouquet" did, counter whites' claims that mute, unbending loyalty will secure blacks' economic, legal, and physical protection. Old Delamere vows that "no faithful servant of mine shall be hanged for a crime he didn't commit, so long as I have a voice to speak or a dollar to spend" (199–200). But despite his status as one of the most respected white men of the community, Delamere proves impotent to forestall plans to lynch Sandy (until the discovery of physical evidence identifying Tom as the culprit). Casting Sandy in the faithful-dog stereotype also enables Chesnutt to engage and refute the argument embedded in the brute beast stereotype about black men's degeneration in freedom. Major Carteret—who had acknowledged Sandy's long history of "doglike fidelity" (24) in the first chapter of the novel and who, as editor of the paper, had the power to print an editorial that could have opposed the white community's growing conviction about Sandy's culpability—readily dismisses Sandy's spotless forty-five-year-record of faithfulness and devotion when circumstantial evidence points to his guilt: "The whole race, in the major's opinion, was morally undeveloped, and only held within bounds by the restraining influence of the white people. Under Mr. Delamere's thumb this Sandy had been a model servant,—faithful, docile, respectful, and self-respecting; but Mr. Delamere had grown old, and had probably lost in a measure his moral influence over his servant. Left to his own degraded ancestral instincts, Sandy has begun to deteriorate, and a rapid decline had culminated in this robbery and murder" (181–82).

Having kept Sandy true to stereotypical portrayals of blacks' dog-like fidelity, Chesnutt transfers white supremacists' arguments about degeneration to the white race. Rather than the stay for Sandy's civilized qualities, the Delamere family is revealed to be degenerating itself, for the theory Carteret espouses applies more properly to white Tom Delamere than to any other character in the novel. When Mr. Delamere's old age prevented him from keeping a close watch on his grandson, the young man began a path (to reuse Carteret's words) of "a rapid decline" that "culminated in . . . robbery and murder." As he redirects the degeneration theory toward white characters, Chesnutt employs the same discourse of undomesticatable animality that animated the brute beast stereotype. Tom Delamere, we are told in his initial description, "was easily the handsomest young man in Wellington. But no discriminating observer would have characterized his beauty as manly. It conveyed no impression of strength, but did possess a certain element, *feline* rather than feminine, which subtly negatived the idea of manliness" (16, emphasis added).

A feline nature is also attributed to Captain McBane, whose uncouthness and undisguised love of violence makes him the novel's other great example of white degeneration. "In works of fiction," the narrator expostulates, "such men are sometimes converted. More often, in real life, they do not change their natures until they are converted into dust. One does well to distrust a tamed tiger" (304). The chapter in which Dr. Miller travels into the center of the mob violence in search of his wife and child bears the title "Into the Lion's Jaws." When the mob's violence reaches its bloodiest culmination, the narrator comments, "In that hour, as in any hour when the depths of race hatred are stirred, a negro was no more than a brute beast, set upon by other brute beasts whose only instinct was to kill and destroy" (307). The sentence's syntax is deceptive, however, for while *Marrow* characterizes both whites and blacks as animals, this gesture is far from equalizing. Instead, it places the white mob in the very same category in which advocates of lynching had placed black men: wild animals or, in Felton's words, "ravening human beasts." Chesnutt literalizes Felton's euphemism "ravening beasts," replacing blacks' alleged appetite for sex with whites' appetite for blood. McBane, Jerry thinks to himself early in the novel, "looks at a nigger lack he could jes' eat 'im alive" (38). The mob he later leads "was merely a white mob thirsting for black blood, with no more conscience or discrimination than would be exercised by a wolf in a sheepfold" (298). In attacking blacks, white men—who "with appetites already whetted by slaughter, saw a chance, welcome rather than not, of shedding more black blood" (299)—become the embodiment of a bestiality that is terrifying and uncontrollable.[71]

In the character of Jerry Letlow, *Marrow* offers another iteration of the black-as-dog narrative that, like Sandy's story, insists on the futility of blacks' dependence on the white community. Though Jerry plays the part of devoted servant as well as Sandy, his display is just an act. Like Grandison's demonstrations of "perfervid loyalty," Jerry's show of devotion represents a calculated strategy for capitalizing on whites' willingness to believe in blacks' gratitude toward them. Not one (in Vest's words) to "kiss the hand that has no food to offer," Jerry decides that he will "stan' in wid de Angry-Saxon race,—ez dey calls deyse'ves nowadays,—an' keep on de right side er my bread an' meat" (90). But as Jerry's surname "Letlow" implies, energies invested in this venture earn a pretty low return. His payoff is limited, for the most part, to the spare change occasionally tossed his way in the course of his duties as Carteret's personal assistant at the newspaper. Thus, though Jerry resembles Grandison in his ability to fool whites with a façade of fidelity, their stories serve very different functions. If, among other things, "The Passing of Grandison" testified to the concealed resentment of slaves for their owners and to the resourcefulness slaves exercised in keeping families together within a system that neither sanctioned nor honored black marriages, Jerry's story, by contrast, suggests that the time for playing the dog to whites has come to an end. Major Carteret tells his obliging housekeeper Jane, "If all the colored people were like you and Jerry . . . there would never be any trouble." Mrs. Carteret follows up by gushing, "Yes, indeed, Mammy Jane . . . you shall never want so long as we have anything. We would share our last crust with you" (44). Yet before the end of the novel, both Jerry and Jane, contrary to Carteret's promise, experience violent deaths at the hands of whites. Jerry is gunned down as he, fleeing the group of black resistors, seeks protection from his white employer: "Jerry's poor flag of truce, his explanations, his reliance upon his white friends, all failed him in the moment of supreme need" (307). Similarly, "not all her reverence for her old mistress, nor all her deference to the whites, nor all their friendship for her, had been able to save [Jane] from this raging devil of race hatred which momentarily possessed the town" (297).

To complement the narratives of Sandy and Jerry, Chesnutt uses Josh Green to propose an alternate recipient of blacks' fabled capacities for fidelity and devotion. When the text introduces Josh, he is, like the shepherd, stowed away on the train's baggage car (though without the conductor's knowledge): "As the train came to a standstill, a huge negro, covered thickly with dust, crawled off one of the rear trucks unobserved, and ran round the rear end of the car to a watering-trough by a neighboring well. Moved either by extreme thirst or by the fear that his time might be too short to permit him to draw a bucket of water, he threw himself down by the trough, drank long and deep, and plunging his head into the water, *shook himself like a wet dog,* and crept furtively back to his dangerous perch" (58–59, emphasis added). Josh's actions—crawling, creeping, shaking—closely resemble canine movements, as does his departure from the train at his final destination: "Stretching and shaking himself with a free gesture, the black man, seeing himself unobserved, moved somewhat stiffly round the edge of the car to the station platform" (62). These associations pave the way for Chesnutt's subsequent use of Josh to redirect the historical associations between black men and dogs. Outwardly defiant toward whites, Josh turns out to be dog-like in his devotion toward other blacks. When Josh learns of the white violence erupting in town, he organizes a force to protect the black community and its property, even though he is not (at that point) in any danger. As Grandison left the safety of Canada to retrieve his family from slave territory, Josh proceeds into the center of the whites' killing spree, intending "to remain quietly and peaceably in the neighborhood of the little group of [black] public institutions, molesting no one, unless first attacked, and merely letting the white people see that they meant to protect their own" (299). To be sure, Chesnutt hardly advocates armed resistance as a viable method of combating racial violence. (Unlike other readers, however, I see this not so much as a sign of Chesnutt's deference to the status quo as a reflection of the fact that—historically—such methods seemed largely ineffectual or countereffectual and resulted, almost without exception, in the deaths of all black combatants.)[72] Josh's heroic if tragic stand demonstrates that blacks' willingness to sacrifice "life itself" could spring from devotion to the black community as well as an obsequious servility toward whites.

The final effect of *Marrow*'s multiple (re)associations of black men and dogs is to link lynching and other forms of racially targeted violence with dog-killing. When protesting the impending lynching of Sandy Campbell, the elder Mr. Delamere exclaims, "I cannot see him killed like a dog, without judge or jury!" (214). This metaphor becomes a refrain throughout the section of the novel describing the Wellington riot. "De w'ite folks are killin' de niggers," Josh tells Dr. Miller, "an' we ain' gwine ter stan' up an' be shot down like dogs. We're gwine ter defen' ou' lives, an' we ain' gwine ter run away f'm no place where we've got a right ter be" (281). An unnamed man in the group of armed black resisters calls out to Miller, "Dey're gwine ter kill us anyhow; an' we're tired,—we read de newspapers,—an we're tired er bein' shot down like dogs, widout jedge er jury" (295). Outside the hospital, McBane calls to the black men trapped inside: "If you surrender and give up your arms, you'll be dealt with leniently,—you may get off with the chain-gang or the penitentiary. If you resist, you'll be shot like dogs" (302). "Dat's no news, Mr. White Man," is Josh's reply. "We're use' ter bein' treated like dogs by men like you." This linkage between lynching and dog-killing clearly reversed the juridical implications of black/animal comparisons, for if the public still supported the expedient killing of wild beasts that threatened human interests, the killing of man's best friend had become for many Americans an act for which few justifications could be imagined. However, the strategic benefits of linking violence against blacks to cruelty toward domesticated animals far exceeded the obvious emotional effects of connecting lynching to something—anything—the public abhorred. In the context of turn-of-the-century U.S. culture, this strategy enabled Chesnutt to present the outbreaks of violence used to suppress blacks' civil rights as not just discrete cases of horrible injustice but rather a real threat to the interests of all Americans and even to the continuation of civilization itself.

This point can best be explained with a momentary excursion backward to "Mars Jeems's Nightmare," one of the conjure tales Chesnutt wrote in the spring of 1898. One purpose of the tale is to revise whites' explanations of blacks' "closeness to nature." The tale opens with John's observations on Julius's intimate knowledge of the nonhuman life of their environs. Julius, he remarks, knew "the qualities of the various soils and what they would produce, and where the best hunting and fishing were to be had. He was a marvelous hand in the management of horses and dogs, with whose mental process he manifested a greater familiarity than mere use would seem to account for, though it was doubtless due to the simplicity of a life that had kept him close to nature."[73] The rest of the story, however, offers a different reason for Julius's uncanny comprehension of animal minds. While John, Annie, and Julius are out for a drive, their neighbor Jeems rushes by in his carriage, furiously whipping his horse until the animal was "rearing and plunging" and "panting and snorting with fear" (57). The tale Julius subsequently tells about Jeems's grandfather—who worked his slaves mercilessly from dusk to dawn, fed them starvation rations, beat them at the slightest provocation, and forbade them to form romantic attachments—belies John's assumption of the "simplicity" of black life in the antebellum South. The story of the elder Jeems's abominable cruelty also suggests that Julius's familiarity with the "mental processes" of horses and his expertise in managing them resulted not from simple-mindedness, but the likelihood of also having been overworked, whipped, beaten, and denied all the while any means of redress. Indeed, as Jeems's overseer Johnson—who had a great reputation for being a "nigger-breaker" (67)—attempts to break in the recalcitrant "noo nigger" (Master Jeems, who has been transformed into a black man through Aunt Peggy's conjuring), he employs tactics commonly used by disreputable horse-breakers to subdue unmanageable equines, including starving their charges to make them too weak to fight back. After beating him thoroughly, Johnson "lock' de noo nigger up in de ba'n, en didn' gib 'im nuffin ter eat fer a day er so, 'tel he got 'im kin'er quiet' down, en he den tu'nt 'im loose en put 'im ter wuk" (62). Sounding very much like one of the villainous horse-breakers reviled in *Black Beauty,* Johnson professes that if he owned the slave himself, he would either "break his sperrit er break 'is neck" (62).

But "Mars Jeems's Nightmare" does more than recite the often-made point that slaves were treated as brutally as animals; it makes the argument that systems of cruelty—whether they be based on hierarchies of race, gender, or species—are interconnected. The event that links the inset story to the framing tales is the sight of the younger Jeems fiercely beating his horse, but this act per se cannot constitute the logical segue from the cruelty of the younger to the elder Jeems, for while Master Jeems senior "nebber 'peared ter hab no feelin' fer nobody," there is no indication that his cruelty manifested itself in abusing horses or other animals. The way Chesnutt accomplishes this transition, then, merits closer attention. After the younger Jeems departs, the two white characters immediately denounce his abuse of his horse. John observes that he "looks as though he were ashamed of himself." In response Annie exclaims indignantly, "I'm sure he ought to be. . . . I think there is no worse sin and no more disgraceful thing than cruelty," to which John replies, "I quite agree with you" (57). The reason why John and Annie (and, more broadly, the class of the educated, white middle-class Americans they represent) agree there was "no worse sin" than cruelty to animals is because, as I explained in the introduction, animal abuse was widely believed to be not just a wrong in and of itself but an act that vitiated the character, led undoubtedly to other acts of violence, and threatened the very future of the nation.

Throughout his four decades of animal activism, George Angell stressed that the success of a liberal democracy depended upon that society's ability and willingness to protect its most vulnerable members—that is, the nonhuman ones. "We speak for those that cannot speak for themselves" was the MSPCA motto. From the beginning of the MSPCA's existence, Angell stressed that the work being conducted by his society would mean, as he stated in a speech first delivered in 1869, "the difference between peace and war, national prosperity and national ruin." "*A government,*" Angell proclaimed, "we must have. Shall it be a government of wise laws, enacted by humane men, administered by an incorruptible judiciary, no wars foreign or domestic, peace, happiness, and prosperity for all? Or shall it be the strong arm of military power, the law of the bayonet, and a great standing army supported by the nation to keep the nation in subjection?"[74] Had Chesnutt read this passage (which was reprinted in the 1884 and 1892 editions of Angell's autobiography), the nightmarish results Angell predicted for a nation without regard for its nonhuman residents might very well have seemed like a prescient and fairly accurate description of a post-Reconstruction Jim Crow South terrorized by the standing army of the Ku Klux Klan. In any event, the problem Chesnutt faced at the turn of the century had clear parallels to the problem Angell faced as he began what he called the SPCA's "great work": how does one rally people to oppose a form of injustice that might seem remote from their interests? Angell's response was to argue that animal welfare did in fact touch on every Americans' interests. "Throw aside all mercy for dumb animals," he suggested, "suppose there were no law to protect them, no penalty for their abuse, no redress for them in this world, and no hope in the next; throw aside all sanitary, financial, and moral considerations; suppose even that you are an atheist, . . . still I say, if you claim to be a good citizen, if you regard the future welfare of your country, *you must provide for the humane education of its children; and that is the grandest feature of our work.*"[75]

In "Mars Jeems's Nightmare," Chesnutt—via Julius—appropriates this strategy. Julius follows John and Annie's repudiation of animal cruelty by arguing, both explicitly and through his story, that cruelty toward nonwhite people also erupts into other forms of violence and oppression. "A man w'at 'buses his hoss," Julius remarks, "is gwine ter be ha'd on de folks w'at wuks fer 'im" (57). As the inset tale reveals, this threat extends to women as well as workers. Libby decides to break off her engagement with Jeems when she discovers his methods for plantation management, for "she des 'lowed she couldn' trus' herse'f wid no sech a man; dat he mought git so useter 'busin' his niggers dat he'd 'mence ter 'buse his wife atter he got useter habbin' her roun' de house" (58). When the reconstructed, posttransformation Jeems abandons his draconian style of plantation management, Libby, in response, renews their engagement. This same principle of structural connections among forms of violence and cruelty governs the logic of the framing tale's resolution.[76] Annie's reaction to Julius's tale—" 'That is a very strange story, Uncle Julius,' observed my wife, smiling" (68)—points to her growing recognition of the tale's other moral about the interconnectedness of cruelty directed against animals, slaves, workers, and women. Just as "a man w'at 'buses his hoss is gwine ter be ha'd on de folks w'at wuks fer 'im" (57), a man allowed to be hard on his workers will eventually become hard on his wife. Annie's decision to rehire Tom in defiance of John's wishes reveals that she, like Libby, has gotten the message: combating her mate's despotism toward blacks is also a matter of self-protection.

The Marrow of Tradition, then, links racial violence to dog-killing for the same reasons that "Mars Jeems" links the cruel treatment of slaves to horse-beating: such strategies enabled Chesnutt to suggest that, if left unchecked, racial oppression threatened to undermine American civilization as surely as indifference to animal cruelty did. Just as *Black Beauty,* through its echoes of *Uncle Tom's Cabin,* successfully tapped into an already established cultural reservoir of feeling, *Marrow* relied on public feelings for animals built up by works such as Sewell's. Thus, rather than an obstacle to Chesnutt's quest to make American readers engage passionately once again with the issue of racial justice, the linkage between racial and animal politics established by texts such as *Black Beauty* facilitated this work.

CONCLUSION

Animal Politics, Affect, and American Studies

Above all I am interested in how agendas in criticism have disguised themselves and, in doing so, impoverished the literature it studies. . . .

If *Sapphira and the Slave Girl* neither pleases nor engages us, it may be enlightening to discover why.

TONI MORRISON, *Playing in the Dark*

IN DISNEY'S motion picture *The Kid* (2000), Bruce Willis stars as Russ Duritz, a Los Angeles–based "image consultant" who has achieved every measure of material success: a high-powered career, influence among the rich and famous, an enormous house in the hills, and a shiny new Porsche. But despite his professional and financial accomplishments, Duritz is a failure. He is selfish and mean-spirited. He has neither friends nor any meaningful familial or romantic attachments. We learn that Duritz has not always been this way when he receives a visit from his eight-year-old self. Initially, eight-year-old Russ is duly impressed with his future self's wealth. He is wowed by Duritz's opulent home, and, upon his arrival, tears off through its expansive rooms excitedly bellowing, "Chester! Chester!" "Who is Chester?" the adult Duritz asks. Chester, the kid explains, is the name he decided he would give to his dog. When Duritz says that he does not have a dog, Russ has a moment of horrible recognition, as the truth of his adult existence suddenly dawns on him. He gasps with a mixture of shock and revulsion: "You mean . . . I'm a loser!" In the rest of the film, the kid helps Willis's character to see emotional connection rather than money and power as the true measure of success. Before the film's end, Duritz has revised his business practices, repaired his relationship with his father, and begun a romance with his employee Amy, who has been convinced all along that beneath Duritz's cynical exterior lay a kinder and gentler self. Duritz's conversion (or reversion) into that self is signaled in the film's final scene, when he arrives at Amy's doorstep. Russ doesn't say anything. He doesn't have to. He is holding in his arms a Golden Retriever puppy, and his embrace of the dog says it all.

The ease with which *The Kid* uses attachment to a dog to symbolize emotional maturity and psychological depth is just one example of the persistence into the current day of ideas and practices analyzed in this book. For the most part, a person's willingness to sympathize with or care for animals remains a *sine qua non* indicator of good character and the ability to form meaningful social relationships. It is because we believe that good pet keeping indicates a person's ability to care well for others that virtually all U.S. presidents of the past 100 years have gone to great lengths to make their companion animals visible to the public.[1] Conversely, the act of abusing or killing a companion animal can mark a person as irreparably evil, as creators of films ranging from *One Hundred and One Dalmatians* (1961; 1996) to *Fatal Attraction* (1987) have found. And just as Americans continue to assign deep significance to a person's feelings for animals, we remain, like our nineteenth-century predecessors, fascinated by the feelings *of* animals as well. Books on this subject appear regularly, are reviewed prominently, and sell well.[2] Stories about feelings of and for animals not only appear regularly in newspapers (as they did a century and a half ago) and the "human" interest segments of television news; they also form a staple of the programming on the popular Animal Planet cable network (which, since 1996, has offered viewers "All animals, all the time"). But it is not just representations of animals that saturate our lives. As development continues to encroach on their habitat, many species of wild animals—including the fox, coyote, mountain lion, and bear—have found ways to live on the perimeters of suburbs and even large urban centers. However, now as in the nineteenth century, Americans interact regularly and primarily with animals that are not free and wild—that is, with the domesticated species we keep for companionship, sport, fiber, or food. Today, there are more than 140 million dogs, cats, and birds in America's homes; the equine population exceeds 5.1 million; and more than 9 billion animals are raised each year for food.[3] Rather than disappearing from life in civilization, animals have become more imbricated in it than ever.

This persistence in contemporary culture of the ideas, cultural practices, and animal populations examined in this book raises some compelling questions. Why have such modes of human-animal interaction as I analyze—those that had strongly affective dimensions and focused on the animals with which humans live—not previously been considered important to the nation's literary, intellectual, and cultural history? Why have scholars of American culture come to believe that wilderness-oriented activities have always been the dominant (and characteristically "American") mode of obtaining morally improving contact with nonhuman nature? These questions deserve to be addressed in far more detail than I can provide in this study. But I will offer, however briefly, an overview of what would constitute a fuller answer to these questions.

At the turn of the twentieth century, many Americans began to reject the idea that civilized creatures were fundamentally different from and superior to savage, wild animals. One expression of this rejection was growing interest in wild animals, which manifested itself (among other ways) in the popularity of fictional and nonfiction accounts of wild animals' lives. This rejection was also expressed in the rise of a competing account of the essential nature of domesticated animals. Americans remained fascinated with "higher" domesticated animals such as horses and dogs, but while many continued to value these animals because of their capacity for such civilized traits as self-discipline, honesty, benevolence, and altruism, others were now praising these creatures on the grounds that they—though long compelled to live within human society—were in fact wild at heart.

Early-twentieth-century receptivity to ideas about the fundamental wildness of even the most ostensibly civilized creatures can be seen in part as a product of complex socioeconomic phenomena that have received substantial critical scrutiny, such as increasing acceptance of evolutionary theory, growing anxieties about the negative effects of modern civilization, and the efforts of middle-class white men to supplant the ideal of manly behavior that reigned in the nineteenth century with a competing version of masculinity better suited to sustaining and extending white men's power in the new social and economic order. As Gail Bederman explains, the ideal of manliness embraced by middle-class men in the nineteenth century placed a strong value on self-restraint, high-mindedness, and benevolent paternalism. "By gaining the manly strength to control himself," Bederman writes, "a man gained the strength, as well as the duty, to protect and direct those weaker than himself: his wife, his children, or his employees."[4] This concept of manliness was highly compatible with appreciating the emotional and moral sensibilities of seemingly civilized animals and defending animals from cruelty and abuse. Such compatibility is evinced in the lionization of George Graham Vest that followed his emotional closing argument in the case against dog-killer Leonidas Hornsby, as well as in the terms in which ASPCA founder Henry Bergh was praised in the 1879 article that appeared in the popular *Scribner's Monthly:* Bergh was "a stalwart hero, a moral reformer worthy of an enlightened and practical epoch" because he was "teaching men to be noble and strong through pity and self restraint."[5]

While some Americans, as Bederman demonstrates, continued "to uphold the long-standing ideologies of upright, civilized 'manliness'" at and after the turn of the century, others became "interested in a quite different type of manhood": "These Americans found a source of powerful manhood in a primal, untamed, 'masculinity,' the opposite of 'civilized manliness.' This primal male power seemed to arise from the 'natural man's' closeness to 'nature.' The 'masculine' strength of the 'natural man' was the sort of strength which *all* men had—civilized and savage. Here was a strength based not on manly self-control but on masculine 'instinct.' It was a violent strength—the strength of a 'savage' or 'carnivore.' This power, unlike that of high-minded 'manliness,' was weakened by civilization's restraining discipline." By the beginning of the twentieth century, "middle-class men were beginning to *like* thinking of themselves as a little bit 'barbarous.' "[6] Because dogs had long been held to be most "like us"— that is, to be, in terms of inner qualities, humans' closest link to the animal world—then to argue that dogs in their "natural" state were guided by instinct, self-preservation, and a desire for dominance rather than discipline, virtue, and benevolent protection of others was also to argue that this was man's natural condition as well.

One of the most significant markers of the cultural reconstruction of canine nature was Jack London's 1903 novel *The Call of the Wild.* By chronicling Buck's transformation from household pet to leader of a pack of wolves roaming the pathless wilderness, London dematerialized the boundary between dog and wolf that—in both the popular imagination and the discourse of natural history—had long been held inviolate. Even more important to Buck's "decivilization" than the development of his physical body is his renunciation of principled high-mindedness associated with the older code of civilized manliness. On Judge Miller's estate, Buck "lived the life of a sated aristocrat."[7] Self-controlled and duty-bound, he acts as the benevolent protector of the Judge's children and property. "He could have died," London writes, "for a moral consideration, say the defence of Judge Miller's riding-whip" (22). In the Yukon, Buck learns to regard his "moral nature" as "a vain thing and a handicap in the ruthless struggle for existence"—to eschew "the law of love and fellowship" in favor of "the law of club and fang" (21). By presenting Buck's transformation as a process of "instincts long dead [becoming] alive again" (22), *Call of the Wild* suggests that what natural historians since Buffon had held to be the dog's essential nature was in fact a suppression of the dog's true nature produced by the artifice of civilization.

The accommodation of canine nature to the new masculine idea that eschewed conventional manly virtue did not, however, necessarily require an association of dogs with wolves or their relocation in wilderness. The popularity of London's dog stories was exceeded by the even greater popularity of the dog paintings Cassius Marcellus Coolidge designed for the Brown and Bigelow printing company's calendars in the first decade of the twentieth century. Rather than emphasizing dogs' kinship with wolves, Coolidge presents dogs in extremely humanized forms. But as much as London's *Call of the Wild,* Coolidge's images undermined the long-standing belief that honesty, self-restraint, and devotion to family were part of the dog's essential nature. Coolidge gives us gaming, smoking, and drinking dogs (generally bulldogs, mastiffs, Great Danes, St. Bernards, and other large or powerful breeds) placed in such traditionally masculine arenas as the card table and sports field. The most famous of these images, *A Friend in Need,* picks up on the familiar idea of canine fidelity, but fidelity in this case is expressed in the morally questionable way of helping a friend to cheat at poker. In a recent interview with the *New York Times,* Coolidge's now ninety-two-year-old daughter Gertrude Marcella Coolidge stated, when asked if she liked her father's paintings, that she did not. "Girls don't like things like that," Ms. Coolidge explained. "It was for boys and men."[8]

If women like Gertrude Coolidge had no interest in images of the kind Coolidge produced, it was not just because these texts endorsed qualities being constructed at that time as specifically masculine. As it established such qualities as pugnacity, physical prowess, and a rejection of high-mindedness as essential male traits, the new discourse of canine nature on which Coolidge drew also denigrated the civilized qualities and feelings previously valued as "manly" by recasting them as feminine and, as such, revolting and even dangerous. *Call of the Wild* contains few female characters of any species. The novel's most prominent female dog, Curly, dies on her first day in the Yukon after she makes an amicable gesture to a canine native. When Curly approaches this husky of the Northland "in her friendly way," he leaps at her without warning, leaving Curly's face "ripped open from eye to jaw." Once the other huskies see that she is wounded, they "closed in upon her, snarling and yelping, and she was buried, screaming with agony, beneath the bristling mass of bodies" (15). Mercedes, the novel's only woman, is almost always depicted crying or whining. When her brother Hal begins to whip his newly purchased dog team, she grabs the whip from his hands crying, "Oh, Hal, you mustn't. . . . The poor dears! Now you must promise you won't be harsh with them for the rest of the trip, or I won't go a step" (48). As the plot unfolds, Mercedes' kindness is painted as more dangerous to Buck and his fellow dogs than any of the club-wielding, whip-slashing men they encounter. When Mercedes cannot cajole Hal into feeding the sled dogs more food, "she stole from the fish-sacks and fed them slyly" (52). As a result of her actions, depletion of the

A Friend in Need (c. 1908) is one of sixteen paintings of dogs that Cassius Marcellus Coolidge created for the Brown and Bigelow printing company in the early twentieth century. Image courtesy of the Archives of Brown and Bigelow, Inc.

dogs' already-low rations occurs at an earlier and even more dangerous part of their journey. In the end, Mercedes succumbs to despair and, instead of walking, "persisted in riding on the sled." The weight of her weak, emotional body becomes the "lusty last straw to the load dragged by the weak and starving animals" (54).

But even without invoking the exigencies of wilderness survival, architects of the new dog found strategies for reconstructing the kind of feelings for animals that were formerly perceived as manly as dangerous and feminine. In O. Henry's 1906 short story "Memoirs of a Yellow Dog," the canine narrator himself denounces tender feelings for animals as disgusting and emasculating. This dog speaks in brash colloquialisms that depart radically from the polite and reserved tone of the animal narrators of books such as *Black Beauty* and

Beautiful Joe. "I don't suppose it will knock any of you people off your perch," he begins, "to read a contribution from an animal." Deliberately rejecting the decorum of earlier animal stories, he tells the reader, "you needn't look for any stuck-up literature in my piece. . . . A yellow dog that's spent most of his life in a cheap New York flat, sleeping in a corner on an old sateen underskirt (the one she spilled port wine on at the Lady 'Longshoremen's banquet), mustn't be expected to perform any tricks with the art of speech."[9] The dog's problem, it turns out, isn't so much the cheapness of the flat as it is that, in it, he is subjected to an unseemly and disgusting femininity. As a puppy, he was purchased by "a fat lady." "From that moment," he laments, "I was a pet—a mamma's own wootsey squidlums. Say, gentle reader, did you ever have a 200-pound woman breathing a flavour of Camembert cheese and Peau d'Espagne pick you up and wallop her nose all over you, remarking all the time in an Emma Eames tone of voice: 'Oh, oo's um oodlum, doodlum, woodlum, toodlum, bitsy-witsy skoodlums?' " (111). So great is this dog's aversion to such sentimentality that he cannot bring himself until two-thirds of the way through his narrative (and then only with great difficulty) to confess that his name is "Lovey." The only comfort he takes in having this "nomenclatural tin can on the tail of [his] self respect" is that his canine neighbor has a far worse one, his being "Tweetness" (115).

The overpowering, feminized affect that stifles the dog has an even more debilitating effect on his mistress's husband. This "little man," Lovey reports, has "sandy hair and whiskers a good deal like mine. . . . We looked so much alike that people noticed it when we went out" (112–13). This physical resemblance between man and dog sets up the story's presentation of them as co-victims of the woman's sentimental, domestic tyranny. "By Sirius!" Lovey exclaims, "there was a biped I felt sorry for. . . . Henpecked?—well, toucans and flamingoes and pelicans all had their bills in him" (112). The chief sign of the husband's pathetic status was that "every evening while she was getting supper she made him take me out on the end of a string for a walk," for "it ain't the nature of a real man to play dry nurse to a dog in public" (112, 114). Lovey so greatly pities this man that he takes it upon himself to unleash some of his repressed masculine nature. While the two are walking one night, Lovey drags him into a saloon. After a great many Hot Scotches, the master throws the dog's leash and collar into the street, exclaiming, "Poor doggie . . . good doggie. She shan't kiss you any more. 'S a darned shame" (116). Lovey becomes even happier when his master announces that he himself will never go back to the flat either, and the two set out at that moment for the Rocky Mountains. But rather than their abandonment of the flat per se, the dog and man's real triumph lies in their abandonment of the highly affective code of human-animal interactions associated with the woman who lives there. The story ends:

> But what pleased me most was when my old man pulled both of my ears until I howled, and said:
>
> "You common, monkey-headed, rat-tailed, sulphur-coloured son of a door mat, do you know what I'm going to call you?"
>
> I thought of "Lovey," and I whined dolefully.
>
> "I'm going to call you 'Pete'," says my master; and if I'd had five tails I couldn't have done enough wagging to do justice to the occasion. (117–18)

Here, pain-inducing physicality (pulling the dog's ears until he howls) is not at odds with caring well for animals, but becomes its highest expression. "Pete" is, of course, a masculine name, and on account of its etymological connection to the word "rock," it communicates a physicality, a hardness, and a naturalness that is opposed to the thoroughly feminized and emasculating world of the flat, a place of flimsy, stained sateen underskirts.

But the changes taking place at this time in the way people wrote about animals reflect not only racial, class, and gender politics—of which we have increasingly sophisticated historical accounts—but also power struggles of which we have only a very impoverished understanding. Bederman has explained that the older code of civilized "manliness" began to falter in the 1890s "partly because economic changes had rendered earlier ideologies of middle-class manhood less plausible" and, "under these changing conditions, manly self-denial grew increasingly unprofitable."[10] The treatment of animals and affect in texts such as *Call of the Wild, A Friend in Need,* and "Memoirs of a Yellow Dog" reflect both this social reality and the fact that, at the same time that self-denial was becoming unprofitable for middle-class men, people also came to realize that the ideas about the moral and emotional qualities of animals that had gained a wide purchase by the end of the nineteenth century could also have exceedingly unprofitable consequences.

The first wave of the backlash against the ideas about animal affect and animal minds that were generating support for animal protection was the scientific community's battle against what was by the early 1890s a quite formidable opposition to the use of animals in scientific research. The most surprising part of this history is not the skill with which scientists rallied support for their cause, but that, in spite of their maneuverings, their triumph over the antivivisectionists was, in the mid-1890s, by no means a foregone conclusion. When, in 1896, Senator James McMillan of Michigan introduced a bill that would regulate animal experimentation in the District of Columbia ("a leading center of American experimental medicine"), "it was endorsed by six sitting judges of the Supreme Court, by the cream of the Washington clergy, by such eminent academics as former president John Bascom of the University of Wisconsin and the Harvard historian Albert Bushnell Hart, and . . . by a long list of practicing physicians."[11] It was in this context that the scientific community closed ranks and denounced as categorically unscientific any statement about nonhuman animals' emotional or moral capacities. To be sure, Descartes had long ago claimed that animals possessed neither emotions, intellect, consciousness, nor even the capacity to feel pain. But even among scientists, few accepted these assertions completely. Buffon, for example, strictly limited soulfulness and reason to human beings, yet he also described animals as having rich emotional lives. Belief in a fundamental similarity between human and nonhuman emotional experience formed a cornerstone of Darwin's theory of evolution, so much so that he devoted an entire book to the subject. This study, however—*The Expression of the Emotions in Man and Animals* (1872)—was all but expunged from the canon of Darwin's works in the wake of the delegitimization of such ideas in the 1890s,[12] which was ushered in by the British scientist C. Lloyd Morgan's 1894 decree on animal behavior: "In no case may we interpret an action as the outcome of the exercise of a higher psychical faculty, if it can be interpreted as the outcome of one which stands lower in the psychological scale."[13]

However, as was the case with Descartes so many years before, the general public did not cease believing animals experienced complex mental phenomena just because some scientists asserted it was not so. At the same time that the foundations of the new theory of animal behavior were being laid, Americans continued to read the narratives about domesticated animals that had been popular for decades and became fascinated, in addition, by stories about wild animals' inner lives. In the preface to one of the most popular of these texts in this genre, *Wild Animals I Have Known* (1898), Ernest Thompson Seton states that his stories illustrate "a moral as old as Scripture—we and the beasts are kin. Man has nothing that the animals have not at least a vestige of, the animals have nothing that man does not in some degree share." Using language straight out of *Descent of Man* (in which Darwin maintains that "the difference in mind between man and the higher animals . . . is certainly one of degree and not of kind"), Seton makes his case for including even predatory animals within the community of beings to whom we give ethical consideration: "Since, then, the animals are creatures with wants and feelings differing in degree only from our own, they surely have their rights."[14] To that end,

Seton's stories attribute to wolves, foxes, rabbits, and other animals whose interests often competed with our own some of the virtue and benevolence that had long been attributed to domesticated animals such as the dog. In addition, by drawing attention to wild animals' point of view, Seton encouraged his readers to question the ethics of our treatment of them. In "Bingo, the Story of My Dog," the wolf-trapping narrator learns what his lupine victims must suffer, when first his right hand and then his right foot become caught in the steel leghold traps he was setting for wolves. As he lies there contemplating a seemingly inevitable death—either a quick one at the jaws of wolves or a lingering one from cold and starvation, "a new thought" occurs to him: "This is how a wolf feels when he is trapped. Oh! what misery have I been responsible for! Now I'm to pay for it. . . . There I lay prone and helpless, wondering if it would not be strictly just that [the wolves] should come and tear me to pieces."[15]

In the first decade of the twentieth century, popular stories like these became a target of a state-sponsored attack that raged for more than five years in the nation's leading magazines and newspapers and came to be known as the "nature faker" controversy.[16] The first strike in this battle came in the form of John Burroughs' essay "Real and Sham Natural History," which appeared in the *Atlantic Monthly* in March 1903. By the 1870s, Burroughs had become the nation's most popular and most profitable writer of nonfiction nature essays, a position he held through the 1880s and '90s.[17] At the turn of the century, however, a number of new writers had made serious encroachments on the turf Burroughs formerly ruled. By the 1890s, many of the nation's schools had officially incorporated humane education into their curricula. As the SPCAs themselves became increasingly vocal advocates of wildlife protection in the 1890s and after, it is not surprising that books encouraging kind treatment to the denizens of fields and forests were fast becoming standard school texts. As those Burroughs attacked were quick to point out, Burroughs' own essays from the 1880s and '90s frequently indulged in the same kind of "anthropomorphizing" against which he now inveighed. Burroughs' allegiances, however, were not to humane education, but to science, and it was by insisting on the "non-scientific" quality of his competitors' writings that he was able to defend the preeminence of his own.

In this cause, Burroughs had a powerful encourager: President of the United States Theodore Roosevelt. Burroughs and Roosevelt had already been corresponding for ten years before 1903, and their friendship deepened considerably after the publication of "Real and Sham Natural History." On March 7, Roosevelt wrote to Burroughs, "I have long wished that something of the kind should be written." At the end of the letter, Roosevelt invited Burroughs to accompany him on a trip to Yellowstone National Park, on which both men were able to indulge in one of Roosevelt's favorite activities: big game hunting. Sensing the impropriety of using his position as president to attack civilian authors, Roosevelt for many years wielded his influence indirectly, via unpublished correspondence with Burroughs and editors of newspapers and magazines. By 1907, Roosevelt could restrain himself no longer, and he allowed his own criticisms of the "nature fakers" to be published in the press. It is no coincidence that, throughout the controversy, the two writers whom Roosevelt and Burroughs most violently attacked—Ernest Thompson Seton and William J. Long—were the ones whose writings most strongly impugned the recreational hunting that, as Bederman has shown, played an essential role in Roosevelt's construction of himself as a masculine man.[18] In a 1907 essay defending himself from the president's attacks on his abilities as a naturalist, Long countered, "The idea of Mr. Roosevelt assuming the part of a naturalist is absurd. He is a hunter." Roosevelt had previously written, "I don't believe for a minute that some of these nature writers [i.e., Long et al.] know the heart of wild things." "As to that," Long cheekily replied, "I find after carefully reading two of his big books that every time Mr. Roosevelt gets near the heart of a wild thing he invariably puts a bullet through it. From his own records I have reckoned a full thousand hearts which he has known thus intimately." Long's essay appeared on June 2, 1907, in newspapers in New York, Chicago, Boston, Philadelphia, and elsewhere, and editorial framing of his argument varied with the politics of each publication. The *Boston Globe* published the piece under the headline: "President a Slayer Not a Lover of Animals."[19]

The threat of an animal politics rooted in feelings of and for animals was not limited to recreational activities (such as sport hunting) newly important to middle-class manhood or to experimental practices (on live animals) that had become newly central to medicine and science. At the end of the nineteenth century and the beginning of the twentieth, the platform advanced by some of the nation's most ambitious and most vocal animal activists challenged with increasing intensity the notion that formed the very core of the laissez-faire capitalism sustaining the growth of robber barons' fortunes and the expansion of the nation's military and industrial power: the notion that, as the unfettered advance of self-interest was "natural," any efforts to regulate the exploitation of the powerless by the powerful constituted a perversion of the natural order. Interpreting Darwinism differently, animal activists such as George Angell rooted their crusade against animal exploitation in the belief that protecting the least powerful members of the community (whether they be human or no) from exploitation at the hands of the powerful was essential to the nation's social, political, and spiritual development. Especially in the 1890s and after, the publications of the organizations Angell superintended until his death in 1908—the MSPCA and AHES—presented cruelty to animals as structurally related to capitalists' exploitation of workers, and they frequently suggested that most instances of the working classes' animal abuse stemmed from capitalists' greed.

In Anna Sewell's *Black Beauty* (600,000 copies of which the AHES distributed in 1890 alone),[20] the impoverished cab driver given the nickname "Seedy Sam" on account of the poor turnout of his horse and his person explains that it is not his lack of compassion but his wage slavery to cab-boss Nicholas Skinner that compels him to treat his horse so badly. When he pulls up to the cab stand with his emaciated horse looking "dreadfully beat" and then flings a tattered rug over the bedraggled animal, another driver criticizes his unkind treatment. To this, Sam replies that his horse's hardships are also his own. The rates he must pay to the cab boss are so high, and the fees paid by wealthy customers are so low, that he, too, lacks a warm coat. "If the horses don't work," Sam says, "we must starve, and I and my children have known what that is before now."[21] Forced to work fourteen-hour days in the bitter cold without any days off, "the shabby, miserable looking driver" suffers an early and unquiet death. His life was "just snuffed out," a fellow driver reports, "he died at four o'clock this morning—raving about Skinner, and having no Sundays. 'I never had a Sunday's rest,' these were his last words" (210). In the following chapter, Sam's dying words are echoed by one of the novel's most sympathetic equine characters, the once-beautiful Ginger whose toils in the cab industry have broken her body and spirit. Like Sam, she endures cruel bosses, long hours, starvation rations, and no rest from her work. "The man who hires me now," Ginger explains to Beauty, "pays a deal of money to the owner every day, and so he has to get it out of me too; and so it's all the week round and round, with never a Sunday rest" (212). Shortly after their meeting, Beauty sees Ginger's corpse carted through the streets; "the head hung out of the cart-tail, the lifeless tongue was slowly dropping with blood" (213).

This same connection between nonhuman and human workers appears throughout the "sequels" to *Black Beauty* whose production Angell solicited with cash prizes and which he then published and distributed through the AHES. Like the other texts in this series, *Strike at Shane's* extends the politics rather than the plot of Sewell's novel. Set on the farm of John Shane in Indiana, the book offers a prescient critique of the forces that have culminated in the current domination of U.S. food production by giants of modern agribusiness: annihilation of traditional agricultural values and methods by efficiency theories developed to increase industrial productivity. Unlike his neighboring farmers, Shane "looks at everything from a money point of view."[22] "He was a hard man to deal with, and always aimed to make a dollar where other people made a dime. It was a favorite maxim of his that nothing should stay on the farm that did not more than pay expenses" (6). As he ran his business, "his only thought was how to get the most work done that day" (11). Shane's wife objects to the harsh use of animals that this theory entails and reminds him "that horses are not machines that can go on forever." But Shane only replies that these "foolish notions . . . won't make any money on the farm; so there's no use discussin' 'em" (33–34). Because Shane views his animals as interchangeable parts, he remains convinced that "it pays better to work a horse for all there is in him, an' when he's wore out shoot him or give him away" (47). Fed up with their abusive treatment, the animals that live on Shane's property—both domestic and wild—hold a meeting to "discuss . . . the best and most convenient remedy for the evils existing on the farm" (24). On the suggestion of a mule who was "formerly employed by a street car company of Indianapolis" and had observed the street car drivers' strategy for remedying labor disputes, the animals decide that they, too, will "all go out on a strike and refuse to work until [they] get better treatment" (20, 25). The horses feign illness, the cow refuses to give milk, and the snakes and toads that eat "noxious insects that . . . injure the crops grown on the farm" (18) take their services elsewhere, as do the birds who eat the worms that devour the seeds the farmer has planted. The animals' strike produces the expected results: without their assistance, the farm is nearly ruined. In the end, Shane "come[s] to the conclusion that we haven't been runnin' the farm on the right principle," and he abandons his bottom-line efficiency theories (77). After he improves his treatment of the animals he owns and ends his persecution of the wildlife, the farm becomes a more prosperous as well as a happier place.

In the 1890s and early 1900s the MSPCA and AHES blanketed the country with these and other publications that placed an increasingly ambitious animal politics at the center of attacks against a broad range of exploitations of the weak by the powerful. Examination of two contiguous articles on Theodore Roosevelt from the January 1901 edition of *Our Dumb Animals* illustrates this connection. At the top of the page is an article titled "Roosevelt" reprinted from *Advocate of Peace* (the publication of the American Peace Society, of which Angell was a vice president). It declares: "The *'strenuous life'* for which he [Roosevelt] pleads is, in its real meaning, a *'warlike'* life." Roosevelt's methods, the writer complains, compel us to "take our place with the nations that make poor China their 'door-mat,' that are ruthlessly over-running the world, stamping into the earth and annihilating native and weaker races. . . . Whoever opposes this, on no matter what high grounds of civilization and Christian principles, must be 'hunted down' in the *Congressional Record* and elsewhere, and repudiated." Immediately below this piece is an article written by Angell that makes a direct connection between Roosevelt's desire to hunt down his liberal-minded political opponents and his desire to hunt down animals. Angell begins by expressing incredulity that the then-governor of New York must

> take the trouble of going all the way to Colorado to *have the fun of shooting, wounding, and killing* such animals as may come within the reach of his gun.
>
> It would seem as though the Governor of New York might find more important business, and if he cannot be satisfied with all the killing of horses and men that have come out of the Cuban war, which *he had as much to do with getting up as any one* (and we think he had more, including the sending of the "Maine" to Havana when we had a large fleet within a few hours of sail of that port, and the President and Secretary Sherman were just closing negotiations with the Spanish Government that would have given freedom to Cuba without the firing of a single gun or the death of a single human being, horse, or mule)—if Mr. Roosevelt cannot be satisfied with all these killings . . . why not arrange with some Albany butcher to help him out.
>
> We are sorry to say that we know of no man in this country whose influence is in our opinion more hostile to the teachings of our "Bands of Mercy" and to the progress of civilization and humanity upon which the future of our country is to so largely depend.
>
> We did all in our power to prevent his appointment as Assistant Secretary of the Navy. . . . If we had succeeded, we think it probable that the "Maine" would never have been sent to Havana and been blown up there—that President McKinley and Secretary Sherman would have induced Spain to give up Cuba without the firing of a single gun, and that the sacrifice of *human and animal life* and the expenditure of millions of dollars (paid and to be paid) for armies, resulting from that war would have been saved.[23]

Elsewhere in *Our Dumb Animals,* we find animal politics juxtaposed or integrated with attacks on: the "yellow dime literature" that encouraged young men to go out West "to fight Indians, who are a hundred times better and more peaceable than the white ruffians that live around them"; the toleration of cruelty and hazing by the administrations of Williams College, West Point

Academy, Northwestern University, and MIT; the invocation of the Monroe Doctrine to legitimate the U.S. military presence at the Panama Canal; and British colonization of India and Africa.[24]

Moreover, by the 1890s, the animal politics promoted by the organizations Angell superintended extended well beyond reducing the suffering of domesticated animals without challenging the status quo. The MSPCA became increasingly aggressive in its denunciation and prosecution of acts of cruelty committed by the rich. In an 1895 article in *Our Dumb Animals,* Angell beamed about the upcoming prosecution of a member of the Myopia polo club who had "struck his pony *eight heavy blows on the head* with his polo mallet" and during the same game left another mount "*bleeding from eleven different places.*" "It is pretty well known to our readers," he stated, "that *polo players who, in violation and defiance of the laws of Massachusetts,* have mutilated their horses for life, *are criminals*—liable at any time to be arrested and imprisoned whenever we can get evidence to convict, and that we have a standing offer of $100 for such evidence."[25] In his "Report of the President for the Year Ending March 1, 1900," Angell relates, "I was called upon *by a Boston club-man* who assured me that while he did not belong to our Massachusetts Societies he did belong to a Society he named in another State. I did not reply that we did not expect from our rich club-men . . . who believe in horse docking, tame fox hunting, shooting of live pigeons from traps for sport, etc. etc., much help in our humane work."[26]

MSPCA and AHES publications opposed all hunting undertaken for recreation, including the hunting of predatory animals such as mountain lions.[27] However, even the killing of animals for food did not go unquestioned. One widely distributed AHES publication—a "sequel" to *Black Beauty* titled *Our Gold Mine at Hollyhurst* (1893)—argued that, although the world was not ready for vegetarianism "yet," it very soon would be. "In the colder regions of the earth," the story's hero, Dr. Edward Gardner, explains, "men are compelled to live on some form of animal diet—there is nothing else to eat—but the vegetable products of the world are increasing and extending over wider areas, and men are learning to make more use of them. . . . Now by the interchange of products between country and country we have an astonishing variety [of vegetable foods], and we shall doubtless use less and less meat."[28] As radical as vegetarianism was at this time, *Our Gold Mine* endorsed changes to humans' relationship with animals far more drastic than abstention from meat. Speaking with Mr. Hibbard about two brothers whose thoughtless treatment of their horses causes them much pain, Gardner laments:

"You may be very sure that I have talked with them repeatedly upon these matters, but without effect apparently. *You see they look upon a horse as so much merchandise—use him up and get another.*"

"They are by no means singular in that opinion."

"Unfortunately, they are not."

"Men buy and sell animals. It seems but natural they should regard them as property."

"But surely we must own our animals. I don't see any other way."

"Neither do I, at present, but I claim that ownership gives us no right to abuse them, or to work them to the verge of distress. In a higher sense we do not own them."

"You say 'at present'?"

"Who can tell what changes may come in the future? You remember what [antislavery activist] Wendell Phillips used to say about agitation. The agitation of this subject has but just begun."[29]

Certainly, every animal protection organization at this time did not endorse, as the MSPCA and AHES did, the abolition of animal experimentation, hunting, meat-eating, and animals' status as property. Though their leaders often attended national conventions, the nation's SPCAs and humane societies for the most part operated independently from each other. The animal movement was not centralized, and neither can we expect to find uniformity in its politics. For a variety of reasons, Henry Bergh and the organization he founded have often been treated as the most influential and the most representative of the nation's SPCAs. Bergh founded the nation's first SPCA, his New York City organization was called the *American* SPCA, and of the three earliest histories of the humane movement, two were published by New York's Columbia University, where Bergh had studied, and the other by the American Humane Association of Albany, New York.[30] Even the latter, however—Sidney H. Coleman's *Humane Society Leaders in America* (1924)—acknowledges (albeit after eighty-eight pages of discussion of Bergh and his successors) that "in the field of animal protection [George Angell] shares with Henry Bergh the title of pioneer." Coleman writes that Angell had "the acumen of a modern advertising specialist. . . . He kept his name before the masses by circulating *Our Dumb Animals* among those who moulded public opinion. Each issue reached every newspaper office in America, every college president, each member of Congress, and, within Massachusetts, every clergyman, lawyer, judge, and state legislator, besides the police force of Boston and thousands of school children scattered throughout America. Whether he was regarded as a fanatic or revered as a leader in a great moral movement, his name came to stand for 'animal protection' and 'humane education.'" "No one else," Coleman observes, "has inspired the writing and caused the distribution of so many pages of humane literature" or "so influenced the trend of constructive humane thought as George Thorndike Angell."[31]

Along with the evidence I discussed in the introduction, this brief survey of widely available humane reform literature reveals how poorly we have been served by existing accounts of animals and American culture. To the extent that it has been studied at all, the animal protection movement has been characterized as a force that extended the social control of elite whites, gave capitalists a means of policing the violent propensities of the working class, and provided "a cathartic outlet" for reformist impulses that was "without social risk."[32] Scholarship on the topic, as well as the lack thereof, tells us that ethical consideration for nonhuman animals has always been marginal in American culture—that the whole movement was inherently conservative—that no one important took it seriously. When Stowe attributed complex mental processes to dogs, she was only joking.[33] When Chesnutt praised an animal protection novel, he was being sarcastic.[34] Twain wrote a story condemning animal experimentation, but his daughter probably made him do it.[35] In chapter 4 I argued that prevailing views have obscured African American interest and participation in animal politics. As the information presented in this conclusion reveals, the story we tell ourselves about the history of animal politics fails us even in its account of what the white folks were up to.

If we are the inheritors of beliefs about the importance of emotional connection to animals generated in the nineteenth century, so too are we heirs to the recognition that, in order to make the most convenient and most profitable use of animals—or merely to maintain our equanimity as we circulate within existing cultural formations—such feelings must be contained, curtailed, and excluded from what counts as the serious, the intellectual, and the academic. The repressions sustaining current narratives about animal politics and animals' significance to American literary and cultural history shield us from distress of the kind experienced by the protagonist of J. M. Coetzee's *The Lives of Animals,* who sees behind the food we eat, the medicines we take, the clothes we wear, and the toiletries we use "crime[s] of stupefying proportions."[36] At the same time, such repressions have significantly impoverished our understanding of the history of our relationship with the nonhuman world and the literary texts that have shaped and been shaped by it.

NOTES

Introduction

Epigraph: Lawrence Buell, *The Environmental Imagination: Thoreau, Nature Writing, and the Formation of American Culture* (Cambridge: The Belknap Press of Harvard University Press, 1995), 33.

1. Since the English language has no single word that refers to "animals other than humans," and since the stylistic infelicities of using "nonhuman animals" in every place I needed to communicate this concept would be so great as to distract the reader from the substance of my argument, I have, with significant regret, resigned myself to the use of "animal" to mean nonhuman animals, unless otherwise indicated.

2. Although most of the creatures I wish to designate as "civilized" were, according to the modern scientific definition, "domesticated," the criteria of this standard do not reflect the precise concerns on which this study will focus (as what follows will make clear). In other words, "domesticated animal" is an important category in my argument, but it is not identical with what I mean by "civilized creatures." For a discussion of the definition of domestication, see the essays by Pierre Ducos, Sandor Bokonyi, and Juliet Clutton-Brock in *The Walking Larder: Patterns of Domestication, Pastoralism, and Predation,* ed. Juliet Clutton-Brock (London: Unwin Hyman, 1989).

3. Leo Marx, *The Machine in the Garden* (New York: Oxford University Press, 1964). "Little Annie's Rambles" was first published in 1835 and appeared in its final form in Hawthorne's 1837 *Twice-Told Tales.*

4. Nathaniel Hawthorne, *The Centenary Edition of the Works of Nathaniel Hawthorne,* 23 vols., ed. William Charvat, Roy Harvey Pearce, and Claude M. Simpson (Columbus: Ohio State University Press, 1962–), 9:121. Further references to this work appear in the text.

5. Carolyn Merchant, *The Columbia Guide to American Environmental History* (New York: Columbia University Press, 2002), 109.

6. During the past three decades, the wilderness romance thesis has been subject to two types of feminist critique. In one camp are the critics who, having observed that this paradigm excludes literature by women and people of color, sought to validate literary traditions (such as the sentimental novel) ostensibly focused on culture, not nature. In "Melodramas of Beset Manhood," *American Quarterly* 33:2 (1981): 123–39, Nina Baym argues that nineteenth century women found little use for the escape-to-the-wilderness fantasy because it insistently cast them as either a threat to be avoided

(in the form of society) or a resource to be dominated and exploited ("the virgin land"). While the work of Baym and others has successfully revalued domestic and sentimental literary traditions that do not fit within the "individual vs. society" model, that critical legacy has not effected a revaluation of the literary function of animals that do not enjoy an existence untrammeled by civilization. Among other critics, Joanne Dobson has defined nineteenth-century American women's literary traditions in terms that exclude, or at the very least shift focus away from, female writers' and readers' interactions with the nonhuman world. In "Reclaiming Sentimental Literature," *American Literature* 69:2 (June 1997): 263–88, Dobson writes: "Literary sentimentalism, I suggest, is premised on an emotional and philosophical ethos that celebrates human connection" (266). In "The American Renaissance Reenvisioned," in *The (Other) American Traditions: Nineteenth-Century Women Writers,* ed. Joyce W. Warren (New Brunswick: Rutgers University Press, 1993), 164–82, Dobson argues that American women's literature written between 1820 and 1870 is preoccupied with "the primacy and power of human affections and affiliations" (167). "I think it is accurate to say," she writes, "that the sentimental imagination at its core manifests an irresistible impulse toward human connection" (170). In three subsequent paragraphs, which extend her definition of sentimentalism, the adjective "human" is used eleven times.

In the other camp are scholars who have endeavored to include women and people of color into the study of the relationship between people and nature. Scholars in this group initially focused on women's relationship with flora and "landscape," rather than fauna. See, for example, Annette Kolodny's *The Land before Her: Fantasy and Experience of the American Frontiers, 1630–1860* (Chapel Hill: University of North Carolina Press, 1984). Studies that do consider women's understandings of their affinities with animals generally disparage domestic culture and assume that the only animals worth identifying with are wild ones. In Vera Norwood's *Made from This Earth: American Women and Nature* (Chapel Hill: University of North Carolina Press, 1993), domestic animals, when they come up at all, are treated as objects of pity associated with women's oppression: "One important effect of [Victorian women's] relegation to home has been to distance women both from their own animal being and from contact with certain classes of animals in nature" (173); "Victorian domesticity sanitized women's sexuality and tamed the animals (human and nonhuman) of home. Euro-American women writers since the late nineteenth century have struggled to reinvest themselves and their animal familiars with a wildness at the center of nature" (176). Norwood's discussion of domesticity focuses on women's separation from wild animals, rather than the potential for new proximities with animals living in domestic space. In her analysis, women's task is not only to liberate themselves from domesticity, but to help their tame and domesticated "animal familiars" to become more wild as well. The terms of her discussion all but preclude reading nineteenth-century women's connection with animals in their home as either liberating or positive. An even more pronounced hostility toward domestic culture and domesticated forms of nature appears in Stacy Alaimo's *Undomesticated Ground: Recasting Nature as Feminist Space* (Ithaca: Cornell University Press, 2000). Alaimo's examination of nature as "an undomesticated space of feminist possibility" suggests that domesticated nature cannot be similarly feminist. Alaimo argues that "nature . . . is undomesticated both in the sense that it figures as a space apart from the domestic and in the sense that it is untamed and thus serves as a model for female insurgency" (16). As the "thus" in this sentence reveals, this study links "female insurgency" to both a rejection of the domestic and an embrace of nature that is not tame. Thus, Alaimo likes Sedgwick's *Hope Leslie* because it "significantly departs from the domestic feminism that reigned during the nineteenth-century" (16), and she praises Mary Austin because she "delights in disrupting domesticity" (21). Chapter 1 of the present study examines in detail how similar views have governed and distorted the criticism on Susan Warner's novel *The Wide, Wide World.*

7. See note 6 above as well as Lesley Ginsberg, " 'The Willing Captive': Narrative Seduction and the Ideology of Love in Hawthorne's *A Wonder Book for Girls and Boys,*" *American Literature* 65:2 (June 1993): 255–73; Rita K. Gollin, "Nathaniel Hawthorne: The Flesh and the Spirit; Or, Gratifying Your Coarsest Animal Needs," *Studies in the Novel* 23:1 (Spring 1991): 82–95; and Mary Allen, *Animals in American Literature* (Urbana: University of Illinois Press, 1983). Allen claims that the animals of American literature "are wild, terrestrial beings. Many are big and violent, though their spirit is more important than their force. . . . They are celibate males, free or fighting to be free. And they are markedly independent. . . . If to be wild is good, to become domesticated is to sell out to a master. Pets are a rarity, and those who do live under a human's roof may yet exhibit wildness—the cat in a deliciously fierce attack" (12–13). The book's introduction concludes: "The animal's integrity rests in his stoic independence. . . . Free of family and culture, such American creations are these. They have no masters" (15–16).

8. Djelal Kadir, "America and Its Studies," *PMLA* 118:1 (January 2003): 15.

9. Henry David Thoreau, *Walden* (1854; reprint, ed. J. Lyndon Shanley, Princeton: Princeton University Press, 1989), 317. Further references to this work appear in the text.

10. In *The Environmental Imagination,* Lawrence Buell observes of Thoreau that "no writer in the literary history of America's dominant subculture comes closer than he to standing for nature in both the scholarly and the popular mind" (2).

11. See Lawrence Buell's chapter, "The Canonization and Recanonization of the Green Thoreau," in *The Environmental Imagination,* 339–69, and Eric Lupfer, "The Emergence of American Nature Writing, 1860–1909: John Burroughs, Henry David Thoreau, and Houghton, Mifflin and Company" (Ph.D. diss., University of Texas at Austin, 2003), 24–76.

12. Lupfer, "The Emergence of American Nature Writing," 56.

13. "Notices of New Books," *New Englander and Yale Review* 24 (1865): 805.

14. Lupfer, "The Emergence of American Nature Writing," 105–6. Lupfer reports

that "in 1891, when a writer named Harriet Clark proposed that the Houghton firm publish a collection of extracts from Thoreau, Scudder recommended against it, arguing that the firm generally avoided such collections and that 'Thoreau is after all so lacking in popularity that it seems scarcely wise to make this exception' " (107).

15. Lupfer, personal communication. Lupfer touches on this point briefly in "The Emergence of American Nature Writing," where, as praise for Burroughs, he cites the poet Edith Thomas's 1886 comment that Burroughs "was loved any place 'where home and homely life are loved' " (107–8).

16. Perry Miller, *Nature's Nation* (Cambridge: The Belknap Press of Harvard University Press, 1967), 199, 197. Further references to this work appear in the text.

17. See, for example, the essays in *Uncommon Ground: Toward Reinventing Nature* (ed. William Cronon, New York: Norton, 1995), especially Cronon's introduction and his own contribution, "The Trouble with Wilderness; or, Getting Back to the Wrong Nature" (69–90). The latter offers a trenchant and lucid critique of conventional equations of "nature" with "wilderness." Yet in the final two paragraphs of this essay, Cronon slips into what I would argue is a no less problematic collapsing of "nature" into the term "wild." See also the essays in the October 1999 *PMLA* "Forum on Literatures of the Environment"; David Mazel, *American Literary Environmentalism* (Athens: University of Georgia Press, 2000); Lawrence Buell, *Writing for an Endangered World: Literature, Culture, and Environment in the U.S. and Beyond* (Cambridge: The Belknap Press of Harvard University Press, 2001); and *Beyond Nature Writing: Expanding the Boundaries of Ecocriticism,* ed. Karla Armbruster and Kathleen R. Wallace (Charlottesville: University of Virginia Press, 2001).

18. This term is taken from Miller's *Nature's Nation:* "This was what America must resist, debauching artificiality" (198).

19. Peter Friederici, *The Suburban Wild* (Athens: University of Georgia Press, 1999); Laure-Anne Bosselaar, *Urban Nature: Poems about Wildlife in the City* (Minneapolis: Milkweed Editions, 2000); Terrell Dixon, *City Wilds: Essays and Stories about Urban Nature* (Athens: University of Georgia Press, 2002). Also relevant is Sam Bass Warner's much earlier *The Urban Wilderness: A History of the American City* (New York: Harper and Rowe, 1972).

20. Aldo Leopold, *A Sand County Almanac* (1949; reprint, New York: Oxford University Press, 1966), xi. In *Wilderness and the American Mind* (New Haven: Yale University Press, 1967), Roderick Nash begins the chapter "Aldo Leopold: Prophet" by casting Leopold as the direct descendant of Thoreau.

21. Carolyn Merchant, *The Columbia Guide to American Environmental History,* 100, 109. Merchant also considers domesticated animals as part of the "pestilent squalor" (106) of low-income housing and examines how the importation of domestic animals by Europeans disrupted the horticultural practices of native peoples and displaced native flora and fauna (28). The number of animals in New York City is recited at the beginning of every episode of the popular Animal Planet cable program *Animal Precinct.*

22. Arnold Williams, *The Common Expositor: An Account of the Commentaries on Genesis, 1527–1633* (Chapel Hill: University of North Carolina Press, 1948), 133–34; Keith Thomas, *Man and the Natural World: Changing Attitudes in England, 1500–1800* (1983; reprint, New York: Oxford University Press, 1996), 17–19, 157.

23. Thomas, *Man and the Natural World,* 17–18.

24. William Perkins, *The Workes of . . . William Perkins* (Cambridge, 1617), quoted in Thomas, *Man and the Natural World,* 157.

25. Andrew Willet, *Hexapla in Genesin* (Cambridge, 1605), quoted in Thomas, *Man and the Natural World,* 19.

26. Ralph Waldo Emerson, *The Collected Works of Ralph Waldo Emerson* (Cambridge: The Belknap Press of Harvard University Press, 1971), 1:39. Further references to this work appear in the text.

27. Janet Davis, *The Circus Age: Culture and Society under the American Big Top* (Chapel Hill: University of North Carolina Press, 2002), 96–98, 161.

28. Aristotle, *Historia Animalium,* reprinted in *The Works of Aristotle,* trans. D'Arcy Wentworth Thompson (Oxford: Clarendon Press, 1910), book 1, 488a.

29. Jacques Roger, *Buffon: A Life in Natural History* (1989; reprint, trans. Sarah Lucille Bonnefoi, Ithaca: Cornell University Press, 1997), 152.

30. Ibid., 228.

31. Georges Louis Leclerc, Count de Buffon, *Natural History, General and Particular,* vol. 4, trans. William Smellie (London: A. Strahan, and T. Cadell, 1791; facsimile reprint, Bristol, UK: Thoemmes Press, 2000), 1–2.

32. Edward Turner Bennett, *Tower Menagerie: Comprising a Natural History of the Animals Contained in that Establishment* (1829), quoted in Harriet Ritvo, *The Platypus and the Mermaid and Other Figments of the Classifying Imagination* (Cambridge: Harvard University Press, 1997), 41.

33. Ritvo, *Platypus and the Mermaid,* 40.

34. Richard Brookes, *New and Accurate System of Natural History* (London: J. Newberry, 1763) 1:xxvi, quoted in Ritvo, *Platypus and the Mermaid,* 39.

35. Ritvo, *Platypus and the Mermaid,* 40.

36. [J. Gregory], *A Comparative View of the State and Faculties of Man with those of the Animal World* (London: J. Dodsley, 1772), 13, quoted in Ritvo, *Platypus and the Mermaid,* 40.

37. Arthur O. Lovejoy, *The Great Chain of Being* (1936; reprint, Cambridge: Harvard University Press, 2001), 90, 92.

38. Richard W. Flint, "American Showmen and European Dealers: Commerce in Wild Animals in Nineteenth-Century America," in *New Worlds, New Animals: From Menagerie to Zoological Park in the Nineteenth Century,* ed. R. J. Hoage and William A. Deiss (Baltimore: John Hopkins University Press, 1996), 98–99. On the publication of guidebooks by British zoos, see Harriet Ritvo, *The Animal Estate: The English and Other Creatures in the Victorian Age* (Cambridge: Harvard University Press, 1987), 216. For a discussion of the ways in which circuses in the late nineteenth and early twenti-

eth centuries constructed their productions as morally improving, see Janet Davis, *The Circus Age,* especially 35 and 82–141.

39. On the formation of zoological gardens, see *New Worlds, New Animals.* On natural history museums, see Donna Haraway, *Primate Visions: Gender, Race, and Nature in the World of Modern Science* (New York: Routledge, 1989), 26–58. For discussions of the role of hunting and physicality in turn-of-the-century masculinity, see Gail Bederman, *Manliness and Civilization: A Cultural History of Gender and Race in the United States, 1880–1917* (Chicago: University of Chicago Press, 1995), especially pp. 170–215, and Mark Seltzer's *Bodies and Machines* (New York: Routledge, 1992), especially pp. 149–72. On the rise of the cult of wilderness in general, see Nash, *Wilderness and the American Mind.*

40. This list, I am sure, is not comprehensive, but it does represent some of the most significant ways in which beliefs in the importance of humans' custodial relations with animals were expressed.

41. Thorstein Veblen, *The Theory of the Leisure Class: An Economic Study of Institutions* (1899; New York: B. W. Huebsch, 1924), 142.

42. In *Desire and Domestic Fiction: A Political History of the Novel* (New York: Oxford University Press, 1987), Armstrong argues that eighteenth- and nineteenth-century conduct books and novels proposed a curriculum for educating daughters that "aimed at producing a woman whose value resided chiefly in her femaleness rather than in traditional signs of status, a woman who possessed psychological depth rather than a physically attractive surface, one who, in other words, excelled in the qualities that differentiated her from the male. As femaleness was redefined in these terms, the woman exalted by an aristocratic tradition of letters ceased to appear so desirable. In becoming the other side of this new sexual coin, the aristocratic woman represented surface instead of depth, embodied material instead of moral value, and displayed idle sensuality instead of constant vigilance and tireless concern for the well-being of others" (20). Armstrong also argues that, though created by and originally directed at women, this concept of a self defined by interior psychological qualities did not remain limited to women but rather came to define understanding of the "modern individual" (8).

43. Philip Fisher makes this point in *Hard Facts: Setting and Form in the American Novel* (New York: Oxford University Press, 1985), 102.

44. Thomas Wentworth Higginson, *Harper's Bazaar* (July 30, 1887), quoted in "Colonel Thomas Wentworth Higginson," *Our Dumb Animals* 20:4 (September 1887): 42.

45. Laurence Hutton, *A Boy I Knew, and Four Dogs* (New York: Harper and Brothers, 1898), 61; Susanna Louise Patteson, *Pussy Meow: The Autobiography of a Cat* (1901; Philadelphia: George W. Jacobs, 1903), 245.

46. C. C. Buel, "Henry Bergh and His Work," *Scribner's Monthly* 17 (April 1879): 884.

47. Ibid., 872.

48. George T. Angell, *Autobiographical Sketches and Personal Recollections* (Boston: American Humane Education Society, [1892?]), 13–14, 90–91. Statistics on nineteenth-century magazine circulation appear in Frank Luther Mott, *A History of American Magazines* (Cambridge: Harvard University Press, 1930), 4:8.

49. William J. Shultz, *The Humane Movement in the United States, 1910–1922* (New York: Columbia University Press, 1924), 35.

50. Although his efforts at humane education intensified in the 1880s, Angell had long considered education about animal cruelty far more important than arresting those who violated animal cruelty laws. In 1864—two years before Bergh founded the ASPCA and four years before the MSPCA's founding—Angell drew up a will stipulating that his trustees should use the remainder of his property to circulate "in common schools, Sabbath schools, or other schools . . . such books, tracts, or pamphlets as in their judgment will tend most to impress upon the minds of youth their duty towards those domestic animals which God may make dependent upon them." Quoted in William Allan Swallow, *Quality of Mercy: History of the Humane Movement in the United States* (Boston: Mary Mitchell Humane Fund, 1963), 9.

51. Angell, *Autobiographical Sketches,* 88–89, 97.

52. George T. Angell, "The American Humane Education Society," *Our Dumb Animals* (September 1889): 43.

53. George T. Angell, "The New Order of Mercy," reprinted in Angell, *Autobiographical Sketches,* p. 29 of the appendix (which has its own pagination).

54. Nathaniel Southgate Shaler, *Domesticated Animals: Their Relation to Man and to His Advancement in Civilization* (New York: Charles Scribner's Sons, 1895), 222, 5–6.

55. This passage originally appeared in the MSPCA's monthly periodical, *Our Dumb Animals,* and was subsequently republished on p. 8 of the appendix of George T. Angell's *Autobiographical Sketches.*

56. George T. Angell, quoted in Francis H. Rowley, *Sixtieth Annual Report of the Massachusetts Society for the Prevention of Cruelty to Animals* (Boston: Massachusetts Society for the Prevention of Cruelty to Animals, 1927), 18, Institutions Collection, American Antiquarian Society.

57. Angell, "The New Order of Mercy," 33.

58. See Harriet Ritvo, "Learning from Animals: Natural History for Children in the Eighteenth and Nineteenth Centuries," *Children's Literature* 13 (1985), 72–93, and James Turner, *Reckoning with the Beast: Animals, Pain, and Humanity in the Victorian Mind* (Baltimore: Johns Hopkins University Press, 1980), 147 n. 73.

59. "Have Animals Souls?" *Putnam's Monthly Magazine* 7:40 (April 1856): 361–71; William Hosea Ballou, "Are the Lower Animals Approaching Man?" *North American Review* 145:372 (November 1887): 516–23; Rev. Charles Josiah Adams, *Where Is My Dog? Or, Is Man Alone Immortal?* (New York: Fowler and Wells, 1892).

60. Rush C. Hawkins, *Better than Men* (New York: J. W. Bouton, 1896), 1–2.

61. This essay was not published during Twain's lifetime and the title he assigned to

it has been lost. The piece appeared in the posthumously published *Letters from the Earth,* ed. Bernard Devoto (New York: Harper and Row, 1962), 222–32, under the title "The Lowest Animal." This same essay is given the title "Man's Place in the Animal World" in *What Is Man? and Other Philosophical Writings,* ed. Paul Baender (Berkeley: University of California Press, 1973), 80–89. For information about the text's composition and publication, see the textual note in this same volume (593–95).

62. Early assertions of the wild nature thesis (in, for example, Roderick Nash's *Wilderness and the American Mind*) and subsequent revisions of it (such as Vera Norwood's *Made from this Earth,* which, like Annette Kolodny's work before it, modifies Nash's thesis to include women) rely extensively on literary texts to argue their point. Even Carolyn Merchant's *The Columbia Guide to American Environmental History* (a history that otherwise has little to say about literature) uses literary texts as the primary sources of evidence for its four-page discussion of "Nature and Ambivalence about the Market Economy" (69–72).

63. *Uncommon Ground,* 25.

64. Donna Haraway's study of (primarily scientific) narratives about primates is both an exception to this statement and an important influence on my own thinking about literary texts. See Haraway, *Primate Visions.* Haraway maintains that the animals scientists study "are material-semiotic actors in the apparatus of bodily production. They are not 'pre-discursive bodies' just waiting to validate or invalidate some discursive practice, nor are they blank screens waiting for people's cultural projections. The animals are active participants in the constitution of what may count as scientific knowledge" (310). For a discussion of the history of the belief that nature would remain homeostatic without the influence of humans, see Michael G. Barbour, "Ecological Fragmentation in the Fifties," in *Uncommon Ground,* 233–55.

65. In "Breaking in Englishness: *Black Beauty* and the Politics of Gender, Race and Class," *Women: A Cultural Review* 5:1 (Spring 1994): 34–52, and *Animal Advocacy and Englishwomen, 1780–1900: Patriots, Nation, and Empire* (Ann Arbor: University of Michigan Press, 1998), Moira Ferguson argues race and slavery rather than horses to be *Black Beauty*'s central concern. Following close on Ferguson's heels, Peter Stoneley argues that Sewell's novel is not about equine bodies but human, masculine ones (or, more specifically, Sewell's conflicting desire for and fear of the latter). See Peter Stoneley, "Sentimental Emasculations: *Uncle Tom's Cabin* and *Black Beauty,*" *Nineteenth-Century Literature* 54:1 (June 1999): 53–72.

66. Vicki Hearne argues eloquently that practices such as horsemanship and dog training are something that humans do along *with* animals—and not something we do *to* them or something they do *for* us. See *Adam's Task: Calling Animals by Name* (New York: Alfred A. Knopf, 1986). For a discussion of Hearne, see Paul Patton, "Language, Power, and the Training of Horses," in *Zoontologies: The Question of the Animal,* ed. Cary Wolfe (Minneapolis: University of Minnesota Press, 2003), 83–99.

67. Louis Legrand Noble, *The Life and Works of Thomas Cole* (1853; reprint, Cambridge: The Belknap Press of Harvard University Press, 1964), 145.

68. Shelley Fisher Fishkin, *Lighting Out for the Territory: Reflections on Mark Twain and American Culture* (New York: Oxford University Press, 1997).

69. Mark Twain, "A Dog's Tale," *Harper's Monthly* 108:643 (December 1903): 11–19; "A Horse's Tale," *Harper's Monthly* 113:676 (September 1906). "A Dog's Tale" was also published in pamphlet form in 1903 by the National Antivivisection Society (with Twain's approval); however, it is not clear whether this publication preceded, followed, or was simultaneous with the story's publication in *Harper's Monthly.* Both "A Dog's Tale" and "A Horse's Tale" were issued in book form (New York: Harper and Brothers, 1904 and 1906, respectively) and are reprinted in *The Complete Short Stories of Mark Twain,* ed. Charles Neider (New York: Bantam Books, 1990), 491–500 and 525–64.

70. Mark Seltzer, *Bodies and Machines,* 153. Roderick Nash also discusses Vest's efforts on behalf of wilderness preservation in *Wilderness and the American Mind* (113–14, 157).

71. William Safire, "Best Speech," *New York Times Magazine* (April 18, 1999), 74.

72. On Houghton Mifflin's shaping and promotion of the genre of nature writing, see Lupfer, "The Emergence of American Nature Writing."

73. "Hon. Henry O. Houghton," *Our Dumb Animals* 28:5 (October 1895): 52. After Houghton's death, Houghton Mifflin published Elizabeth Stuart Phelps's antivivisection novella *Loveliness: A Story* (Boston: Houghton Mifflin, 1899).

74. Merchant, *The Columbia Guide to American Environmental History,* 77.

75. Buel, "Henry Bergh and His Work," 879.

76. Turner, *Reckoning with the Beast,* 95, 114.

77. "The Great Kansas City 'Band of Mercy' Meeting," *Our Dumb Animals* 32:1 (June 1899): 4.

78. George T. Angell, "Report of the President for the Year Ending March 1, 1900," *Our Dumb Animals* 32:11 (April 1900): 138. By 1925, the number of Bands of Mercy grew to 150,000, and its membership to 5 million (Massachusetts Society for the Prevention of Cruelty to Animals, "The American Humane Education Society Past, Present, Future." MSPCA Archives, photocopy, n.d.).

Chapter One. Animal Bodies

Epigraph: Susan Warner, journal, quoted in Anna Warner, *Susan Warner ("Elizabeth Wetherell")* (New York: G. P. Putnam's Sons, 1909), 284–85.

1. Nina Baym, *Women's Fiction: A Guide to Novels by and about Women in America, 1820–70* (Ithaca: Cornell University Press, 1978; 2nd ed., Urbana: University of Illinois Press, 1993), 141.

2. Readings of horses and horsemanship figure prominently in Joanne Dobson, "The Hidden Hand: Subversion of Cultural Ideology in Three Mid-Nineteenth-Century American Women's Novels," *American Quarterly* 38:2 (1986): 223–42; G. M. Goshgarian, *To Kiss the Chastening Rod: Domestic Fiction and Sexual Ideology in the American Renaissance* (Ithaca: Cornell University Press, 1992), 76–120; Catharine

O'Connell, "'We *Must* Sorrow': Silence, Suffering, and Sentimentality in Susan Warner's *The Wide, Wide World,*" *Studies in American Fiction* 25:1 (1997): 21–39; and Marianne Noble, "An Ecstasy of Apprehension: The Gothic Pleasures of Sentimental Fiction," in *American Gothic: New Interventions in a National Narrative,* ed. Robert K. Martin and Eric Savoy (Iowa City: University of Iowa Press, 1998), 163–82. See also Mary Hiatt, "Susan Warner's Subtext: The Other Side of Piety," *Journal of Evolutionary Psychology* 8 (1987): 257; Jane Tompkins, afterword to *The Wide, Wide World,* by Susan Warner, ed. Tompkins (New York: The Feminist Press, 1987), 600; Isabelle White, "Anti-Individualism, Authority, and Identity: Susan Warner's Contradictions in *The Wide, Wide World,*" *American Studies* 31:2 (1990): 33; Susan S. Williams, "Widening the World: Susan Warner, Her Readers, and the Assumption of Authorship," *American Quarterly* 42:4 (1990): 572; and Erica R. Bauermeister, "*The Lamplighter, The Wide, Wide World,* and *Hope Leslie:* Reconsidering the Recipes for Nineteenth-Century American Women's Novels," *Legacy* 8:1 (1991): 22.

3. White, "Anti-Individualism, Authority, and Identity," 33.

4. Goshgarian, *To Kiss the Chastening Rod,* 112.

5. Dobson, "The Hidden Hand," 231.

6. Noble contends that "the violence that is consistently inflicted upon horses during the course of the book, then, can be read as coded representations of the violence done to women during the course of their acculturation" (175). In addition to noting Ellen's connection to horses in general, critics have remarked especially on the connections between Ellen and John's horse the Black Prince. O'Connell identifies this link as crucial to Ellen's understanding of her own subjection: "Ellen . . . finds this story [of John's first ride on the Black Prince] distressing, and the other women laughingly recognize that Ellen is making the connection between herself and the horse" (31). Noble claims that by associating Ellen with the Black Prince, "Warner draws an implicit comparison between Ellen's body and Satan, suggesting that the female body is a reservoir of sinfulness within female nature" (176).

7. Joanne Dobson and Isabelle White, for example, see Ellen (at least in terms of her outward behavior) as completely broken, while Goshgarian views Ellen as a perpetually rebellious horse who misbehaves every time the master steps away. Ellen, Goshgarian alleges, is "*quite unable to keep herself right*" (109, emphasis in original).

8. Goshgarian, *To Kiss the Chastening Rod,* 115, 112, 107.

9. Tompkins explains the novel as "a kind of bildungsroman in reverse" and claims that "the ideal to which the novel educates its heroine and its readers is the opposite of self-development and self-realization, it is to become empty of self" (598). According to O'Connell, "There is fundamental narrative tension between the sentimental construction of Ellen Montgomery's subjectivity through her passionate emotional life and the directive from every authority figure in the novel to abandon her sense of self and live for the will of others" (24). Even though O'Connell suggests that Ellen does achieve subjectivity through her expression of her suffering, her essay rings with nostalgia and lament for a former, untamed, and unoppressed self. These assumptions

about subject formation infuse a range of Warner criticism, reaching an apex perhaps in "The Wild Side of *The Wide, Wide World,*" *Legacy* 11:1 (1994): 1–16, in which Veronica Stewart argues that "Nancy, as trickster, specifically as Ellen's suppressed nature, reveals the heroine's internalized predisposition to escape oppressive social conventions by tapping a sense of connection with nature's beauty" (7).

10. Williams uses this term as she summarizes critical consensus on John Humphreys (572). Her own argument, however, does not take up the issue of his horsemanship.

11. Tompkins, afterword, 600.

12. See Hiatt, "Susan Warner's Subtext," 257; Dobson, "The Hidden Hand," 227, 231–32; Goshgarian, *To Kiss the Chastening Rod,* 104–11; O'Connell, "We Must Sorrow," 22–23, 29–33; and Noble, "An Ecstasy of Apprehension," 174–78. O'Connell succinctly explains how central a negative evaluation of John is to the argument that Warner opposed domestic ideology. *The Wide, Wide World,* she writes, "undercuts its own endorsement of female submission by subtly rendering grotesque the moral features of its primary patriarchal authority figure, John Humphreys" (22); "The delegitimation of John Humphreys is crucial to the novel's validation of Ellen's perspective and experience. . . . If the novel is seen as depicting his control as right and good, then the ending appears definitively to settle all questions of appropriate female behavior" (29).

13. For a discussion of class (but not horsemanship) in *The Wide, Wide World,* see Richard Brodhead, "Sparing the Rod: Discipline and Fiction in Antebellum America," in *Cultures of Letters: Scenes of Reading and Writing in Nineteenth-Century America* (Chicago: University of Chicago Press, 1993), 13–47

14. Throughout this chapter, I will discuss a Western/European and then a specifically Anglo-American discourse of horsemanship. While the riding practices and culture of the American Southwest were influenced by Central and South American equestrian traditions (which themselves came from Spain and Portugal), equestrianism in the northeastern United States developed primarily from the British tradition; still practiced as the dominant form of recreational riding in that area today, it is called "English" riding. Since the history of horsemanship in other regions of the country differs significantly from that of the East Coast world in which Warner's novel takes place, it will not be considered here.

15. Thomas Blundeville, *The Arte of Ryding and Breakinge Greate Horses* (London, 1560; New York: Da Capo Press, 1969), bk. 3, C1r-v.

16. See Michel Foucault, *Discipline and Punish: The Birth of the Prison,* trans. Alan Sheridan (New York: Vintage Books, 1977), 3–6. Further references to this work appear in the text.

17. John Astley, *The Art of Riding* (London: Henrie Denham, 1584), 6.

18. Renaissance beliefs about equine nature were informed by such classical texts as Plato's *Phaedrus.* There, Plato likened the human soul to a team of horses—one white and one black—and their charioteer. The charioteer must manage the two horses,

who pull in opposite directions. While the white horse complies with the charioteer's wishes and tries to pull him upward to heaven, the black horse resists his commands, and pulls downward toward earth and, particularly, toward the bodies of young boys. As soon as he sees an attractive youth, the black horse plunges on a descent away from nobler ideals and toward the instant gratification of bodily lusts. This horse "no longer responds to the whip or the goad of the charioteer; it leaps violently forward and does everything to aggravate its yokemate and its charioteer, trying to make them go up to the boy and to suggest the pleasures of sex" (*Plato: Complete Works,* ed. John M. Cooper, Indianapolis: Hacket, 1997, 254a). It is this equine archetype that gained particular currency in the Renaissance, especially as it (along with many other classical tropes) was recycled in love poetry. For additional examples of the paralleling of horse/human passion on the one hand, and horseman/restraining reason on the other, see Shakespeare's sonnets 50 and 51 and *Venus and Adonis* lines 390–400.

19. William Shakespeare, *Venus and Adonis,* in *The Riverside Shakespeare,* ed. G. Blackmore Evans (Boston: Houghton Mifflin, 1974), lines 260–70.

20. On the domestication of horses and development of horsemanship, see Stephen Budiansky's *The Nature of Horses: Their Evolution, Intelligence, and Behavior* (London: Phoenix, 1998), especially pp. 40–54.

21. Charles Chenevix-Trench, *A History of Horsemanship* (Garden City, NY: Doubleday, 1970), 101.

22. Vladimir S. Littauer, *The Development of Modern Riding* (1962; reprint, New York: Howell Book House, 1991), 41.

23. Writers offered gentlemen instruction on horsemanship both in books devoted exclusively to riding—such as Markham Gervase's *A Discource of Horsemanshippe* (London: J. C. for Richard Smith, 1593) and Nicholas Morgan's *The Perfection of Horsemanship, Drawne from Nature Art, and Practice* (London: Printed for Edward White, 1609)—and in more general texts, such as Georges Guillet de Saint-Georges' *The Gentleman's Dictionary* (London: Printed for H. Bonwincke, 1705) and Richard Blome's *The Gentleman's Recreation* (London: S. Roycroft, 1686).

24. Astley, *The Art of Riding,* A2r.

25. William Hope, *The Complete Horseman,* quoted in Littauer, *The Development of Modern Riding,* 32.

26. Richard Berenger, *The History and Art of Horsemanship* (London: printed for T. Davies, 1771), 2:19.

27. Again, my analysis applies specifically to prevailing trends in the Anglo-American horsemanship that was so important to the northeastern United States where Warner's novel is set. Alternate aesthetics of horsemanship developed, on an alternate timetable, in other regions of the United States (particularly in the American southwest), and these merit separate analyses. Though horsemanship rooted in the principles of psychological discipline has—since the late eighteenth century—increasingly dominated both actual training practices and cultural discourses, it did not completely displace violent and brutal equestrian practices. And while the majority of

nineteenth-century horsemanship manuals advocated training methods that motivate the animal through gentleness and rewards, there were notable exceptions. For an example of a particularly violent nineteenth-century methodology, see York and Williams, *The Horseman's Guide and Farrier* (Montpelier, VT: Argus and Patriot Job Printing House, 1865).

28. A. H. Rockwell, *The Improved and Practical System of Educating the Horse* (New York: Fisher, 1872), 6, 52; the *Tribune* reporter's remarks are quoted on p. 11.

29. Colonel J. C. Battersby, *The Bridle Bits: A Treatise on Practical Horsemanship* (New York: Orange Judd Company, 1886), 138, 5.

30. Anthony Dent, *The Reign of the Horse* (Washington, DC: Folger Library Publications, 1991), 8.

31. Thomas Wise, *The Newest Young Man's Companion,* 13th ed. (London: J. and H. Taylor, 1782).

32. Harry Hieover [Charles Bindley], *Practical Horsemanship* (London: Longman, Brown, Green, and Longmans, 1850), viii.

33. For the history of sidesaddle riding, see Lida Fleitmann Bloodgood's *The Saddle Queens: The Story of the Side-saddle* (London: J. A. Allen, 1959), especially pp. 1–47.

34. Susan Warner, *The Wide, Wide World* (1850; reprint, New York: The Feminist Press, 1987), 385. Further references to this work appear in the text.

35. For a discussion of the affective nature of discipline in nineteenth-century American culture, see Richard Brodhead, *Cultures of Letters,* 13–47. While in Foucault's theory, anonymous, interchangeable personnel execute the disciplinary function, the power Brodhead describes results from an affective and intimate relationship with a particular authority figure, who on account of that relationship, will be equally effective in controlling the reader/child/student when present as when absent. Once the subject is trained, or disciplined, in this manner, disciplinary power is easily transferred to other authority figures with whom the subject establishes affective ties.

36. Lora Romero, *Home Fronts: Domesticity and Its Critics in the Antebellum United States* (Durham: Duke University Press, 1997), 46.

37. Charles Butler, *The American Lady* (Philadelphia: Hogan and Thompson, 1836), 66–67. Further references to this work appear in the text.

38. As an advertisement printed in the back of the 1869 *American Woman's Home* explains, *Principles of Domestic Science* was "*The American Woman's Home* revised, rearranged, and adapted with much new matter, for use in schools, academies and colleges for young women." The passages of *Principles* quoted here appear verbatim in *The American Woman's Home* (itself based on Beecher's 1841 *Treatise on Domestic Economy*). I quote from the 1870 textbook to demonstrate that Beecher and Stowe's ideas were promoted and received as a theory of female education. Further references to this work appear in the text.

39. Edward Stanley, *The Young Horsewoman's Compendium to the Modern Art of Riding* (London: James Ridgeway, 1827), vi.

40. *Young Lady's Equestrian Manual* (London: Whitehead and Company, 1838), vii.

41. "The Exercise of Riding," *American Magazine of Useful and Entertaining Knowledge* 2 (1835): 82 (emphasis in original).

42. Ghislani Durant, *Horse-Back Riding from a Medical Point of View* (New York: Cassell, Petter and Galpin, 1878), 111. For an American monograph on riding for women, see Elizabeth Karr, *The American Horsewoman* (Boston: Houghton Mifflin, 1884). Karr claims that "ladies throughout the country, and especially in our large cities and towns, are apparently awakening to an appreciation of the importance of out-door amusement and exercise in securing and prolonging health, strength, beauty, and symmetry of form, and that horseback riding is rapidly becoming the favorite form of such exercise" (v).

43. See [Mrs. J. Stirling Clarke,] "Hints on Equestrianism for the Fair Sex," *Godey's Lady's Book,* 37 (1848), 45–48, 108–9, 169–71, 240–41, 303–4, 361–62. Further references to this work appear in the text.

44. Nancy Armstrong, *Desire and Domestic Fiction: A Political History of the Novel* (New York: Oxford University Press, 1987), 8. Further references to this work appear in the text.

45. My insistence on the decidedly corporeal dimension of Ellen's development marks another point of departure from Noble, whose reading of the novel is premised on the claim that domestic ideology called for an "erasure of the female corporeality" (166).

46. Thus the practice of middle-class horsewomanship complicates the notion of a nineteenth-century world rigidly bifurcated into female, domestic, sentimental and male, nondomestic, nonsentimental spheres. Although Clarke distinguishes between masculine and feminine styles of riding in the passage that follows, the strategies of psychologically oriented control that she attributes to (and were indeed taken up by) women originated in an almost exclusively male tradition of horsemanship.

47. Beecher and Stowe illustrate the fatiguing effect of mindless exercise with the following example: "let a person go shopping with a friend, and have nothing to do but look on. How soon do the continuous walking and standing weary! But, suppose one, thus wearied, hears of the arrival of a very dear friend: she can instantly walk off a mile or two to meet her, without the least feeling of fatigue" (105–6). Almira H. Lincoln Phelps, vice principal of Troy Female Seminary (who also believed that "*Mind* is ultimately the object to be acted upon, in physical as in other branches of education," emphasis in the original), warned specifically against riding for the mere purpose of display in *Lectures to Young Ladies, Comprising Outlines and Applications of the Different Branches of Female Education* (1833): "Riding on horseback is a very healthful as well as graceful exercise; yet it is somewhat questionable whether there is not too much the appearance of display in a young lady's prancing through the most public streets of a city. A rural excursion on horseback is more safe and proper" (49, 55).

48. When horses canter, their legs move in one of two possible sequences, one of which terminates with the right front leg, the other with the left (equaling the right and left lead, respectively). When cantering on an arc, the horse may become unbal-

anced if the rider does not make sure the leg closest to the inside of the curve is the "leading" leg. Also, when cantering for long periods of time cross country on a straightway, the rider must take care to switch the horse's lead periodically so that one side of the horse's body does not fatigue more than the other. As rural areas were increasingly cordoned off with fences, hedges, and ditches, jumping also became a practical equestrian skill.

49. Alice Hayes, *The Horsewoman: A Practical Guide to Side-Saddle Riding* (London: W. Thacker and Company, 1893), 2, 185.

50. Mrs. J. Stirling Clarke, *The Habit and the Horse; A Treatise on Female Education* (London: Smith Elder and Company, 1857), 25–26.

51. Many critics ignore Alice's speech; others, such as O'Connell, have charged that Alice's estimation of John disqualifies her as a credible character witness (30–31). But is it within Alice's character to lie on any, or anyone's, account? Hasn't Alice proven herself both an accomplished horsewoman and a lover of animals—especially by her decision to save Captain Parry in the snowstorm at risk to her own life?

52. See Romero, *Home Fronts,* 50–51.

53. See Goshgarian, *To Kiss the Chastening Rod,* 100–111.

54. Dobson, "The Hidden Hand," 227, 231.

55. Michel Foucault, "The Ethic of Care for the Self as Practice of Freedom: An Interview," in *The Final Foucault,* ed. James Bernauer and David Rasmussen, (Cambridge: MIT Press, 1988), 11. Romero quotes this passage (87) as she argues that Stowe's use of domestic ideology as resistance was not a transcendence of power relations but rather an engagement with them.

56. Anna Warner, *Susan Warner* (New York: Knickerbocker Press, 1909), 284–85, 352, 375, emphasis in original.

57. Williams, "Widening the World," 567.

58. Anna Warner, *Susan Warner,* 408.

59. Grace Greenwood, "Grace Greenwood as a Groom," *Our Dumb Animals* 2:5 (October 1869): 47, emphasis in original.

Chapter Two. Animal Transformations

Epigraph: Walt Whitman, "Song of Myself," *Leaves of Grass and Other Writings,* ed. Michael Moon (New York: Norton, 2002), 52.

1. F. O. Mattheissen, *The American Renaissance* (1941; reprint, New York: Oxford University Press, 1972), 238, 238n (page citations are to reprint edition).

2. Hawthorne receives one paragraph, for example, in Roderick Nash's *Wilderness and the American Mind* (New Haven: Yale University Press, 1967; 1982), just long enough for Nash to use him as evidence for the "persistence into the nineteenth century" of Puritan attitudes toward nature (39).

3. See Rita K. Gollin, "Nathaniel Hawthorne: The Flesh and the Spirit; Or, 'Gratifying Your Coarsest Animal Needs,' " *Studies in the Novel* 23:1 (Spring 1991): 82–95; Les-

ley Ginsberg, " 'The Willing Captive': Narrative Seduction and the Ideology of Love in Hawthorne's *A Wonder Book for Girls and Boys,*" *American Literature* 65:2 (June 1993): 255–73; and Nancy Bentley, "Slaves and Fauns: Hawthorne and the Uses of Primitivism," *ELH* 57 (1990): 901–37. Bentley's essay will be discussed in more detail below.

4. Here and throughout, I am using "evolution" to refer to the general theory of species transformation, not Darwin's theory of natural selection. As Peter J. Bowler has demonstrated, "The theory of the transmutation of species was not commonly called the 'theory of evolution' until late in the nineteenth century. . . . The terms 'evolution' or 'evolved' do not occur very often in Darwin's writings and although he seems to have been prepared to regard the overall development of life as an 'evolution,' he did not use the word in the sense of the evolution of one particular form from another." "The Changing Meaning of 'Evolution,' " *Journal of the History of Ideas* 36:1 (1975): 100–103.

5. Nathaniel Hawthorne, *The Centenary Edition of the Works of Nathaniel Hawthorne,* 23 vols., ed. William Charvat, Roy Harvey Pearce, and Claude M. Simpson (Columbus: Ohio State University Press, 1962–), 18:262–63; this edition is hereafter cited in the text as *CE,* followed by the volume and page number.

6. See, in addition to my discussion of this topic in the introduction, Thoreau's nearly paranoid reaction to John Field's chickens, which "stalked about the room like members of the family" and "stood and looked in my eye or pecked at my shoe significantly." *Walden* (1854; reprint, ed. J. Lyndon Shanley, Princeton: Princeton University Press, 1989), 204.

7. See the discussion of Thoreau's attitude toward dogs in the introduction.

8. See the discussion of pet keeping that appears in the introduction.

9. Hawthorne was born Nathaniel Hathorne, Jr. He added the "w" to his family name when he began to publish.

10. See *CE* 15:659 and 674.

11. As jarring as the idea of drowning Bunny may be to our sensibilities, it is important to note that Hawthorne's contemplation of this act actually aligns him with contemporary humane thinking, as drowning (done quickly, by an adult) was the method of euthanasia advocated by animal welfare activists. When the Hawthornes return to the Old Manse after a trip to Salem in November of 1842 and find their cat Pigwiggen "almost starved, and very melancholy," he considers euthanizing her by drowning to prevent her suffering (*CE* 15:659). Hawthorne's feelings on the subject become even more clear in his response to Mrs. Tappan's suggestion that Bunny "might be turned out into the woods, to shift for himself." Hawthorne writes: "There is something characteristic in this idea; it shows the sort of sensitiveness, that finds the pain and misery of other people disagreeable, just as a bad scent, but is perfectly at ease when once they are removed from her sphere. I suppose she would not for the world have killed Bunny, although she would have exposed him to the certainty of lingering starvation, without scruple or remorse" (*CE* 8:451).

12. Nathaniel Hawthorne, *The Marble Faun* (1860; reprint, vol. 4 of *The Centenary*

Edition of the Works of Nathaniel Hawthorne, and New York: Penguin, 1990), 235. The text and pagination of the *Centenary* and Penguin editions are identical. Further references are to these editions and appear in the text. As Lawrence Buell points out, several nineteenth-century readers of *The Marble Faun* claimed that Donatello was modeled on Thoreau, as each possessed the ability "to associate himself with the wild things of the forest." See *The Environmental Imagination: Thoreau, Nature Writing, and the Formation of American Culture* (Cambridge: The Belknap Press of Harvard University Press, 1995), 329–30. To me, such assertions seem less suggestive of any actual linkage between Donatello and Thoreau on Hawthorne's part, than they are of the efforts of Thoreau's acquaintances and supporters to downplay Thoreau's contrarian tendencies by drawing attention to those behaviors that appeared more socially acceptable. In the context of emerging ideas about the importance of kindness to animals, insisting, as Emerson did, that Thoreau "took foxes under his protection from the hunters" (quoted in Buell 330) made his bizarre relation to the wilderness appear more intelligible and more admirable. But Thoreau's own words leave us in doubt as to whether or not he would have acted as Emerson suggested. In *Walden,* Thoreau laments the fact that fewer boys take up hunting now than formerly, and he attributes this change "not to an increased humanity, but to an increased scarcity of game, for perhaps the hunter is the greatest friend of the animals hunted, not excepting the Humane Society" (211). In any event, I see significant differences between Thoreau's interest in associating with wild creatures on their turf and terms and Hawthorne's and Donatello's interests, which (in their ultimate expressions) involve the animals' abandonment of the wild in order to assume the status of pet (a condition anathema to Thoreau). For discussions of nineteenth-century efforts to construct a more socially acceptable Thoreau, see Buell, *Environmental Imagination,* 339–55, and Eric Lupfer, "The Emergence of American Nature Writing, 1860–1909: John Burroughs, Henry David Thoreau, and Houghton, Mifflin and Company" (Ph.D. diss., University of Texas at Austin, 2003), 105–14.

13. Richard Harter Fogle, *Hawthorne's Fiction: The Light and the Dark* (Norman: University of Oklahoma Press, 1952), 191. Evan Carton offers a lucid survey of the twentieth-century criticism treating *The Marble Faun* as an allegory for the Fall of Man and an illuminating discussion of the problems with these arguments in *"The Marble Faun": Hawthorne's Transformations* (New York: Twayne Publishers, 1992), 27–44.

14. Evan Carton, *"The Marble Faun": Hawthorne's Transformations,* 34.

15. On anti-Catholic sentiment in *The Marble Faun,* see Robert S. Levine, " 'Antebellum Rome' in *The Marble Faun,*" *American Literary History* 2:1 (Spring 1990): 19–38, and Carton, *"The Marble Faun": Hawthorne's Transformations,* 45–69. On the novel's treatment of racial mixing, see Bentley, "Slaves and Fauns: Hawthorne and the Uses of Primitivism," 901–37; Carton, *"The Marble Faun": Hawthorne's Transformations,* 97–121; and Blythe Ann Tellefsen, " 'The Case with My Dear Native Land': Nathaniel Hawthorne's Vision of America in *The Marble Faun,*" *Nineteenth-Century Literature* (March 2000): 455–79. On the novel's treatment of art and aesthetics, see chapter 7 of Richard H. Millington's *Practicing Romance: Narrative Form and Cultural Engagement*

in Hawthorne's Fiction (Princeton: Princeton University Press, 1992) and Carton, *"The Marble Faun": Hawthorne's Transformations,* 45–69. On *The Marble Faun* and the role of the literary artist in nineteenth-century culture, see Carton, *"The Marble Faun": Hawthorne's Transformations,* 70–96, and Emily Schiller, "The Choice of Innocence: Hilda in *The Marble Faun,*" *Studies in the Novel* 26:4 (Winter 1994): 372–91. For a discussion of the congruence between thermodynamic theory and the aesthetics and politics of *The Marble Faun,* see Martin Kevorkian, "'Within the Domain of Chaos': Nathaniel Hawthorne, Lucretian Physics, and Martial Logic," *Studies in the Novel* 31:2 (Summer 1999): 178–201. In "Dread and Desire: 'Europe' in Hawthorne's *The Marble Faun,*" *Essays in Literature* 21:1 (Spring 1994): 54–67, Udo Natterman analyzes the novel as a reflection of contemporary U.S. anxieties about the foreign.

16. Carton, *"The Marble Faun": Hawthorne's Transformations,* 39; Fogle, *Hawthorne's Fiction,* 191.

17. Richard H. Brodhead, *The School of Hawthorne* (New York: Oxford University Press, 1986), 77.

18. See Bentley, "Slaves and Fauns: Hawthorne and the Uses of Primitivism," 901–37, and Tellefsen, "The Case with My Dear Native Land," 455–79. Going further than Bentley, Tellefsen claims that *The Marble Faun* advances the argument that the racial inferiorities of African Americans pose ineluctable obstacles to their assimilation into U.S. culture.

19. Charles Darwin, *The Origin of Species* (1859; reprint, New York: Penguin, 1985), 271. Though Darwin did not ascribe to this theory generally, he allowed that it might be true in the case of the dog, which could, he thought, have descended from the wolf and the fox.

20. Peter J. Bowler, *Evolution: The History of an Idea* (1983; rev. ed., Berkeley: University of California Press, 1989), 56.

21. Charles White, *An Account of the Regular Gradation in Man, and in Different Animals and Vegetables, and from the Former to the Latter* (1799), quoted in Harriet Ritvo, *The Platypus and the Mermaid and Other Figments of the Classifying Imagination* (Cambridge: Harvard University Press, 1997), 92.

22. Robert Rosenblum and H. W. Janson, *Nineteenth-Century Art* (New York: Harry N. Adams, 1984), 468. Frémiet's 1859 sculpture was rejected by the salon and subsequently destroyed, but he produced another version of *Gorilla Carrying Off a Woman* in 1887, which was received enthusiastically. Films such as *King Kong* (1933; 1976) and *Mighty Joe Young* (1949; 1999) attest to continued interest in this theme.

23. Jan Bondeson and A. E. W. Miles, "Julia Pastrana, the Nondescript: An Example of Congenital, Generalized Hypertrichosis Terminalis with Gingival Hyperplasia," *American Journal of Medical Genetics* 47 (1993): 199.

24. See also Hawthorne's retelling of Europa's story in *Tanglewood Tales* (1853) and his story about the Minotaur (another human-animal hybrid) in the same volume (*CE* 7:234–64 and 183–212).

25. Hawthorne's discomfort with women who defied conventional gender roles

may also have contributed to his feelings about Pastrana. Since the Middle Ages, women who transgressed gender norms have been depicted either as monsters or as the breeders of monsters. See Gesa Mackenthun, "A Monstrous Race for Possession: Discourses of Monstrosity in *The Tempest* and Early British America," in *Writing and Race*, ed. Tim Youngs (New York: Longman, 1997), 52–79. And as Harriet Ritvo has explained, in the nineteenth century bearded women "were . . . appreciated as incipient hermaphrodites" and these "individuals of apparently mixed sex threatened to unsettle human gender categories" (*Platypus and the Mermaid*, 170–71). Evan Carton has argued that Hawthorne's sharp criticism of women who failed to conform to culturally sanctioned feminine roles reflected his own troubled sense that—in pursuing a poorly remunerative and house-bound career as a writer—he himself had violated codes of masculinity. See *"The Marble Faun": Hawthorne's Transformations*, 70–96.

26. Nathaniel Hawthorne, "Our Predecessor," *American Magazine of Useful and Entertaining Knowledge* 2:7 (March 1836): 312.

27. "The Female Orang Outang.—[Simia Satyrus, vel Satyrus Troglodytis]," *American Magazine of Useful and Entertaining Knowledge* 2:4 (December 1835): 143.

28. "Species of Men," *American Magazine of Useful and Entertaining Knowledge* 2:12 (August 1836): 515.

29. "Cuvier's Animal Kingdom," *American Magazine of Useful and Entertaining Knowledge* 2:12 (August 1836): 514.

30. "Mischievousness of Monkeys," *American Magazine of Useful and Entertaining Knowledge* 2:12 (August 1836): 485.

31. "Orang Outang, Or Wild Man of the Woods. / *Simia Satyrus of Linneus; Pitheus Satyrus of Cuvier*," *American Magazine of Useful and Entertaining Knowledge* 3:2 (November 1836): 53; "Orang-Outang. (*Satyrus.*)," *American Magazine of Useful and Entertaining Knowledge* 3:6 (March 1837): 246.

32. Hawthorne momentarily engages in a more sympathetic consideration of monkeys after a visit to London's Regent Park Zoo on September 8, 1855. The following day, Hawthorne wrote in his journal, "At the moment, I do not distinctly remember anything that interested me, except a sick monkey—a very large monkey, and elderly, he seemed to be, and with a rear worn quite bare, by much sitting upon it." A zookeeper offered the ailing animal food,

> But the poor monkey shook his head, slowly, and with the most pitiable expression I ever saw, at the same time extending his hand to take the keeper's, as if claiming his sympathy and friendship. By and by, the keeper (who was rather a surly fellow) essayed harsher measures, and insisted that the monkey should eat what had been brought for him; and hereupon ensued somewhat of a struggle. . . . Then the keeper scolded the monkey, and seizing him by one arm, drew him out of his little bedroom into the larger cage, upon which the wronged monkey began a loud, harsh, reproachful chatter, more expressive of a sense of injury than any words could be. Observing the spectators in front of the cage, he seemed to appeal to them, and

> addressed his chatter thitherward, and stretched out his long, lean arm, and black hand, between the bars, as if claiming the grasp of any one friend he might have in the whole world. (*CE* 21:314–15)

Yet even here his sympathies fail to override his original convictions about monkeys' grotesqueness. "In a future state of being" (i.e., in the afterlife), he writes at the end of this entry, "I think it will be one of my enquiries, in reference to the mysteries of this present state, why monkies [*sic*] were made. The Creator could not surely have meant to ridicule his own work. It might rather be supposed that Satan had perpetrated monkies, with a malicious purpose of parodying the master-piece of creation" (*CE* 21:315). The resemblance between humans and primates, Hawthorne concludes, must be the result of diabolical machination.

33. Lovejoy, *The Great Chain of Being* (1936; reprint, Cambridge: Harvard University Press, 2001), 59.

34. Georges Louis Leclerc, Count de Buffon, *Natural History, General and Particular,* vol. 4, trans. William Smellie (London: A. Strahan, and T. Cadell, 1791; facsimile reprint, Bristol, UK: Thoemmes Press, 2000), 2. See also the discussion of Buffon's *Natural History* in the introduction.

35. "The Female Orang Outang," 143; "The Dog Keeper," *American Magazine of Useful and Entertaining Knowledge* 2:4 (December 1835): 248.

36. "The Dog," *American Magazine of Useful and Entertaining Knowledge* 2:9 (May 1836): 397.

37. Anthony Trollope, "The Genius of Nathaniel Hawthorne," *North American Review* 129 (September 1879): 220–22, quoted in *The Merrill Studies in "The Marble Faun,"* ed. David B. Kesterson (Columbus, Ohio: Charles E. Merrill Publishing Company, 1971), 12.

38. Jean-Baptiste Lamarck, *Zoological Philosophy,* trans. Hugh Elliot (Chicago: University of Chicago Press, 1984), 126. Further references to this work appear in the text.

39. Chroniclers of evolutionary thought have long done injustice to Lamarck by insisting that his work was immediately discredited and forgotten and completely mischaracterizing the nature of Lamarck's hypothesis. Contrary to the accounts of him offered in most science textbooks and not a few more authoritative sources, Lamarck did not develop the theory of acquired characteristics. The belief that characteristics an organism developed during its lifetime could be passed on to its offspring was "universally accepted from the ancients to the nineteenth century" (Ernst Mayr, *The Growth of Biological Thought: Diversity, Evolution, and Inheritance,* Cambridge: The Belknap Press of Harvard University Press, 1982, 356). Lamarck's acceptance of this belief neither defined his theory of evolution, nor distinguished it from that of Darwin, who "never denied the possibility that the inheritance of acquired characters might act alongside natural selection in the evolutionary process" (Peter J. Bowler, "Lamarckism," in *Keywords in Evolutionary Biology,* ed. Evelyn Fox Keller and Elisabeth A. Lloyd, Cambridge: Harvard University Press, 1992, 189). This erroneous attri-

bution had, until fairly recently, completely eclipsed Lamarck's actual and highly significant contributions to nineteenth-century science. We now know that Lamarck's theory of *transformisme* had a continuous influence after its publication in 1809 and was certainly widely known in the 1850s. Ernst Mayr observes, "From the date of publication (1809) of Lamarck's *Philosophie zoologique* on, no one discussing species, faunas, distributions, fossils, extinction, or any other aspect of organic diversity could afford any longer to ignore the possibility of evolution. And it was not ignored, as the frequent references to Lamarck or to 'development' clearly document. It was because he was aware of the 'threat' of evolutionism that Lyell devoted so many chapters of the *Principles of Geology* to its refutation" (*The Growth of Biological Thought,* 391).

40. L. J. Jordanova, *Lamarck* (New York: Oxford University Press, 1984), 96.

41. Ibid., 84, 90–91.

42. See Harriet Ritvo, "Classification and Continuity in *The Origin of Species,*" in *Charles Darwin's "The Origin of Species": New Interdisciplinary Essays,* ed. David Amigoni and Jeff Wallace (New York: Manchester University Press, 1995), 62–63.

43. Charles Lyell, *Principles of Geology,* vol. 2 (1832; reprint, Chicago: University of Chicago Press, 1991), 26–27. Further references to this work appear in the text.

44. See Harriet Ritvo's discussion of domesticated animals in *The Platypus and the Mermaid,* 51–130

45. Peter Benes, "To the Curious: Bird and Animal Exhibitions in New England, 1716–1825," in *New England's Creatures: 1400–1900* (Boston: Boston University, 1995), 148.

46. Ibid., 156; Isaac W. Merrill's diary is quoted in ibid., 157.

47. "The Dog," 397.

48. "Species of Men," 515.

49. "Have Animals Souls?" *Putnam's Monthly Magazine* 7:40 (April 1856): 361–71. See also William Hosea Ballou, "Are the Lower Animals Approaching Man?" *North American Review* 145:372 (November 1887): 516–23; Rev. Charles Josiah Adams, *Where Is My Dog? Or, Is Man Alone Immortal?* (New York: Fowler and Wells, 1892).

50. [Robert Chambers,] *Vestiges of the Natural History of Creation* (1844; reprint, Chicago: University of Chicago Press, 1994), 347. Further references to this work appear in the text.

51. Adam Sedgwick, "'Vestiges of the Natural History of Creation,'" *The Edinburgh Review* 82:165 (July 1845): 11. Further references to this work appear in the text.

52. James A. Secord, introduction to *Vestiges of the Natural History of Creation,* [by Robert Chambers], xxvi.

53. Bowler, *Evolution,* 142.

54. While *Zoological Philosophy,* like *Vestiges,* was controversial, the former carried more authority by virtue of being authored by an internationally recognized scientist; *Vestiges,* in contrast, was published anonymously, and the identity of its author was not revealed until 1884.

55. Mayr, *The Growth of Biological Thought,* 357.

56. Carton, *"The Marble Faun": Hawthorne's Transformations,* 103.

57. In his discussion, Carton considers satyrs and fauns to be identical—the latter being only the Roman name for the former. Satyrs "were often confounded with the fauns" by the Roman poets, according to the 1910 edition of *Encyclopedia Britannica,* 11th ed. (New York: Encyclopaedia Brittanica, Inc.), 234. But the creatures were not identical, and Hawthorne, at least, did not consider them so. See note 59 below.

58. "The Female Orang Outang," 144. The other two articles are "Orang Outang, Or Wild Man of the Woods. / *Simia Satyrus of Linneus; Pitheus Satyrus of Cuvier,*" 3:2 (November 1836): 53, and "Orang-Outang. (*Satyrus.*)," 3:6 (March 1837): 246.

59. "The Pomegranate Seeds" clearly distinguishes between satyrs and fauns. The full passage tells us that, during her search for Proserpina, Ceres

> often . . . encountered fauns, who looked like sun-burnt country people, except that they had hairy ears, and little horns upon their foreheads, and the hinder legs of goats, on which they gambolled merrily about the woods and fields. They were a frolicksome kind of creature, but grew as sad as their cheerful dispositions would allow, when Ceres inquired for her daughter, and they had no good news to tell. But, sometimes, she came suddenly upon a rude gang of satyrs, who had faces like monkeys, and horses' tails behind them, and who were generally dancing in a very boisterous manner, with shouts of noisy laughter. When she stopt to question them, they would only laugh the louder, and make new merriment out of the lone woman's distress. How unkind of those ugly satyrs! (*CE* 7:310)

In this description, Hawthorne demonstrates his knowledge that, in earlier Greek art, satyrs appear old and ugly, with the ears and tail of a horse (and an erect phallus, though this detail, for obvious reasons, does not work its way into his children's story). Praxiteles' sculpture was, as Carton points out, originally titled *Resting Satyr,* and the statue that Hawthorne saw was in fact a Roman copy of this Greek work. Praxiteles' sculpture, however, marked a departure from the original artistic depiction of satyrs, in that his satyr was young, graceful, and handsome and had only vestigial animal traits. The incongruence between Praxiteles' statue and traditional conceptions of the satyr's appearance and character explains, most likely, subsequent generations' insistence on calling the statue *The Faun.* I have found no evidence that Hawthorne knew the original title of Praxiteles' work.

60. See Louise E. Robbins, *Elephant Slaves and Pampered Parrots: Exotic Animals in Eighteenth-Century Paris* (Baltimore: Johns Hopkins University Press, 2002), 130.

61. On Hawthorne's association of monkeys with the devil, see n. 32 above. In *The Marble Faun,* Hawthorne describes the priesthood as "pampered, sensual, with red and bloated cheeks, and carnal eyes" and attributes to them an "apparently . . . grosser development of animal life than most men" (411).

62. Carton, *"The Marble Faun": Hawthorne's Transformations,* 103.

63. See Charles Darwin, *The Descent of Man, and Selection in Relation to Sex* (1871; reprint, Princeton: Princeton University Press, 1981). The assertion in chapter 2 that

"the lower animals are excited by the same emotions as ourselves," for example, is supported first with a discussion of the range of emotions dogs and horses experience and an observation on the many and well-known anecdotes that testify to the "love of a dog for his master." In the next paragraph, Darwin shifts to a discussion of tender feelings of monkeys, which attributes to them the qualities long associated with dogs. "Monkeys," Darwin writes, "will also, according to Brehm, defend their master when attacked by any one" (39–41). The move from dogs to monkeys often occurs within the same sentence: "Every one has seen how jealous a dog is of his master's affection, if lavished on any other creature; and I have observed the same fact with monkeys" (41–42); "Animals manifestly enjoy excitement and suffer from ennui, as may be seen with dogs, and, according to Rengger, with monkeys" (42).

64. Charles Darwin, *The Expression of the Emotions in Man and Animals* (1872; reprint, New York: Oxford University Press, 1998), 116.

65. Carton, *"The Marble Faun": Hawthorne's Transformations,* 33.

66. Bowler, *Evolution,* 147, 82, 22, 82.

67. Ibid., 5, emphasis in original.

68. See Marion L. Kesselring, *Hawthorne's Reading: 1828–1850* (New York: New York Public Library, 1949), 49.

69. Among other factors, Hawthorne's own impromptu prayer to the cloud in the shape of a dog in *Mosses from an Old Manse* (discussed earlier in the chapter) indicates that his thoughts on this matter do not coincide with Hilda's.

70. While "Chiefly about War Matters" associates a group of fleeing slaves with animals (by comparing them, in one much-discussed passage, to fauns), the essay also positions animality as something with which all humans must contend. Several pages after the comparison of the escaping slaves to fauns, Hawthorne describes the captured white Confederate soldiers held prisoner by the Union Army in Harper's Ferry. Hawthorne's initial description of the prisoners echoes his descriptions of animals he observed in the London Zoological Gardens: the men "lay on heaps of straw, asleep, or, at all events, giving no sign of consciousness; others sat in the corners of the room, huddled close together, and staring with a lazy kind of interest at the visitors" (*CE* 23:428). "Almost to a man," Hawthorne continues, "they were simple bumpkin-like fellows . . . with faces singularly vacant of meaning" (*CE* 23:429). "It is my belief," he writes, "that not a single bumpkin of them all . . . had the remotest comprehension of what they had been fighting for, or how they had deserved to be shut up in that dreary hole; nor, possibly did they care to inquire into this latter mystery, but took it as a god-send to be . . . well warmed and well foddered to day, and without the necessity of bothering themselves about the possible hunger and cold of tomorrow. Their dark prison-life may have seemed to them the sunshine of all their lifetime" (*CE* 23:429).

Of all the men in this "semi-barbarous moral state," there was "one poor wretch, a wild beast of a man" who was "a horror to all beholders." This shocking individual had beaten to death, at the close of a battle, a wounded Northern soldier who had crawled to him "on hands and knees" begging for assistance. Hawthorne wonders to himself if the unmerciful soldier now "beheld a continual portraiture of his victim's horror-stricken agonies," but concludes: "I rather fancy, however, that his moral sense was yet too torpid to trouble him with such remorseful visions, and that, for his own part, he might have had very agreeable reminiscences of the soldier's death, if other eyes had not been bent reproachfully upon him and warned him that something was amiss" (*CE* 23:429–30). Unlike Donatello's murder of the Model, this murder awakens no latent moral sensibilities in the murderer. But despite the soldier's unregeneracy, Hawthorne insists on an unbroken continuity between him and civilized humankind, and expresses his hope for the regeneration of the rest of Southern whites: "He [the rebel soldier] was a wild beast, as I began with saying; an unsophisticated wild beast, while the rest of us are partially tamed, though still the scent of blood excites some of the savage instincts of our nature. What this wretch needed in order to make him capable of the degree of mercy and benevolence that exists in us, was simply such a measure of moral and intellectual developement [*sic*] as we have received; and, in my mind, the present war is so well justified by no other consideration as by the probability that it will free this class of southern whites from a thraldom, in which they scarcely begin to be responsible beings" (*CE* 23:430).

The best, though unexpected, result of the Civil War, Hawthorne suggests, will be the "humanization" of the animal-like white Southerners. Even the eminently civilized readers of the *Atlantic Monthly* ("the rest of us") are addressed as "partially tamed" beings whose "savage instincts" have been checked but not erased. We all, Hawthorne suggests, are like fauns in that the "coarser, animal portion of [our] nature might eventually be thrown into the back-ground, though never utterly expelled" (*Marble Faun,* 9).

71. Herbert Spencer, "Progress: Its Law and Cause" (1857; reprinted in *Essays: Scientific, Political, and Speculative,* by Herbert Spencer, London: Williams and Norgate, 1868, 3).

72. See notes 13 and 15 above. *The Marble Faun*'s treatment of the evolution from childhood to adulthood is discussed in Millington, *Practicing Romance,* 177–206, and Carton, *"The Marble Faun": Hawthorne's Transformations,* 70–96; the evolution from Catholicism to Puritanism and that of Old World authoritarian regimes into New World democracy are discussed in Levine, " 'Antebellum Rome' in *The Marble Faun*"; the evolution from Renaissance art to Protestant aesthetics is discussed in Carton, *"The Marble Faun": Hawthorne's Transformations,* 45–69.

73. Hawthorne's skepticism about the progressive nature of natural and social history represents a significant revision of an earlier position. In his 1852 campaign biography of Franklin Pierce, Hawthorne had expressed unbridled optimism in divine Providence and the inevitable progress of human civilization. Then, he wrote that the alternative view to organized abolition, which was "probably a wise one" (and which was definitely Pierce's),

> looks upon Slavery as one of those evils, which Divine Providence does not leave to be remedied by human contrivances, but which, in its own good time, by some

means impossible to be anticipated, but of the simplest and easiest operation, when all its uses shall have been fulfilled, it causes to vanish like a dream. There is no instance, in all history, of the human will and intellect having perfected any great moral reform by methods which it adapted to that end; but the progress of the world, at every step, leaves some evil or wrong on the path behind it, which the wisest of mankind, of their own set purpose, could never have found the way to rectify. (*CE* 23:352)

Here we see that Hawthorne's characteristic lack of faith in human "contrivances" is coupled with the insistence that "Divine Providence" will cause "evils" to "vanish like a dream"—that "the progress of the world, at every step, leaves some evil or wrong on the path behind it." By the end of the decade, what Hawthorne found to be vanishing was not slavery but his belief that history followed some ever-improving path. In "Chiefly about War Matters" (1862), for example, his description of the Union troops at General McClellan's camp begins optimistically enough, but quickly slips into an exposition of his fears that rather than a linear path of steadily diminishing evils, the trail of civilization seems to be a maze in which we are liable at any moment to return to our starting point.

> The enervating effects of centuries of civilization vanish at once, and leave these young men to enjoy a life of hardship, and the exhilarating sense of danger—to kill men blamelessly, or to be killed gloriously—and to be happy in following out their native instincts of destruction. . . . One touch of nature makes not only the whole world, but all time akin. Set men face to face, with weapons in their hands, and they are as ready to slaughter one another, now, after playing at peace and good-will for so many years, as in the rudest ages, that never heard of peace-societies, and thought no wine so delicious as what they quaffed from an enemy's skull! . . . We measure our advances from barbarism, and find ourselves just here! (*CE* 23:421–22)

74. Georges Cuvier, "Biographical Memoir of M. de Lamarck" (1836), reprint, *Zoological Philosophy,* by Jean-Baptiste Lamarck, trans. Hugh Elliot (Chicago: University of Chicago Press, 1984), 434. Further references to this work appear in the text. See also Jordanova, *Lamarck,* 102.

75. Within the novel Hawthorne also attacks the attitudes espoused by Cuvier, in his treatment of Kenyon. Like Cuvier, Kenyon (at least initially) believes that things should not transgress fixed categories. He dislikes the statue *Dying Gladiator* because he finds himself "getting weary and annoyed that the man should be such a length of time leaning on his arm, in the very act of death. . . . Flitting moments—imminent emergencies—imperceptible intervals between two breaths—ought not to be incrusted with the eternal repose of marble; in any sculptural subject, there should be a moral standstill, since there must of necessity be a physical one. Otherwise, it is like flinging a block of marble up into the air, and, by some trick or enchantment, causing it to stick there. You feel that it ought to come down, and are dissatisfied that it does not

obey the natural law." Miriam responds, "You think that sculpture should be a sort of fossilizing process" (16). Kenyon's preference for "fossilizing" art further links him to Cuvier, as Cuvier was and is regarded as the father of paleontology. Indeed Kenyon's artistic activity even begins to look like paleontological practice when he digs up an "earth-stained" and "slightly corroded" statue of the Venus de' Medici from an excavation site outside of Rome (423). The irreconcilability of Cuvierian aesthetics and Hawthorne's ideal of artistic creativity is also illustrated in Kenyon's initial failure to sculpt a bust of Donatello: "If, at one sitting, he caught a glimpse of *what appeared to be a genuine and permanent trait,* it would probably be less perceptible, on a second occasion, and perhaps have vanished entirely, at a third. So evanescent a show of character threw the sculptor into despair" (270–71, emphasis added). Kenyon succeeds only after he gives up "all pre-conceptions about the character of his subject" (271). Finally, in the Carnival Kenyon is surrounded and attacked by a "whole host of absurd figures" (446) that embody the kind of permeability between species against which Cuvier inveighed: "A biped, with an ass's snout" (445), "Clowns and parti-colored harlequins; orang-outangs; bear-headed, bull-headed, and dog-headed individuals . . . and all other imaginable kinds of monstrosity and exaggeration" (446).

Hawthorne may have considered satirizing Cuvier in his fiction as early as 1842. A notebook entry for June 1 of that year records the following idea for a story: "A young man finds a portion of the skeleton of a Mammoth; he begins by degrees to become interested in completing it; searches round the world for the means of doing so; spends youth and manhood in this pursuit; and in old age has nothing to show for his life, but this skeleton" (*CE* 8:243). One of Cuvier's great claims to fame was his naming and study of the mastodon, as Hawthorne himself notes in "Extinct Animals," *American Magazine of Useful and Entertaining Knowledge* 2:10 (June 1836): 407–8.

76. Lovejoy, *The Great Chain of Being,* 43.

77. Jonathan Edwards, *On the End in Creation,* quoted in ibid., 43–44.

78. Lovejoy, *The Great Chain of Being,* 296.

79. See Evan Carton's discussion of the connections among Miriam's art, patricide, and Hawthorne's choice of an artistic career in *"The Marble Faun": Hawthorne's Transformations,* 70–98.

80. Lovejoy explains that when "the idea of God . . . [became] predominantly this-worldly, tending towards a fusion with the conception of 'Nature' infinitely various in its manifestations and endlessly active in the production of differing kinds of beings. . . . When the Chain of Being—in other words, the entire created universe—came to be explicitly conceived, no longer as complete once for all and everlastingly the same in the kinds of its components, but as gradually evolving from a less to a greater degree of fullness and excellence, the question inevitably arose whether a God eternally complete and immutable could be supposed to be manifested in such a universe" (*The Great Chain of Being,* 316–17).

Chapter Three. The Domestic ~~Angel~~ Animal

Epigraph: Harriet Beecher Stowe, *My Wife and I; Or, Harry Henderson's History*, vol. 12 of *The Writings of Harriet Beecher Stowe* (New York: AMS Press, 1967), 322.

1. Arthur Riss, "Racial Essentialism and Family Values in *Uncle Tom's Cabin,*" *American Quarterly* 46:4 (December 1994): 529. Further references to this work appear in the text.

2. Elizabeth Barnes, *States of Sympathy: Seduction and Democracy in the American Novel* (New York: Columbia University Press, 1997), 92. Further references to this work appear in the text. Barnes's reading is both indebted to and critical of Karen Sánchez-Eppler's "Bodily Bonds: The Intersecting Rhetorics of Feminism and Abolition," in *Touching Liberty: Abolition, Feminism, and the Politics of the Body* (Berkeley: University of California Press, 1993). While Sánchez-Eppler argues (in Barnes's words) that "sentimental fiction relies on the body as the privileged site of communication," Barnes counters that "both the physical and the fictional body must always be read as projections of the sympathetic reader" (95). "Sentimental works," Barnes insists "do not differentiate between real and fictional characters for the simple reason that, based on the principles of sympathy, other people become real to us through our projected sentiments, not by their objective presence in the world" (96). In Stowe's work, Barnes contends, "bodies are treated as primarily affective rather than material" (96).

3. See, for example, Peter Stoneley's "Sentimental Emasculations: *Uncle Tom's Cabin* and *Black Beauty,*" *Nineteenth-Century Literature* 54:1 (June 1999): 53–72, and Karen Sánchez-Eppler's *Touching Liberty.* Stoneley argues that black male bodies in *Uncle Tom's Cabin* are associated with animality and "an unavoidable physiological destiny" (61)—thus implying that other bodies are not. Though critics have traditionally argued that Stowe assigns only African American characters "animal" bodies whose influences they cannot escape, the list of those to whom Stowe allegedly consigns to their embodied selves is growing. For example, in "Benevolent Maternalism and Physically Disabled Figures: Dilemmas of Female Embodiment in Stowe, Davis, and Phelps," *American Literature* 68:3 (September 1996): 555–87, Rosemarie Garland Thompson suggests that novels by Harriet Beecher Stowe, Rebecca Harding Davis, and Elizabeth Stuart Phelps define their disembodied, benevolent, and white heroines who "stand as apotheoses of womanly physicality" (569) against physically disabled figures who function as "the perilously corporeal female Other" (558) and "whose dependence is secured by disability, blackness, and/or lower-class status" (565). Discussing *Oldtown Folks,* Kathryn R. Kent argues that only the confirmed spinster Miss Asphyxia and "people of color . . . embody 'animality' or brute force." "'Single White Female': The Sexual Politics of Spinsterhood in Harriet Beecher Stowe's *Oldtown Folks,*" *American Literature* 69:1 (March 1997): 49.

Sánchez-Eppler argues that Stowe's "celebration of Tom's soul serves to erase his flesh" (47). Like other antislavery writers, Stowe, she contends, saw the "obliteration of black bodies as the only solution to the problem of slavery" (48). These ideas about

Stowe's erasure of black embodiment and sexuality can be traced back to James Baldwin's scurrilous "Everybody's Protest Novel" (1949), which claims: "Here, black equates with evil and white with grace; if, being mindful of the necessity of good works, she could not cast out the blacks—a wretched, huddled mass, apparently, claiming, like an obsession, her inner eye—she could not embrace them either without purifying them of sin. She must cover their intimidating nakedness, robe them in white, the garments of salvation; only thus could she herself be delivered from ever-present sin, only thus could she bury, as St. Paul demanded, 'the carnal man, the man of the flesh.' Tom, therefore, her only black man, has been robbed of his humanity and divested of his sex" (reprinted in *Uncle Tom's Cabin: A Norton Critical Edition,* ed. Elizabeth Ammons, New York: Norton, 1994, 498).

4. Sánchez-Eppler, *Touching Liberty,* 27; Robert S. Levine, *Martin Delany, Frederick Douglass, and the Politics of Representative Identity* (Chapel Hill: University of North Carolina Press, 1997), 146.

5. Michael D. Pierson has recently examined the arguments against slavery contained in *The Minister's Wooing* (1859) and *Agnes of Sorrento* (1862), countering the long-standing belief that, in writing these New England novels, Stowe abandoned her concern with slavery to address issues of gender and religion. By analyzing the ways in which *Wooing* and *Sorrento* echo the antislavery arguments circulating in the late 1850s and early 1860s, Pierson demonstrates that "Stowe remained engaged with antislavery politics throughout the last years of slavery in the United States" (22). However, Pierson's argument is that these two novels contain an extension of the antislavery arguments that are central to *Uncle Tom* and *Dred.* He does not suggest that examining *Wooing* or *Pearl* fundamentally challenges the understanding of Stowe's position on race or slavery derived from study of her earlier works, nor does he focus on her conception of race or racial difference per se. See "Antislavery Politics in Harriet Beecher Stowe's *The Minister's Wooing* and *The Pearl of Orr's Island,*" *American Nineteenth Century History* 3:2 (Summer 2002): 1–24.

6. Susan Marie Neurnberg, "The Rhetoric of Race," in *The Stowe Debate: Rhetorical Strategies in Uncle Tom's Cabin,* ed. Mason I. Lowance, Jr., Ellen E. Westbrook, R. C. DeProspo (Amherst: University of Massachusetts Press, 1994), 256–57. Further references to this work appear in the text.

7. See Robert J. C. Young, *Colonial Desire: Hybridity in Theory, Culture, and Race* (New York: Routledge, 1995).

8. Neurnberg, "The Rhetoric of Race," 267.

9. Levine, *Martin Delany, Frederick Douglass, and the Politics of Representative Identity,* 146–48.

10. Harriet Beecher Stowe, "Sojourner Truth, the Libyan Sibyl," *Atlantic Monthly* 11 (April 1863): 480.

11. Hawthorne states that, after viewing the band of fleeing slaves, his "prevalent idea was, that, whoever may be benefitted by the results of this war, it will not be the present generation of negroes, the childhood of whose race is now gone forever, and

who must henceforth fight a hard battle with the world, on very unequal terms. On behalf of my own race, I am glad, and can only hope that an inscrutable Providence means good to both parties." *The Centenary Edition of the Works of Nathaniel Hawthorne*, 23 vols., ed. William Charvat, Roy Harvey Pearce, and Claude M. Simpson (Columbus: Ohio State University Press, 1962–): 23:420. See the discussion of "Chiefly about War Matters" in chapter 2, nn. 70, 73.

12. Harriet Beecher Stowe, "Our Dogs," reprinted in *Queer Little People* (1867; *Stories and Sketches for the Young,* vol. 16 of *The Writings of Harriet Beecher Stowe,* New York: AMS Press, Inc., 1967, 66). Further references to *Queer Little People* are to this edition and appear in the text.

13. Harriet Beecher Stowe, *My Wife and I,* 439. Further references to this work appear in the text.

14. Harriet Beecher Stowe, *Poganuc People: Their Loves and Lives* (1879; reprint, Hartford, CT: The Stowe-Day Foundation, 1987), 40.

15. Stowe, *Queer Little People,* 110.

16. Ibid., 114–20. On natural history and children's reading, see Harriet Ritvo, "Learning from Animals: Natural History for Children in the Eighteenth and Nineteenth Centuries," *Children's Literature* 13 (1985): 72–93.

17. See Stowe's "Hum, the Son of Buz," in *Queer Little People,* 49–57. In 1869, Stowe published an article supporting the newly formed animal welfare organizations in *Hearth and Home* (January 2, 1869), 24. Another early reference to humane societies appears in Henry David Thoreau's 1854 *Walden*: "perhaps the hunter is the greatest friend of the animals hunted, not excepting the Humane Society" (ed. J. Lyndon Shanley, Princeton: Princeton University Press, 1989, 211). For more on the rise of animal welfare organizations in the United States, see the introduction.

18. Harriet Beecher Stowe, "Dogs and Cats," *Queer Little People,* 107–8.

19. Matthew Senior, " 'When the Beasts Spoke': Animal Speech and Classical Reason in Descartes and La Fontaine," in *Animal Acts: Configuring the Human in Western History,* ed. Jennifer Ham and Matthew Senior (New York: Routledge, 1997), 62.

20. Keith Thomas, *Man and the Natural World: Changing Attitudes in England: 1500–1800* (1983; New York: Oxford University Press, 1996), 33.

21. Harriet Beecher Stowe, "A Talk about Birds," in *Our Charley and the Stories Told Him,* reprinted in vol. 16 of *The Writings of Harriet Beecher Stowe,* 332, emphasis in original.

22. Harriet Beecher Stowe, *The Minister's Wooing* (1859; reprint, Hartford, CT: The Stowe-Day Foundation, 1994), 360. Further references to this work appear in the text.

23. Harriet Beecher Stowe, *Dred: A Tale of the Great Dismal Swamp* (1856; reprint, Edinburgh: Edinburgh University Press, 1999), 359.

24. Harriet Beecher Stowe, "Our Country Neighbors," *Queer Little People,* 65. Prior to its publication in *Queer Little People,* this essay appeared in the juvenile periodical *Our Young Folks.*

25. Harriet Beecher Stowe, "The Grand Tour Up River," originally published in *Christian Union* in 1872 and reprinted in *Palmetto Leaves* (1873; reprint, Gainesville: University of Florida Press, 1999), 258–61, emphasis in original. Further references to this work appear in the text.

26. Stowe, *Dred,* 560. Dred's conviction that "the elect shall talk with the birds and beasts" after the day of judgment reflects the long-standing Christian belief (discussed in the introduction) that humans and animals lived in perfect harmony and understanding in the Garden of Eden.

27. Harriet Beecher Stowe, *We and Our Neighbors; Or, the Records of an Unfashionable Street* (1875; reprinted in vol. 13 of *The Writings of Harriet Beecher Stowe*), 296.

28. Harriet Beecher Stowe, *A Dog's Mission, or, The Story of Old Avery House, and Other Stories* (1884; reprinted in vol. 16 of *The Writings of Harriet Beecher Stowe*), 259.

29. Harriet Beecher Stowe, "Bodily Religion: A Sermon on Good Health" (1868; reprinted in vol. 8 of *The Writings of Harriet Beecher Stowe*), 344. Further references to this work appear in the text.

30. Harriet Beecher Stowe, *Little Foxes* (1865; reprinted in vol. 14 of *The Writings of Harriet Beecher Stowe*), 352–53. Further references to this work appear in the text.

31. Carroll Smith-Rosenberg and Charles Rosenberg, "The Female Animal: Medical and Biological Views of Woman and Her Role in Nineteenth-Century America," *Journal of American History* 60 (September 1973): 333–34.

32. Ibid., 335. As the authors explain, nineteenth-century medical experts believed that "any imbalance, exhaustion, infection, or other disorders of the reproductive organs could cause pathological reactions in parts of the body seemingly remote" (335).

33. See *Primary Geography for Children, on an Improved Plan with Eleven Maps and Numerous Engravings* (Cincinnati: Corey and Fairbank, 1833).

34. See Harriet Beecher Stowe, *The Pearl of Orr's Island: A Story of the Coast of Maine* (1862; reprint, Boston: Houghton Mifflin, 2001); *Oldtown Folks* (1869; reprint, New Brunswick: Rutgers University Press, 1987); and *Pink and White Tyranny: A Society Novel* (1871; reprinted in vol. 11 of *The Writings of Harriet Beecher Stowe*). "The Laborers of the South" appeared in the *Christian Era* in 1872 and was republished the following year in Stowe's *Palmetto Leaves.* Citations for other texts appear above.

35. Lydia Huntley Sigourney, *Letters to Mothers,* quoted in Ann Douglas, *The Feminization of American Culture* (New York: Alfred A. Knopf, 1977; London: Papermac, 1996), 75.

36. For additional evidence of this point, see the description of Moses and Mara's Latin lessons in *Pearl of Orr's Island* and the description of Tina's training by Miss Asphyxia in *Oldtown Folks.*

37. Stowe undoubtedly spoke from personal experience on the issue of blame assigned to mothers for children's shortcomings. Most of the Stowes' own children chose paths that she and Calvin certainly would not have chosen for them. By the late 1850s her son Fred had a serious problem with alcoholism, and early in the summer of 1864 (shortly before "Intolerance" was published in the *Christian Union*) her son

Charley ran away from boarding school and took a job as a sailor (Joan D. Hedrick, *Harriet Beecher Stowe: A Life,* New York: Oxford University Press, 1994, 308–9).

38. In discussing Stowe's strategic essentialism, I am not suggesting that Stowe uses essentialism in the way that Gayatri Spivak advocates in "Subaltern Studies: Deconstructing Historiography," *In Other Worlds: Essays in Cultural Politics* (New York: Methuen, 1987), 197–221, and in a subsequent interview with Ellen Rooney, "In a Word: Interview," *Outside in the Teaching Machine* (New York: Routledge, 1993), 1–23. In these pieces, Spivak proposes that it is sometimes necessary for activist intellectuals to adopt "what may seem to be essentialist positions" for the purposes of political mobilization, even though they believe positivist essentialism to be "theoretically nonviable" ("Interview," 3; "Subaltern," 207). Stowe does not share Spivak's suspicion of foundationalist epistemology.

39. Stowe acknowledges the differences within as well as among breeds of dogs. Both Prince and Rover in "Our Dogs" are Newfoundlands, but they have very different "personalities."

40. Barnes's quote continues: "Insofar as democracy implies the representation of individual difference, sentimental politics reveals itself to be a politics of affinity rather than of democracy. Individual material differences are elided through models of sympathy that teach readers to view other 'selves' as projections of their own and to care for others in proportion to how convincingly those others can be shown as related to oneself" (98).

41. Stowe's refusal to believe in a hierarchy among humans parallels, in many ways, her refusal to schematize her world according to the hierarchical models of either the Great Chain of Being or Enlightenment science.

42. Many readers remain stubbornly wedded to the belief that Stowe wanted an all-white America, despite recent studies of *Dred* that contradict that notion. The best of these, Robert Levine's chapter, "The African American Presence in Stowe's *Dred,*" in *Martin Delany, Frederick Douglass, and the Politics of Representative Identity,* reads *Dred* "as an African American–inspired revision of *Uncle Tom's Cabin*" (146). There Levine thoroughly debunks the theory that Stowe wanted all Africans to emigrate from the United States. *Dred,* he argues, "explodes critical myths about her purported blindness to African American realities" (147). Levine's close reading of the novel reveals that the portrayal of Tiff "mocks the notion of blood as a determinant of character" (157). He points out that "Milly's social-reform work in New York City . . . conveys [Stowe's] post-1852 conviction that the free blacks did have an important role to play in the United States" (173). And he convincingly reads Tiff and Milly's transracial love as a sign of Stowe's hopefulness for racial integration (174).

43. As Susan L. Roberson has revealed, Warner's original manuscript for *The Wide, Wide World* included several scenes—later excised because of her publisher's complaints about the novel's length—that draw attention on the intersection between racial and gendered politics. See "Ellen Montgomery's Other Friend: Race Relations in an Expunged Episode of Warner's *Wide, Wide World,*" *ESQ* 45:1:1–31.

44. Harriet Beecher Stowe, *Uncle Tom's Cabin* (1852; reprint, New York: Norton, 1994), 196.

45. Elsewhere, Stowe insists that any similarities between blacks and animals were produced by the treatment to which whites subjected them. Blacks are not brutes, but humans who have been "imbruted": "treated in every way like brutes, [the slaves on Legree's plantation] had sunk as nearly to their level as it was possible for human beings to do" (*Uncle Tom's Cabin,* 301).

Chapter Four. Animal Justice

Epigraphs: Mark Twain, *Pudd'nhead Wilson's Calendar for 1894* (New York: Century Company, 1893); Charles W. Chesnutt, *The Quarry* (Princeton: Princeton University Press, 1999), 58–59.

1. Elizabeth Dodd, "Forum on Literatures of the Environment," *PMLA* 114:5 (October 1999): 1095. Other observations of the relative absence of black writers from literature and environment studies appear in Cheryll Glotfelty's introduction to *The Ecocriticism Reader: Landmarks in Literary Ecology,* ed. Cheryll Glotfelty and Harold Fromm (Athens: The University of Georgia Press, 1996), xxv, and the introduction to *The Norton Book of Nature Writing,* ed. Robert Finch and John Elder (college edition, New York: Norton, 2002), 17.

2. Lawrence Buell, *The Environmental Imagination: Thoreau, Nature Writing, and the Formation of American Culture* (Cambridge: The Belknap Press of Harvard University Press, 1995), 18. In his recent examination of antipastoralism in Frederick Douglass's 1845 *Narrative,* Michael Bennett argues convincingly that "a main current within African American culture has, from Frederick Douglass to Toni Morrison, expressed a profound antipathy toward the ecological niches usually focused on in ecocriticism: pastoral space and wilderness" ("Anti-Pastoralism, Frederick Douglass, and the Nature of Slavery," in *Beyond Nature Writing: Expanding the Boundaries of Ecocriticism,* ed. Karla Armbruster and Kathleen R. Wallace, Charlottesville: University of Virginia Press, 2001, 208). For a discussion of factors that made nineteenth-century women of color unlikely to write about their affinities with wild animals, see Vera Norwood, in *Made from This Earth: American Women and Nature* (Chapel Hill: University of North Carolina Press, 1993), especially the chapter, "Writing Animal Presence: Nature in Euro-American, African-American, and American Indian Fiction" (172–208).

3. Dodd, "Forum on Literatures of the Environment," 1095.

4. Bennett, "Anti-Pastoralism, Frederick Douglass, and the Nature of Slavery," 195.

5. Edward Bruce Hamley, *Our Poor Relations: A Philozoic Essay* (Boston: J. E. Tilton and Company), 1872.

6. See, for example, Melvin Dixon, *Ride Out the Wilderness: Geography and Identity in Afro-American Literature* (Urbana: University of Illinois Press, 1987), and Michael Bennett, "Anti-Pastoralism, Frederick Douglass, and the Nature of Slavery."

7. James Turner, *Reckoning with the Beast: Animals, Pain, and Humanity in the Victorian Mind* (Baltimore: Johns Hopkins University Press, 1980), 54.

8. Angell also replaced *The Liberator's* cross-holding redeemer figure with an angel, a move that illustrated both Angell's sense of the divine dimensions of the SPCA cause and his proclivities for wild self-aggrandizement. In an even more dramatic allusion to Garrison's periodical, the British Union for the Abolition of Vivisection titled their newsletter, begun in 1898, *The Abolitionist,* and then subsequently changed its name to *The Liberator.* See Marjorie Spiegel, *The Dreaded Comparison: Human and Animal Slavery* (New York: Mirror Books, 1996), 100–101.

9. C. C. Buel, "Henry Bergh and His Work," *Scribner's Monthly* 17 (April 1879): 884. Angell's *Our Dumb Animals* even attempted to retroactively claim Lincoln himself as a supporter of the humane cause. The May 1903 edition of the periodical features a large picture of Lincoln with the caption: "A man who never in his whole life was present at a *gambling* football game—or a *gambling* polo game—or a *gambling* steeple-chase—or ever thought it *fun* to wound or kill harmless creatures" (35:12:145, emphasis in original). This praise for Lincoln was also intended as a criticism of the current president, Theodore Roosevelt, who engaged in all of these activities.

10. *"To Be an Author": Letters of Charles W. Chesnutt, 1889–1905,* ed. Joseph R. McElrath, Jr., and Robert C. Leitz III (Princeton: Princeton University Press, 1997), 162. *Uncle Tom's Cabin* had long been both a favorite book of Charles W. Chesnutt and a personal symbol of his literary ambitions; see Helen M. Chesnutt, *Charles Waddell Chesnutt: Pioneer of the Color Line* (Chapel Hill: University of North Carolina Press, 1952), 10. In a journal entry recorded when he was twenty-three and still unpublished, Chesnutt mused, "why could not such a man [like himself], if he possessed the same ability, write a far better book about the South than Judge Tourgee or Mrs. Stowe has written?" (*The Journals of Charles W. Chesnutt,* ed. Richard H. Brodhead, Durham: Duke University Press, 1993, 125). In 1900, John P. Green (state representative in Ohio and cousin of Chesnutt), either by chance or perhaps out of awareness of his cousin's regard for Stowe, compared *The House Behind the Cedars* (1900) to *Uncle Tom.* Chesnutt responded with voluble thanks, writing: "If I could write a book that would stir the waters in any appreciable degree like that famous book, I would feel that I had vindicated my right to live & the right of a whole race" (*"To Be an Author,"* 156). Thus, when Chesnutt's editors at Houghton Mifflin wrote to him of their plans to promote his new novel, *The Marrow of Tradition* (1901), by comparing it to *Uncle Tom,* he was delighted. "There is to be a splendid production of *Uncle Tom's Cabin* at the Boston Theatre for the next two weeks," his editors wrote on October 21, 1901, "and beside the regular advertising, we are taking a page in their programme connecting your book with *Uncle Tom's Cabin* in such a way as to encourage the sale of it, we hope" (quoted in Helen Chesnutt, *Charles Waddell Chesnutt,* 175). Chesnutt promptly replied that it would be "very gratifying" to see his novel "lodged in the popular mind as the legitimate successor of *Uncle Tom's Cabin*" (*"To Be an Author,"* 162).

11. The first of the follow-ups to *Uncle Tom's Cabin* appeared before the novel was

even fully in print. While *Uncle Tom's Cabin* was still being serialized in *The National Era,* John P. Owens of Baltimore produced a proslavery drama titled *The Southern Uncle Tom,* which repudiated the abolitionist argument of Stowe's text. Textual responses to the novel ranged from jubilantly pro-abolitionist poems, with which Northern newspapers were sprinkled, to acrid antiabolitionist novels, such as *Aunt Phillis's Cabin, Or, Southern Life as It Is* (1852), *Uncle Tom in England* (1852), *Uncle Tom's Cabin in Ruins* (1853), and *Uncle Robin in His Cabin in Virginia and Tom Without One in Boston* (1853), to name only a few. However, spin-offs of *Uncle Tom's Cabin* were not limited to literary and dramatic formats. Stowe's novel inspired a spate of poetry and sheet music (both lyric and instrumental), as well as several dioramas, a card game, children's picture books, and commemorative plates, spoons, bowls, ladies' scarves, and figurines made of china bisque. See Stephen A. Hirsch, "Uncle Tomitudes: The Popular Reaction to *Uncle Tom's Cabin,*" *Studies in the American Renaissance* (1978), 303–30.

12. See Harriet Beecher Stowe, *Uncle Tom's Cabin* (1852; New York: Norton, 1994), and Anna Sewell, *Black Beauty* (1877; New York: Penguin, 1994). At the opening of each text, the black hero (Black Beauty in Sewell and Uncle Tom in Stowe) contentedly labors under a benevolent and paternal country master. Unexpected hardship soon launches each protagonist out of his domestic circle and into the marketplace. There he is initially sold to a very wealthy master who treats him well, even though that relationship lacks the extreme intimacy shared with the first master. Eventually both Beauty and Tom end up on downward trajectories in which they are sold at public auction, separated from family, and finally purchased by taskmasters who intend to work them to death. Along the way, Beauty encounters several characters with analogs in *Uncle Tom.* Like Topsy, the horse Ginger was separated from her mother before her memory and subjected to such physical torture that she now disobeys her masters despite any amount of beating. Cab boss Nicholas Skinner shares Simon Legree's belief in a capitalist ethic unmediated by human sympathy. (But while Legree can't "sell dead niggers" [363], Skinner can work his horses as hard and "as long as they'll go and then sell 'em for what they'll fetch, at the knackers or elsewhere" [254].) At the end of his respective story, each hero is reunited with a male representative from his former "home" who was just a child at the time the protagonist had left it. In Beauty's case, it is the adult Joe Green, and for Tom, the matured George Shelby. Shelby cannot save Tom from his tragic end, but Beauty is returned to a loving, permanent home from which he will never be sold again.

My reading of *Black Beauty* differs from that of Moira Ferguson and Peter Stoneley, in that I see Sewell drawing on ideas about slaves to talk about horses, whereas Ferguson and Stoneley suggest that Sewell was not, ultimately, as interested in horses as she was in issues of race and gender. As I explain in the introduction, one of the aims of this book is to correct the misreadings resulting from this modern tendency to read animals as primarily a screen for something else. See Moira Ferguson, "Breaking in Englishness: *Black Beauty* and the Politics of Gender, Race and Class," *Women: A Cul-*

tural Review 5:1 (Spring 1994): 34–52; Peter Stoneley, "Sentimental Emasculations: *Uncle Tom's Cabin* and *Black Beauty*," *Nineteenth-Century Literature* 54:1 (June 1999): 53–72.

13. George T. Angell, *Autobiographical Sketches and Personal Recollections* (Boston: American Humane Education Society, [1892?]), 94–99 and 36 of the second pagination series. *Black Beauty* was originally published in England in 1877, but the book sold slowly at first. Having no idea how popular her book would become, Sewell sold the novel outright for twenty pounds to a small publishing house in Norwich, England. The firm, which specialized in religious works, did little to promote the text, and Sewell herself died three months after its publication. In the 1880s, MSPCA president George Angell began searching for a book that would do for animal welfare what *Uncle Tom's Cabin* had done for abolition, and he printed ads soliciting the production of such a work. Angell found what he was looking for when, in early 1890, an American who had read *Black Beauty* forwarded Angell a copy of the text.

14. Henry Louis Gates, Jr., *The Signifying Monkey: A Theory of Afro-American Literary Criticism* (New York: Oxford University Press, 1988), 123.

15. As I discuss in more detail later in this chapter, both animal trickster figures from African American folklore and the mode of signifyin(g) associated with them have been acknowledged to be central to Chesnutt's craft. But as those animal figures are fully anthropomorphized, to observe that characters such as Uncle Julius are modeled on Br'er Rabbit hardly implies a connection between blacks and animals per se.

16. *The Narrative of the Life of Frederick Douglass,* reprinted in *The Classic Slave Narratives,* ed. Henry Louis Gates, Jr. (New York: Mentor, 1987), 255, 271, 282.

17. This rhetorical strategy also appears in Douglass's fiction. In his 1853 novel *The Heroic Slave,* Madison Washington's opening soliloquy turns on the same logic of human superiority. "What, then, is life to me?" the enslaved protagonist exclaims, "it is aimless and worthless, and worse than worthless. Those birds, perched on yon swinging boughs . . . are still my superiors. . . . How mean a thing am I. That accursed and crawling snake, that miserable reptile . . . is freer and better off than I. . . . He is my superior, and scorns to own me as his master, or to stop to take my blows. When he saw my uplifted arm, he darted beyond my reach, and turned to give me battle. I dare not do as much as that" (reprinted in *The Classic African-American Novels,* ed. William L. Andrews, New York: Mentor, 1990, 26–27). Here, meaningful human existence is registered as the ability to have dominion over animals.

18. Eric Sundquist, *To Wake the Nations: Race in the Making of American Literature* (Cambridge: The Belknap Press of Harvard University Press, 1993), 315–16 and 373–74. Writing on "The Conjurer's Revenge," for example, Sundquist argues convincingly that the incomplete transformation of Primus from a mule back into a man at the story's end (leaving him with a clubfoot) symbolizes both the dehumanizing aspects of slavery and the social inequities of the late-nineteenth-century South. "Crippled by generations of bondage," Sundquist writes, "not yet fully a 'man,' first legally defined as a laboring animal and still characterized as 'bestial' by postbellum

racist theory, the Negro has not yet fully escaped the white man's legal conjure known first as slavery and now as Jim Crow" (374). Regarding "Tobe's Tribulations" (in which a black man seeking to escape slavery is transformed permanently into a frog) Sundquist observes, "Like other animal transformation tales in Chesnutt's repertoire, 'Tobe's Tribulation' plays upon the degrading effects of slavery and contemporary racist laws of natural hierarchy: Tobe is still waiting after forty years to be turned back into a man" (315).

19. Charles W. Chesnutt, "The Bouquet," in *The Wife of His Youth and Other Stories of the Color Line* (1899; reprint, Ann Arbor: The University of Michigan Press, 2002), 277. Further references to this work appear in the text. On the date of composition for "The Bouquet," see Joseph R. McElrath, Jr., and Robert C. Leitz III, eds., *"To Be an Author,"* 101 n. 1.

20. Reprinted in Susy Platt, ed., *Respectfully Quoted: A Dictionary of Quotations from the Library of Congress* (Washington, DC: Congressional Quarterly, Inc., 1992), 88–89. See also Daisy Kramer, *Old Drum, Being an Account of George Graham Vest & His Now Famous Eulogy to the Dog* (Kirkwood, MO: The Printery, 1970), and William Safire, "Best Speech," *New York Times Magazine* (April 18, 1999), 72–74.

21. *The Journals of Charles W. Chesnutt,* 52–53.

22. Rush C. Hawkins, *Better than Men* (New York: J. W. Bouton, 1896), 1–2.

23. Thomas Wentworth Higginson, *Harper's Bazaar* (July 30, 1887), quoted in "Colonel Thomas Wentworth Higginson," *Our Dumb Animals* 20:4 (September 1887): 42.

24. Frederick Douglass, quoted in Marjorie Spiegel, *The Dreaded Comparison,* 109. Douglass's 1853 novel *The Heroic Slave* details fugitive slaves' terrifying experiences of being pursued by slave catchers' bloodhounds, whose presence protagonist Madison Washington associates with both the near certainty of being recaptured and the likeliness of being "torn . . . to pieces" (56). Yet the novel also offers an alternate account of canine nature that calls to mind the role that the dog Bobby plays in Emmanuel Levinas's account of his imprisonment in Nazi concentration camps. When the runaway Washington arrives at night at the home of white abolitionists Mrs. and Mr. Listwell, their "faithful dog" Monte begins barking ferociously at the sound of the stranger's advance (32). (Washington had never been to their home before.) The barking, however, soon ceases, "for, with true canine instinct, Monte quickly discovered that a friend, not an enemy of the family, was coming to the house, and instead of rushing to repel the supposed intruder, he was now at the door, whimpering and dancing for the admission of himself and his newly made friend" (32). The Listwells' dog instinctively recognizes Washington's humanity as he approaches the house.

25. Harriet E. Wilson, *Our Nig: or, Sketches from the Life of a Free Black* (1859; reprint, New York: Vintage, 1983), 41–42, 61.

26. J. G. T., "Blood-Hounds and Slavery," *Our Dumb Animals* 1:12 (May 1869): 92, emphasis in original.

27. *Our Dumb Animals* regularly published the names of the persons from whom

they had received donations as well as the towns in which new Bands of Mercy were formed. This data would provide a starting point for investigations of contributors' racial identities.

28. Hawkins, *Better than Men,* 11.

29. Charles W. Chesnutt, "McDugald's Mule," reprinted in *The Short Fiction of Charles W. Chesnutt,* ed. Sylvia Lyons Render (Washington, DC: Howard University Press, 1981), 183–85. In the last passage quoted, Chesnutt seems to be signifyin(g) on the controversial passage in *Huckleberry Finn,* in which Aunt Sally asks Huck if anybody was hurt in the (spurious) steamboat accident, and he responds, "No'm. Killed a nigger."

30. Ibid., 184.

31. See my discussion of the animal protection movement in the introduction and the conclusion.

32. The editors of *Charles W. Chesnutt: Essays and Speeches,* ed. Joseph R. McElrath, Jr., Robert C. Leitz III, and Jessie S. Crisler (Stanford: Stanford University Press, 1999), note, "While meeting the exacting demands of his 1899–1902 belletristic schedule and those of a highly successful stenographic career before and after, he continued his self-education regimen, systematically surveyed the evidence in periodicals of the state of race relations in the United States, participated in local civic affairs and national organizations advancing the African American cause, and in what time remained frequented the Cleveland Public Library to perform the research requisite for writing and speaking" ("Editorial Note," xx).

33. Sarah Knowles Bolton, introduction to *Pussy Meow: The Autobiography of a Cat,* by Susanna Louise Patteson, quoted in *Charles W. Chesnutt: Essays and Speeches,* 173 n. 3. Marshall Saunders' *Beautiful Joe* (1893) was also modeled on *Black Beauty* and, like Sewell's novel, published by George Angell's American Humane Education Society. Hezekiah Butterworth's 1993 introduction describes *Beautiful Joe* as a follow-up to *Black Beauty,* and, in the first chapter of the novel, the canine narrator describes his familiarity with Sewell's text: "I have seen my mistress laughing and crying over a little book that she says is a story of a horse's life, and sometimes she puts the book down close to my nose to let me see the pictures" (reprint, Bedford, MA: Applewood Books, 1999, 14).

34. *Charles W. Chesnutt: Essays and Speeches,* 172.

35. *"To Be an Author,"* 65, 67. The June 5 draft of Chesnutt's letter to Cable appears in full in Helen M. Chesnutt, *Charles Waddell Chesnutt,* 57–59.

36. On Chesnutt's use of the regional dialect tale, see Richard H. Brodhead, *Cultures of Letters: Scenes of Reading and Writing in Nineteenth-Century America* (Chicago: University of Chicago Press, 1993), 177–210; of the plantation romance, see Eric J. Sundquist, *To Wake the Nations,* 271–454; of the discourse of white heteronormativity, see Mason Stokes, *The Color of Sex: Whiteness, Heterosexuality, and the Fictions of White Supremacy* (Durham: Duke University Press, 2001), 108–32.

37. See Sundquist, *To Wake the Nations,* 333.

38. Charles W. Chesnutt, "The Passing of Grandison," in *The Wife of His Youth and Other Stories of the Color Line,* 200. Further references to this work appear in the text.

39. Jeffrey Moussaieff Masson, *Dogs Never Lie about Love: Reflections on the Emotional World of Dogs* (New York: Crown Publishers, 1997).

40. See John W. Roberts, "The African American Animal Trickster as Hero," in *Redefining American Literary History,* ed. A. LaVonne Brown Ruoff and Jerry W. Ward (New York: Modern Language Association of America, 1990), 100–111. As Roberts explains, the strategies Br'er Rabbit employs reflected the limited options open to enslaved African Americans: "Like their animal trickster, [slaves] were in a contest of indeterminate duration for their survival with a limited number of ways for securing it. Therefore, they had to rely to great extent on their ingenuity to develop endless variations on a single theme: the transcendent power of wit" (111). The African American animal trickster tale was used "to promote cleverness, guile, and wit as the most advantageous behavioral options for dealing with the slave masters in certain generic situations" (110).

41. Georges Cuvier, *The Animal Kingdom* (1817; trans. Edward Blythe et al., Boston: Etes and Lauriat, 1878), 78.

42. In addition to placating white Northerners, comparisons between slaves and faithful dogs were also designed to reassure Southern whites that slavery could be maintained without the threat of a violent black uprising. Abolitionists, in turn, specifically targeted the image of the slave as contented, deferential dog in an attempt to undermine white Southerners' confidence in their ability to hold blacks in servitude and escape reprisal. In Melville's *Benito Cereno,* Captain Delano's assumption of blacks' dog-like fidelity makes him blind and vulnerable to the rebellion and aggression of the blacks onboard the *San Dominick.*

43. Notable examples include Thomas Nelson Page, *In Ole Virginia; or, Marse Chan, and Other Stories* (New York: C. Scribner's Sons, 1887), and Joel Chandler Harris, *Uncle Remus, His Songs and His Sayings* (New York: D. Appleton and Company, 1880).

44. William Swainson, *On the Natural History and Classification of Quadrupeds,* quoted in Harriet Ritvo, *The Platypus and the Mermaid and Other Figments of the Classifying Imagination* (Cambridge: Harvard University Press, 1997), 40.

45. Quoted in Ritvo, *Platypus and the Mermaid,* 191.

46. Quoted in Ida B. Wells, *Southern Horrors and Other Writings: The Anti-Lynching Campaign of Ida B. Wells, 1892–1900,* ed. Jacqueline Jones Royster (Boston: Bedford, 1997), 62.

47. James K. Vardaman, quoted in Albert D. Kirwan, *Revolt of the Rednecks: Mississippi Politics: 1867–1925* (Lexington: University of Kentucky Press, 1951), 146–47.

48. George M. Fredrickson, *The Black Image in the White Mind: The Debate on Afro-American Character and Destiny, 1817–1914* (New York: Harper and Row, 1971), 278.

49. Nathaniel Southgate Shaler, "The Negro Problem," *Atlantic Monthly* 54 (November 1884): 708, 703.

50. Ibid., 701.

51. Nathaniel Southgate Shaler, "The Nature of the Negro," *Arena* 3 (December 1890): 33, 34.

52. Shaler, "The Negro Problem," 703.

53. Fredrickson, *The Black Image in the White Mind,* 278. Fredrickson notes that while the theory of black as dangerous brute does counter the image of African Americans advanced previously, this view, which rose to prominence in the 1890s, did have roots in antebellum defenses of slavery. "The proslavery theorists," Fredrickson explains, "had argued that the 'brute' propensities of the blacks were kept in check only as a result of the absolute white control made possible by slavery and that emancipation in the South would bring the same 'reversion to savagery' that had allegedly taken place after the blacks had been freed in Haiti and the British West Indies" (259).

54. Edward H. Forbush, *The Domestic Cat; Bird Killer, Mouser, and Destroyer of Wildlife; Means of Utilizing and Controlling It* (Boston: Wright and Potter Printing Company, 1916). On nineteenth-century cat breeds and breeding, see Harriet Ritvo, *The Animal Estate: The English and Other Creatures in the Victorian Age* (Cambridge: Harvard University Press, 1987), 115–21.

55. Georges Louis Leclerc, Count de Buffon, *Natural History, General and Particular,* vol. 4, trans. William Smellie (London: A. Strahan, and T. Cadell, 1791; facsimile reprint, Bristol, UK: Thoemmes Press, 2000), 60.

56. Henry David Thoreau, *Walden* (1854; reprint, ed. J. Lyndon Shanley, Princeton: Princeton University Press, 1989), 232. Similarly, Harriet Beecher Stowe makes the unalterability of feline nature a central trope of her 1872 novel *Pink and White Tyranny,* which satirizes John Seymour's naïve belief that he can remake the frivolous socialite Lillie Ellis into a domestic angel. See Harriet Beecher Stowe, *Pink and White Tyranny: A Society Novel* (1871; reprinted in vol. 11 of *The Writings of Harriet Beecher Stowe,* New York: AMS Press, Inc., 1967), especially pp. 286, 353, 366, and 371–72.

57. Nathaniel Southgate Shaler, *Domesticated Animals: Their Relation to Man and to His Advancement in Civilization* (New York: Charles Scribner's Sons, 1895), 50–51, 55. Further references to this work appear in the text. See also Wallace Rice, *Animals: A Popular Natural History of Wild Beasts* (Chicago: Herbert S. Stone and Company, 1901), which asserts, "The domestic cat readily runs wild and is often confounded with its untamed cousins in many parts of the world" (103).

58. For a discussion of tigers in medieval bestiaries, see Margaret Haist, "The Lion, Bloodline, and Kinship," in *The Mark of the Beast,* ed. Debra Hassig (New York: Routledge, 1999). Harriet Ritvo discusses depictions of tigers and other wild cats in eighteenth- and nineteenth-century natural history books in "Learning from Animals: Natural History for Children in the Eighteenth and Nineteenth Centuries," *Children's Literature* 13 (1985): 85–88.

59. William Holloway and John Branch, *The British Museum; or Elegant Repository of Natural History,* 2 vols. (London: John Babcock, 1803), quoted in Ritvo, "Learning from Animals," 88. S. S. Smith, *Illustrated History of Wild Animals and Other Curiosi-*

ties Contained in P. T. Barnum's New and Greatest Show on Earth, Museum, Menagerie, Polytechnic Institute, and International Zoological Garden (New York: Press of Wynkoop and Hallenbeck, 1878), 10. In the late-nineteenth-century United States, such beliefs were dramatized for the public regularly in circuses' so-called tamed tiger acts. As circus historian Alex Kerr explains, nineteenth-century "tamed tigers" were "by no means 'tame.'" "In those days . . . a flaming barrier kept the lions at one end of the cage until the 'tamer' had entered, and once these red-hot bars were withdrawn, the uncontrolled beasts attacked him on sight. He stayed inside to defend himself against their fury for as long as he dared. The public did not expect to see the animals perform; they were only interested in whether the man came out alive or dead" (*No Bars Between,* London: Cassell and Company Ltd., 1957, xv, xiii).

60. Thomas Dixon, Jr., *The Leopard's Spots: A Romance of the White Man's Burden, 1865–1900* (1902; reprint, Ridgewood, NJ: The Gregg Press, Inc., 1967), 49–50. Thomas Dixon, Jr., *The Clansman: An Historical Romance of the Ku Klux Klan* (1905; reprint, Lexington: University Press of Kentucky, 1970), 283, 304.

61. *The People's Natural History,* vol. 1, ed. Charles John Cornish (New York: The University Society, 1903), 101.

62. James Watson, *The Dog Book: A Popular History of the Dog . . .* (New York: Doubleday, Page and Company, 1905). In *Anecdotes of Dogs* (London: Bell and Daldy, 1867; reprint, 1870), Edward Jesse finds the theory of dogs' descent from wolves

> not convincing, the dog having characters which do not belong to the wolf. The dog, for instance, guards property with strictest vigilance, which has been entrusted to his charge. . . . His courage is unbounded, a property not possessed by the wolf: he appears never to forget a kindness, but soon loses the recollections of an injury, if received by one he loves, but resents it if offered by a stranger. His docility and mental pliability exceed those of any other animal; his habits are social, and his fidelity not to be shaken; hunger cannot weaken, nor old age impair it. His discrimination is equal, in many respects, to human intelligence. If he commits a fault, he is sensible to it and shows pleasure when commended. These, and many other qualities, which might have been enumerated, are distinct from those possessed by the wolf. It may be said that domestication might produce them in the latter. This may be doubted, and is not likely to be proved. (14)

See also the discussion of eighteenth- and nineteenth-century natural history writing on the dog in the introduction.

63. See the discussion of the kidnapping of Elizabeth Barrett Browning's dog in Virginia Woolf, *Flush: A Biography* (London: L. and V. Woolf at the Hogarth Press, 1933). See also Elizabeth Stuart Phelps, *Loveliness: A Story* (Boston: Houghton Mifflin, 1899); Henry Mahew, "Of the Former Street-Sellers, 'Finders,' Stealers, and Restorers of Dogs," reprinted in *Faithful Friends: Dogs in Life and Literature,* ed. Frank Jackson (New York: Carroll and Graf Publishers, 1997), 440–42; and the March 1934 *London Times* article on dog-stealing reprinted on p. 447 of the same volume.

64. *Dog Stories from "The Spectator,"* ed. John St. Loe Strachey (New York: Macmillan, 1895), 252–53.

65. Sarah Knowles Bolton, *Our Devoted Friend, the Dog* (1901; reprint, Boston: L. C. Page and Company, 1902).

66. "Editorial Note," in *Charles W. Chesnutt: Essays and Speeches,* xx. See also Richard Brodhead, *Cultures of Letters,* especially pp. 195–210. As Brodhead argues, the *Atlantic* defined literature, authorship, and literary achievement for many of this period's writers—Chesnutt included.

67. Shaler, "The Negro Problem," 702.

68. Eric J. Sundquist, introduction to *The Marrow of Tradition,* by Charles W. Chesnutt (New York: Penguin, 1993), xvii, xviii, xxxviii. See this essay for a more detailed account of the events on which *Marrow* is based.

69. Charles W. Chesnutt, *The Marrow of Tradition* (1901; reprint, New York: Penguin, 1993), 60. Further references to this work appear in the text.

70. Quoted in Helen M. Chesnutt, *Charles Waddell Chesnutt,* 57. This sentence appears in the first draft of the letter Chesnutt composed, but not in the revised draft he sent to Cable.

71. Here, too, Chesnutt is developing strategies with which earlier African American writers had experimented. Recognizing the central role that the rhetoric of uncivilized animality played in justifications for lynching, Ida B. Wells presents white lynchers as "brutal" and their acts as the "last relic of barbarism and savagery" (*Southern Horrors and Other Writings,* 65, 72). (In *Manliness and Civilization: A Cultural History of Gender and Race in the United States, 1880–1917,* Chicago: University of Chicago Press, 1995, Gail Bederman argues that Ida B. Wells's *Southern Horrors* presents the lynch mob and its supporters as uncivilized people. Bederman's analysis does not, however, take into account the ways in which ideas about animality function in Wells's text.) In *Iola Leroy* (1892), Francis Harper uses a similar strategy for redirecting the rhetoric of "rapacious beasts" by casting the white man as the ravenous beast who preys carnally/sexually on black women. Dr. Latimer tells Iola that she is "like a tender lamb snatched from the jaws of a hungry wolf, but who still needs protecting, loving care" (*Iola Leroy, Or, Shadows Uplifted,* Boston: Beacon Press, 1987, 273).

72. Chesnutt makes this point himself on pp. 295–96 of the novel.

73. Charles W. Chesnutt, *The Conjure Woman and Other Conjure Tales* (1899; reprint, ed. Richard H. Brodhead, Durham: Duke University Press, 1993), 55. See pp. 23–24 of this volume for the chronology of the conjure tale's composition. Further references to this work appear in the text.

74. Angell, "Will It Pay?" originally published in the February 1869 edition of *Our Dumb Animals,* and reprinted in the appendix of Angell's *Autobiographical Sketches,* 7 (second pagination series).

75. Ibid., 8, emphasis in original.

76. In *To Wake the Nations,* Eric Sundquist describes "Mars Jeems's Nightmare" as a rare case in which the ultimate moral of the conjure tale is "clear," for "more often in

the conjure tales, Julius's ulterior motive functions as much to camouflage as to reveal the interior significance of the conjure, which appears in symbolic language" (371). Here, Sundquist contends, "Julius is so forward with the moral of his tale in this case—white folks must make allowances for 'po' ign'ant niggers w'at ain' had no chanst ter l'arn'—that the discrepancy between John's and Annie's separate recognitions of it hardly matters" (334). In contrast, I would suggest that the moral Julius states does not clarify the entire didactic purpose of the tale and that Annie and John's separate responses are essential elements of the text's argument.

Conclusion

Epigraph: Toni Morrison, *Playing in the Dark* (Cambridge: Harvard University Press, 1990), 8–9, 19.

1. Recent presidents have gone well beyond their predecessors' strategy of making sure images of their animals reach the voting public; savvy first ladies now assist White House pets in production of their own monographs. See Barbara Bush, *Millie's Book: As Dictated to Barbara Bush* (New York: William Morrow, 1990), and Hillary Rodham Clinton, *Dear Socks, Dear Buddy: Kids' Letters to the First Pets* (New York: Simon and Schuster, 1998).

2. See, for example, Elizabeth Marshall Thomas, *The Hidden Life of Dogs* (Boston: Houghton Mifflin, 1993); Jeffrey Moussaieff Masson and Susan McCarthy, *When Elephants Weep: The Emotional Lives of Animals* (New York: Delacorte Press, 1995); Jeffrey Moussaieff Masson, *Dogs Never Lie about Love: Reflections on the Emotional World of Dogs* (New York: Crown Publishers, 1997); and Marc Bekoff, *Minding Animals: Awareness, Emotions, and Heart* (New York: Oxford University Press, 2002).

3. American Veterinary Medical Association, *U.S. Pet Ownership and Demographics Sourcebook* (Schaumburg, IL: American Veterinary Medical Association, 2002), 2. The April 2003 edition of *Meat Animals Production, Disposition, and Income* (a publication of the United States Department of Agriculture) reports the number of cattle, pigs, sheep, turkeys, and chickens raised annually for meat as 9,024,901,000.

4. Gail Bederman, *Manliness and Civilization: A Cultural History of Gender and Race in the United States, 1880–1917* (Chicago: University of Chicago Press, 1995), 12.

5. C. C. Buel, "Henry Bergh and His Work," *Scribner's Monthly* 17 (April 1879): 872, 884.

6. Bederman, *Manliness and Civilization,* 74.

7. Jack London, *The Call of the Wild* (1903; reprinted in *The Call of the Wild, White Fang, and Other Stories,* ed. Earl Labor and Robert C. Leitz III, New York: Oxford University Press, 1990), 6. Further references to this work appear in the text.

8. Dan Barry, "Artist's Fame Is Fleeting, but Dog Poker Is Forever," *New York Times,* June 14, 2002: A1, 32.

9. O. Henry [William Sydney Porter], *The Four Million* (1906; facsimile reprint,

Amsterdam: Fredonia Books, 2000), 110. Further references to this work appear in the text.

10. Bederman, *Manliness and Civilization,* 12–13.

11. James Turner, *Reckoning with the Beast: Animals, Pain, and Humanity in the Victorian Mind* (Baltimore: Johns Hopkins University Press, 1980), 95.

12. On the reception history of this book, see Paul Ekman, introduction to *The Expression of the Emotions in Man and Animals* (New York: Oxford University Press, 1998).

13. C. Lloyd Morgan, quoted in Turner, *Reckoning with the Beast,* 64.

14. Charles Darwin, *The Descent of Man, and Selection in Relation to Sex* (1871; reprint, Princeton: Princeton University Press, 1981), 105; Ernest Thompson Seton, *Wild Animals I Have Known* (1898; reprint, Toronto: McClelland and Stewart, Inc., 1991), 15.

15. Seton, *Wild Animals I have Known,* 124.

16. See Ralph H. Lutts, *The Nature Fakers: Wildlife, Science, and Sentiment* (1990; reprint, Charlottesville: University Press of Virginia, 2001), for a detailed account of this controversy. Roosevelt's March 7, 1907, letter to Burroughs is quoted on p. 42 of this text.

17. See Eric Lupfer, "The Emergence of American Nature Writing, 1860–1909: John Burroughs, Henry David Thoreau, and Houghton, Mifflin and Company" (Ph.D. diss., University of Texas at Austin, 2003).

18. See Bederman, *Manliness and Civilization,* 170–215.

19. Lutts, *The Nature Fakers,* 112–13.

20. George T. Angell, *Autobiographical Sketches and Personal Recollections* (Boston: American Humane Education Society, [1892?]), 98.

21. Anna Sewell, *Black Beauty* (1877; reprint, New York: Penguin, 1994), 207. Further references to this work appear in the text.

22. *Strike at Shane's* (Boston: American Humane Education Society, 1893; reprint, Bedford, MA: Applewood Books, 1999), 50. Further references to this work appear in the text.

23. "Roosevelt," *Our Dumb Animals* 33:8 (January 1901): 88, emphasis in original; George T. Angell, "Roosevelt Going a Hunting," *Our Dumb Animals* 33:8 (January 1901): 88, emphasis in original.

24. See George T. Angell, ["Yellow Dime Literature"], *Our Dumb Animals* 28:5 (October 1895): 50; George T. Angell, "Williams College," *Our Dumb Animals* 26:7 (December 1893): 77; "Strenuous Life," *Our Dumb Animals* 33:8 (January 1901): 89, "More Brutal Hazing," *Our Dumb Animals* 33:8 (January 1901): 89; George T. Angell, "Hazing at West Point," *Our Dumb Animals* 33:8 (January 1901): 89; George T. Angell, "About Fortifying the Nicaragua Canal," *Our Dumb Animals* 33:8 (January 1901): 88; George T. Angell, "The New King," *Our Dumb Animals* 33:10 (March 1901): 114; George T. Angell, "If a Few Thousand Boers," *Our Dumb Animals* 33:12 (May 1901): 146.

25. George T. Angell, "The Game of Polo," *Our Dumb Animals* 28:5 (October 1895): 50, emphasis in original. This same page also contains four other articles criticizing polo. Another attack on polo appears in George T. Angell, "Whose Fault Is It?" *Our Dumb Animals* 32:1 (June 1899): 5.

26. Angell, "Report of the President for the Year Ending March 1, 1900," *Our Dumb Animals* 32:11 (April 1900): 138, emphasis in original.

27. For a critique of Roosevelt's hunting of mountain lions, see "The President's Dog," *Our Dumb Animals* 34:7 (December 1901): 78. For other critiques of the killing of wildlife, see "Protect the Toads," *Our Dumb Animals* 28:12 (May 1896): 146; George T. Angell, "In the Wilderness," *Our Dumb Animals* 33:12 (May 1901): 146; "The Killing of Seals," *Our Dumb Animals* 33:12 (May 1901): 146; J. H. Kellogg, ["Hunting or Fishing for Sport"], *Our Dumb Animals* 33:12 (May 1901): 146; George T. Angell, "Protection of Birds," *Our Dumb Animals* 32:1 (June 1899): 5.

28. *Our Gold Mine at Hollyhurst* (Boston: American Humane Education Society, 1893), 134.

29. Ibid., 80–81, emphasis in original.

30. Roswell C. McCrea, *The Humane Movement: A Descriptive Survey* (New York: Columbia University Press, 1910); William J. Shultz, *The Humane Movement in the United States, 1910–1922* (New York: Columbia University Press, 1924); Sydney H. Coleman, *Humane Society Leaders in America* (Albany, NY: American Humane Association, 1924). The title page of McCrea's *The Humane Movement,* states that the volume was "prepared on the Henry Bergh Foundation for the Promotion of Humane Education in Columbia University."

31. Coleman, *Humane Society Leaders in America,* 89–91.

32. Turner, *Reckoning with the Beast,* 54.

33. In *Touching Liberty: Abolition, Feminism, and the Politics of the Body* (Berkeley: University of California Press, 1993), Karen Sánchez-Eppler writes that the ability of Nina (in Stowe's novel *Dred*) to read the signs that indicate a person's moral character is "jokingly shared with dogs" (28). As examination of Stowe's other writings on the canine mind indicates, Stowe was not joking.

34. In the introduction to *Charles W. Chesnutt: Essays and Speeches,* ed. Joseph R. McElrath, Jr., Robert C. Leitz III, and Jessie S. Crisler (Stanford: Stanford University Press, 1999), the editors cite Chesnutt's review of Patteson's animal protection novel as evidence that he occasionally abandoned the "earnestness and high seriousness" that characterized most of his nonfiction writing. "This is the Chesnutt," the editors write, "who, when reviewing *Pussy Meow,* a book written by a cat lover and for others similarly enamored, had the temerity to observe, tongue-in-cheek, that it 'will appeal to all lovers of dumb animals'—he himself apparently not being among their number" (xxxiii–xxxiv). No evidence is offered to support this last assumption.

35. In *The Short Works of Mark Twain: A Critical Study* (Philadelphia: University of Pennsylvania Press, 2001), Peter Messent claims that "A Dog's Tale" "was apparently

written to support his daughter Jean's antivivisectionist sympathies." Messent offers no evidence that Jean had a role in the composition of the story or that the story's politics are not Twain's own. He does, however, assert that "the cloying sentimentality of the story is its most noticeable feature" (194).

36. J. M. Coetzee, *The Lives of Animals* (Princeton: Princeton University Press, 1999), 69.

INDEX